Covering the Enviro

Covering the Environment serves as a primer for future and current journalists reporting on environmental issues across all types of media. This practical resource explains the primary issues in writing on the environment, identifies who to go to and where to find sources, and offers examples on writing and reporting the beat. It also provides background to help environmental journalists identify their audiences and anticipate reactions to environmental news.

This primer emphasizes the role of environmental journalists not as environmental advocates but as reporters attempting to accurately and fairly report the news. Contents include:

- an overview and history of the environment and journalism, spotlighting the most significant issues in the beat;
- guidance on understanding environmental and health science, ranging from issues of risk, to scientific research and studies, to interviewing scientists;
- insights into government and regulatory communities and environmental advocates on all sides of the political spectrum;
- assistance in accessing public records and conducting computer-assisted reporting;
- guidance in writing the story for print, broadcast and Internet audiences;
- an examination of the future of journalism and coverage of the environment.

Observations and story excerpts from experienced journalists provide a "real world" component, illuminating the practice of environmental journalism. Additional features in each chapter include study questions, story assignments and resources for more information. The book also provides a glossary of environmental, science, regulator and journalism terms, as well as a reference section and index.

This resource has been developed to train advanced undergraduate and graduate journalism students to cover the science and environment community, writing print and broadcast stories to a general audience. It also serves as a guide for working journalists who cover the environment as part of their work.

Author **Bob Wyss** has worked as a journalist for over 35 years, and has covered environmental and energy issues for a variety of publications, including the *Providence Journal*, the *Boston Globe*, the *New York Times*, and *E* magazine. He has taught journalism, including environmental journalism, at Michigan State University and the University of Connecticut.

LEA's communication series

Jennings Bryant/Dolf Zillmann, General Editors

Selected titles in Journalism (Maxwell McCombs, Advisory Editor) include:

Real Feature Writing, Second Edition
Aamidor

Media Coverage of New and Controversial Science
Communicating Uncertainty
Friedman/Dunwoody/Rogers

Professional Feature Writing, Fourth Edition
Garrison

The Troubles of Journalism
A Critical Look at What's Right and Wrong with the Press, Third Edition
Hachten

Internet Newspapers
The Making of a Mainstream Medium
Li

The Two W's of Journalism
The Why and What of Public Affairs Reporting
Merritt/McCombs

The American Journalist in the 21st Century
U.S. News People at the Dawn of a New Millennium
Weaver/Beam/Brownlee/Voakes/Wilhoit

Covering the Environment

How Journalists Work the Green Beat

Bob Wyss

Routledge
Taylor & Francis Group

NEW YORK AND LONDON

First published 2008
by Routledge
270 Madison Ave, New York, NY 10016

Simultaneously published in the UK
by Routledge
2 Park Square, Milton Park, Abingdon, Oxon OX14 4RN

Routledge is an imprint of the Taylor & Francis Group, an informa business

Typeset in Sabon by Wearset Ltd, Boldon, Tyne and Wear
Printed and bound in the United States of America on acid-
free paper by Walsworth Publishing Company, Marceline, MO

Library of Congress Cataloging in Publication Data
Wyss, Bob.
Covering the environment: how journalists work the green
beat/by Bob Wyss.
p. cm.
Includes bibliographical references and index.
1. Environmental protection Press coverage. 2. Mass media
and the environment. I. Title.
PN4888.E65W97 2007
070.4'493337–dc22
2007019662

British Library Cataloguing in Publication Data
A catalogue record for this book is available from the British
Library

ISBN10: 0-8058-5768-0 (hbk)
ISBN10: 0-8058-5769-9 (pbk)
ISBN10: 0-203-92760-5 (ebk)
ISBN13: 978-0-8058-5768-9 (hbk)
ISBN13: 978-0-8058-5769-6 (pbk)
ISBN13: 978-0-203-92760-1 (ebk)

Contents

PART III
Writing the beat   137

PART IV
Understanding the beat   229

Figures

Preface

Covering the Environment is for students and professionals who want to learn how to report and communicate about the environment. When I taught my first environmental journalism class in 1993 I was surprised that there was no comprehensive textbook teaching students and professionals how to cover the environment. The situation has not changed since then. There are a number of excellent books and anthologies that address specific subjects that are in this text. However, there is no book like *Covering the Environment* that offers a comprehensive and professional approach to environmental journalism.

This absence comes at a time when the number of journalists who cover the environmental beat is significant. While formal coverage began in the late 1960s with a handful of news organizations, more than 1,400 journalists have identified themselves as environmental journalists in the United States (SEJ, 2005b). Another 7,500 journalists in 110 other countries have said that they cover the environment (IFEJ, 2001). Not all of the journalists in either of these groups cover the environment for a major news organization. Some work the beat part-time along with other duties. Others may be freelance journalists or educators. But the numbers do demonstrate how the beat has been developing and growing. Coverage has grown along with news consumer interest in the field. Science is indicating that the environment will be an ever increasing element of future news coverage. There is a scientific consensus that the climate is warming and dramatically changing the earth's environment. The story of global warming too often has been wrapped in misconceptions or scare tactics. *Covering the Environment* is designed to serve as a primer to help current and future journalists report on this and other environmental issues.

The book is intended to provide readers with guidance in how to understand the beat by explaining the primary issues, identifying who and where to find sources and providing examples on how to write and report the beat. It also provides some background to help would-be environmental journalists identify their audience and how they react to environmental news. However, the book is not aimed at communication scholars who analyze the role of the news media in covering the environment. Readers interested in that topic should be able to find what they need in a range of excellent academic journals.

Intended audience

Covering the Environment instructs advanced undergraduate and graduate journalism students about how to cover the science and environment community and then write and broadcast stories to a general audience. At the same time it is versatile enough to be used in a range of interdisciplinary courses so that scientists and the environmental community can learn how to communicate with journalists and the general public. It also serves as a primer for thousands of working journalists who need to cover the environment on a regular or occasional basis. Finally, international journalism students and professionals can find most of the principles helpful in how they would approach the beat even if some of the regulatory and government structures are slightly different.

Overview of content

Covering the Environment is designed as a guidebook to help teach journalists, writers, scientists, environmentalists and others how to communicate. The primary text explains the gulf that exists at times between journalists and scientists and it shows how to interview and obtain information from officials, records and research papers. It then details how to write or broadcast that information in a way to be understood by the general public. It features invaluable tools such as a glossary and an extensive reference section.

Book structure

This book is organized into four parts. The first chapters provide an overview of the environment and journalism. Chapter 1 offers background on how journalists are covering the environment and spotlights the most significant issues in the beat. Chapter 2 is a history of how various observers have communicated about the environment. The second part offers information on how to report about the environment. Chapters 3 through 5 provide guidance on how to understand environmental and health science, ranging from issues of risk, scientific research and studies, to interviewing scientists. Chapters 6 and 7 offer background into the government and regulatory community and the environmental advocates on all sides of the political spectrum. Chapter

8 assists in understanding such reporting tools as how to access public records and how to conduct computer-assisted reporting. The third part is devoted to writing the story for print, broadcast and Internet audiences. Chapters 9 through 11 deal with print stories, beginning with short, breaking news stories and covering longer, developed and narrative stories. One chapter examines specialized beat writing, including nature, travel and agriculture journalism. Another explains how to write opinion columns and editorials about the environment. Chapter 13 is about broadcast news writing on the environment and Chapter 14 discusses online environmental journalism. The last two chapters are in the fourth and final part. Chapter 15 centers on how environmental journalists are not environmental advocates but reporters attempting to accurately and fairly report the news. Chapter 16 examines the future of journalism and coverage of the environment.

As the author, I arranged the chapters in what I felt was the most logical, linear order. However, instructors and students are free to read the chapters in whatever order they find most useful. Chapter 15 addresses some misconceptions some students and observers have about environmental journalism. Some may find it helpful to read this chapter earlier.

Special features

Covering the Environment has several special features. The end of each chapter includes study questions, story assignments and where to find additional information. The book also has a glossary of environmental, science, regulator and journalism terms, as well as a reference section and index. The most important features are the words and the stories of the many journalists who cover the environment. The observations and story excerpts include Mark Schleifstein of the *New Orleans Times-Picayune*, who covered Hurricane Katrina; Dan Fagin, formerly of *Newsday* and now with New York University, who wrote about cancer clusters on Long Island, NY; Dina Cappiello of the *Houston Chronicle*, who designed an air toxic test that showed the air in Houston was far more dangerous than what had been reported by Texas state officials; Ken Ward Jr. of the *Charleston Gazette*, who studied government documents and found that the state had erroneously allowed a coal silo to hover over an elementary school; Candace Page of the *Burlington Free Press*, whose narrative environmental stories entertained readers; Peter Lord of the *Providence Journal*, who made the plight of lead paint poisoning so humanly poignant by portraying young children permanently impaired by the pollution; Steve Grant of the *Hartford Courant*, who demonstrated how a canoe trip can capture the imagination of readers; and Tom Philp of the *Sacramento Bee*, whose editorial crusade to open the Hetch Hetchy reservoir in Yosemite brought new insight to local residents. Those are to name a few.

Covering the Environment is a culmination of my professional experiences over more than 35 years. I covered environmental and energy issues from 1984 to 1997 for the *Providence Journal*. I attended and presented at the Society of Environmental Journalists inaugural annual conference in Boulder, CO in October, 1991. In the fall of 1993, while on leave from the newspaper, I was a visiting professor at Michigan State University, where I helped establish the forerunner of a major environmental journalism program that is now led by Jim Detjen. Since beginning as an assistant professor of journalism at the University of Connecticut, in 2002, I have written about the environment for a variety of publications including the *Boston Globe*, the *New York Times*, and *E* magazine.

Acknowledgments

I wish to acknowledge and thank everyone who assisted in this venture. Among them are: Dan Fagin, New York University; Mark Neuzil, University of St. Thomas; Bill Kovarik, Radford University; Sharon Friedman, Lehigh University; Boyce Rensberger, Massachusetts Institute of Technology; Len Ackland, University of Colorado; Emelia Askari, *Detroit Free Press*; Bill Allen, University of Missouri; Chris Burnett, California State University, Long Beach; Bud Ward, *Environment Writer*; Candace Page, *Burlington Free Press*; Peter Lord, *Providence Journal*; Jocelyn Steinke, Western Michigan University; David Ropeik, of Concord, MA; Rob Taylor, International Center for Journalism; Linda Callahan, North Carolina A&T State University; Dale Willman, Field Notes Productions; Mark Schleifstein, *New Orleans Times-Picayune*; Peyton Fleming, Ceres; Steve Batt, University of Connecticut; Monica Allen, *New Bedford Standard-Times*; Steve Schneider, Stanford University; Ken Ward Jr., *Charleston Gazette*; Seth Borenstein, Associated Press; Tim Wheeler, *Baltimore Sun*; JoAnn Valenti, Brigham Young University; Tom Meersman, *Minneapolis Star Tribune*; Dina Cappiello, *Houston Chronicle*; Steve Grant, *Hartford Courant*; Tom Philp, *Sacramento Bee*; Amanda Griscom Little, *Grist*; Vince Patton, KGW-TV; Peter Dykstra, CNN; Christy George, Oregon Public Broadcasting; Matt Hammill, WQAD-TV; Ira Chinoy, University of Maryland; Kodi Barth, University of Connecticut; Amy Gahran, Boulder, CO; Vicki Monks, Oklahoma City, OK, Joseph A. Davis, Washington, DC, Wendee Holtcamp, Houston, TX, and S. Robert Chiappinelli and Robert Frederiksen, both of Providence, RI.

The University of Connecticut Department of Journalism provided invaluable support. I wish to thank Maureen Croteau, department chair, Wayne Worcester, Marcel Dufresne and Tim Kenny.

At Routledge I would like to thank Linda Bathgate, senior editor, and Kerry Breen, senior editorial assistant. The professional reviewers who also assisted were Sharon Dunwoody, University of Wisconsin Madison, Carolyn Johnsen, University of Nebraska, Bill Kovarik,

Radford University, Mark Neuzil, University of St. Thomas, Joann M. Valenti, Brigham Young University and Kristopher Wilson, Emory University.

Special thanks and assistance in reviewing the manuscript is made to Laura Sprague, Catherine Paolino and especially my partner Dianne Sprague.

The following news organizations gave permission to excerpt portions of several stories: *Baltimore Sun* for the Howard Street tunnel fire story; McClatchy Newspapers for the story on clean coal technology; and the *Sacramento Bee* for the Hetch Hetchy editorials.

This book is dedicated to two great journalism teachers: Ben Cunningham, former journalism professor at California State University, Long Beach, and Al Johnson, former reporter and editor at the *Providence Journal*. They continue to influence my work on a daily basis.

Part I

Introducing the beat

Chapter 1

Covering the environment

Mark Schleifstein was worried. As the environmental reporter for the *New Orleans Times-Picayune*, he had often been asked to write about the hurricanes that in late summer and early fall were striking the southeast coast of the U.S. He was skilled at clearly describing the natural phenomena of a major storm and translating the technical language of the climatologist into understandable terms for the average reader. After years of covering the storms he was concerned that people were becoming complacent, that they did not understand the potential force of a major hurricane. "I always felt we needed to improve our coverage," he explained. "Around 1992, before Hurricane Andrew hit Florida, I began to feel strongly that more needed to be done to warn and prepare people for the consequences of a major hurricane" (Schleifstein, 2005b). He believed that New Orleans was especially in grave danger. For years engineers had built levees on the Mississippi River and elsewhere to protect the region from flooding and to keep shipping flowing. The flooding had stopped, but so had the sediment build-up that sustained South Louisiana's estuaries. Now New Orleans was actually below sea level and the once vibrant wetlands that had protected the city from an ocean assault were sinking into the salt water. Plus the levees were aging and engineers were worried about their reliability. Schleifstein knew these environmental hazards. He had written stories that ranged from the bayou's vanishing wetlands to toxic chemicals in Louisiana's air. In 1997 he was part of a *Times-Picayune* team that won a Pulitzer Prize for a series about how the oceans were being overfished (Pulitzer.org, 2006).

He proposed a series about the hazards New Orleans faced from a major hurricane. At first editors were not interested, even when Schleifstein presented them with detailed proposals that clearly laid out the threat from the "Big One." Editors were cynical of Schleifstein's premise that New Orleans was in serious danger. Schleifstein remembered one editor who suggested that the environmental writer was engaging in "disaster porn." Schleifstein remained persistent and after several years he finally convinced the newspaper to allow him to work on the 2002 series that was called "Washing Away" (Schleifstein, 2005b).

Written with colleague John McQuaid, one portion began: "A major hurricane could decimate the region but flooding from even a moderate storm could kill thousands. It's just a matter of time." The series predicted that flooding could be widespread, hundreds of thousands would be left homeless, and it could take months for the area to dry out. It predicted that up to 200,000 people would be left behind and one of the few shelters available would be the Superdome in downtown New Orleans. The series said "Thousands will drown in homes or cars from the flooding, which most likely would come from a storm surge but might come from the collapse of a levee" (Schleifstein & McQuaid, 2002, p. 4).

No one disputed the stories, which were based on extensive research with scientists, engineers and public officials. Similar stories were reported also in 2002 by the *New York Times* and National Public Radio's "All Things Considered." But few took heed. Between 2002 and 2005 one reporter counted nine more *Times-Picayune* stories on the Bush Administration's decision not to allocate more federal money for New Orleans hurricane protection (Rutten, 2005).

The storm strikes

Time to prepare ran out in the summer of 2005. A tropical depression developed off Africa, built in power as it crossed the Atlantic, and swept into the Gulf of Mexico. By Sunday, August 28 it was heading towards Louisiana and had been upgraded to an extremely dangerous Category 4 storm. Called Hurricane Katrina, this is how Schleifstein described the storm in his page one story that Sunday:

> Katrina could turn out to be the perfect hurricane, much to the dismay of south Louisiana residents.
> Not only is there little to keep it from strengthening on a dangerous scale, but it is expected to create a dome of storm surge that could flood much of eastern New Orleans, the 9th Ward, and Mid-City in New Orleans, swamp much of the West Bank and Plaquermines and St. Bernard parishes, and flood north shore areas.
> (Schleifstein, 2005a, p. 1)

Journalists have a responsibility to find a line between reporting the worst-case situation and not alarming people. It could be the equivalent of shouting fire in a crowded theater. As he was writing this, Schleifstein, based on his interviews with climatologists and engineers, saw no need to hedge.

It was extremely clear to me that the storm would do more damage than what we were reporting, I was pretty conservative in what I was reporting. This was a Category 4 storm that was out in the ocean with a significant storm surge. I could not be an alarmist if I wanted to be. I wanted to scare the hell out of people so that they would get out of the city.

Later, an editor told Schleifstein that the reporter looked as white as a sheet in the days before Katrina arrived whenever anyone asked him about the storm. At synagogue one day that weekend he saw a friend who indicated he was wavering on whether to leave. Schleifstein told him to get the hell out of town (Schleifstein, 2005b).

The storm struck the Gulf Coast and then New Orleans the next morning, Monday, August 29. It arrived with winds of 100 miles per hour and heavy bands of rain that bent trees and blew off a portion of the roof of the Superdome where 10,000 people had sought refuge. It appeared that New Orleans may have missed the brunt of the attack until the levees gave way. By afternoon the storm was gone but the flooding in New Orleans was worsening. Rescuers began finding people clinging to porches and waiting in attics or atop roofs to be plucked to safety.

Tuesday morning Schleifstein awoke underneath his newsroom desk. He had sought refuge the night before, after covering the story for nearly 36 hours. The news that morning was grim. The *Times-Picayune* had lost its electricity along with everyone else in the path of the storm but the newspaper's emergency generator power enabled reporters to continue producing stories for the paper's sister news organization, NOLA.org. The online news described the flooding, the tens of thousands of people still trapped, and the fear that thousands may have died. Schleifstein realized his New Orleans house had to be underwater, but he knew his family was safe. That was when the editors decided that they needed to evacuate the newspaper building, where 220 employees and family members had stayed through the storm. The flood waters were still rising and if the trucks did not leave soon, they might become stranded.

Employees scampered aboard the newspaper's delivery trucks and each vehicle left rapidly. The trucks maneuvered around swamped cars stuck in the road and soon the vehicles were on the Crescent City Connection bridge over the Mississippi River. Schleifstein listened to the patter coming from WWL-AM. The radio station had set up in an emergency operations center and had access to a range of local officials discussing the gravity of the flooding spreading across the city. It was one of the few journalistic voices the day after the storm. Besides the crippled *Times-Picayune*, three out of the city's four television stations

Figure 1.1 Much of New Orleans is flooded in the aftermath of Hurricane Katrina that struck the Gulf Coast, August 29, 2005. Environmental news reporters for years had been warning that such a flood was a good possibility (source: courtesy Federal Emergency Management Administration).

had been knocked off the air by the storm. From the open back doors of the truck Schleifstein and his colleagues could see smoke rising from buildings that were on fire and marooned in the flooding from firefighters.

It took days for the world to understand the full horror of the disaster. Up to 80 percent of New Orleans was flooded, more than 100,000 structures destroyed and property damage was estimated at up to $100 billion (O. Johnson, 2006). The death toll for Louisiana was more than 1,500 (Hunter, 2006). But the greatest horror may have been the inability of local, state and federal officials to help the trapped and homeless of New Orleans. Tens of thousands of poor people were unable to leave the city, many trapped at the Superdome and the city's convention center. Dead bodies were left in open streets for days or trapped in fetid attics for weeks or months.

Schleifstein was exhausted, not just physically but emotionally. "It was a frustrating experience and a number of times reporters were overcome by what they were reporting," he said. "I was one of them. It became clear to me that people were going to be dying from this storm. And as bad as it was, it was not as big a storm as we had feared. It could have been worse" (Schleifstein, 2005b).

He had difficulty accepting praise for his earlier stories warning how vulnerable New Orleans and the Gulf Coast was to a major hurricane. "Yeah, we were right, but what does that mean?" Schleifstein told Alex Martin of the *Irish Times*. "The part that everybody failed was getting the people out" (Martin, 2005, p. 1).

Many believed he was too harsh. Joseph A. Davis, a freelance writer in Washington, DC said:

> Mark S. and John McQuaid probably saved tens of thousands of lives with their visionary, monumental and courageous series "Washing Away." As bad as the preparedness and response to Katrina was, it seems to me likely it would have been far worse without the kick-in-the-butt this series provided. Evacuation saved lots of lives. No journalism award on the planet is worth as much as that.
>
> (Davis, 2006)

Schleifstein and the rest of the staff of the *Times-Picayune* continued to produce news stories from remote locations through online blogs and eventually through the published newspaper back in New Orleans. In April, 2006 the *Times-Picayune* was awarded two Pulitzer Prizes. It shared the Public Service award with the *Biloxi-Gulfport Sun Herald* and it was awarded the Breaking News Reporting award, both for coverage of Katrina (Pulitzer.org, 2006).

Who makes and reports the news

Schleifstein is an environmental reporter. It is a comparatively new beat. But so is the interest in the environment.

In the past 50 years both the U.S. and the world have experienced a profound change in how they value the environment. The revision occurred when society said it would no longer accept the pollution and environmental harm that had always been a part of civilization. At first the public, and the news media, focused on obvious and easy targets, such as automobile exhaust that choked the air of cities such as Los Angeles, toxic waste that sickened residents in neighborhoods such as Love Canal and polluted rivers such as the Cuyahoga in Cleveland that were so foul that they caught on fire. As resolutions to these problems were found, the remaining issues became more daunting.

The environmental challenges of the twenty-first century will be far more subtle, demanding and global. They range from questions on how chemicals may be altering our genetic make-up to the long-term ramifications of how humans have caused the planet's temperatures to rise. As the potential impacts have increased, so have the stakes. Journalists today have greater tools and better understanding of how to address and communicate environmental problems. The issues are more complex and the number of advocates with competing stakes make it more difficult to communicate what is happening to the environment. Understanding the facts and making judgments on them becomes critical.

Environmental stories rarely are as dramatic as they were in the summer of 2005 when Hurricane Katrina struck Louisiana. More often, they have lacked drama. Rather than striking with a fury, some ooze, seep, or bubble silently and are often unseen. Or the story might change so imperceptibly as to nearly be invisible, such as the disappearance of another animal or plant species. But Katrina began to shock people into taking the environment more seriously. A Gallup Poll conducted in March, 2006 showed that Americans had growing concerns about the environment. The poll found that 67 percent of the respondents believed that the environment was getting worse, compared to 54 percent who had answered that way in 2002 (PollingReport.com, 2006). A few months later *Newsweek* magazine reported that "the task of avoiding ecological disaster (from climate change) may seem hopeless, and some environmental scientists have, quietly, concluded that it is. But Americans are notoriously reluctant to surrender their fates to the impersonal outcomes of an equation" (Adler, 2006, p. 43). The "New Greening of America" described how Americans individually were trying to make a difference against waste and pollution.

Not everyone has believed that journalists have been getting all of the facts about the environment to the public. A poll by Harris Interactive reported that 44 percent of those questioned felt that the media was not doing enough to reduce environmental problems (Harris Interactive, 2005). The 2006 Gallup Poll indicated that 58 percent believed that global warming was already occurring. Yet many seemed confused, ranking global warming as a lower priority than toxic waste or water pollution, problems where controls have been in place for years. In addition, 30 percent of those polled by Gallup believed that news of global warming had been exaggerated (PollingReport.com, 2006).

The environmental beat is relatively young. In 1973 *Editor & Publisher* listed 95 newspaper reporters who identified themselves as specialists covering the environment (Detjen *et al.*, 2000). Thirty years later the Society of Environmental Journalists reported that 1,400 journalists covered the environment either for a news organization or as a freelancer (SEJ, 2005b). Meanwhile the International Federation of Environmental Journalists, created in the early 1990s, said it represented more than 7,500 environmental journalists, in 117 countries, who work in what they report is every type of medium and includes scientific authors and filmmakers (IFEJ, 2001).

The number of U.S. journalists who are actively working for news-papers and television stations may be somewhat smaller, according to four studies undertaken between 2000 and 2003. Researchers identified 364 reporters located in four regions of the country who reported on the environment on a regular basis. The studies, while confined to 28 states in New England, the Mountain West, the Pacific Northwest and the South, found more similarities than differences, prompting the researchers to suggest that there may be a national norm for covering the environment (Sachsman *et al.*, 2006).

The studies found that newspapers were far more likely than a television station to have an environmental reporter. Researchers reported that 46.9 percent of all newspapers and 13 percent of television stations assigned reporters to the environmental beat. Newspapers with circulations of less than 14,000 were not likely to have an environmental reporter while 85 percent of dailies with a circulation of 60,000 or more had one. While these reporters carried the title, most reported that they were not guaranteed to be able to write exclusively about their beat. Reporters spent anywhere from 53.7 percent of their time in the Pacific Northwest region to a low of 37.9 percent for those in New England on environmental stories. Sometimes the alternate assignments were science or health related but they could also range over a variety of subjects. Despite these alternate tasks, environmental reporters also expressed strong satisfaction towards their job and one primary reason was the degree of autonomy they were given. One reason may be that environmental reporters are also veterans of the newsroom. The studies indicated that on average they had spent between 13.5 and 15.8 years in journalism (Sachsman *et al.*, 2006).

The journalists interviewed in these studies virtually all agreed that environmental reporters need to be objective in their coverage and fair in dealing with both corporations and environmental organizations. Most also believed it was not their role to work with community leaders in solving environmental problems. Many did worry that too many of their environmental journalism colleagues did slant stories towards environmental proponents and advocates. They also expressed concern that too many stories concentrated on environmental problems and pollution rather than working to help readers understand the growing complexity of environmental issues (Sachsman *et al.*, 2006).

Issues of tomorrow

The challenge in the future for environmental journalists will be to help people understand how humans have been affecting our planet. Accomplishing that will not be easy. Hurricane Katrina caused one of the worst natural disasters in U.S. history. It followed by a few months an earthquake and tsunami in the Indian Ocean that devastated South Asia, killing more than 200,000 people ("The Human," n.d.). The 2005 U.S. hurricane season was one of the most active in a century, with 28 named storms, 15 hurricanes and seven storms intense enough to earn a Category 3 or higher designation (NOAA, 2005). All of this climate activity prompted a number of news organizations to ask if climate change was behind so many natural disasters. Science and the environment rarely have such simple, concrete answers. It would be difficult to compare a tsunami caused by an Indian Ocean earthquake with the rise in the number of tropical disturbances in the North Atlantic. Over time researchers may be able to link a rise in violent storms with global warming, but such a finding would take time.

Climate change was at the top of a select list of potential and emerging issues that are likely to dominate the discussion of environmental news both in the U.S. and the world in the coming years. Other major issues include diminishing water supplies in many regions of both the U.S. and the world, the impacts from a growing population, and the threat of extinction faced by many species because of environmental changes. Journalists need to understand these issues because the public looks to them for guidance. Also, the press loses credibility when reporters misunderstand or misdirect attention from what is important. As residents of New Orleans found, some issues have been so important that there was no limit on how many times they should have been addressed.

Climate change

The terms climate change and global warming are sometimes used interchangeably to describe a build-up in global temperature produced by human activity. Climate change can also mean global cooling and either increases or decreases in global temperature can be spawned by natural events or forces. Scientists have agreed that the earth's temperature has been rising dramatically and that human activity is the most likely cause. Numerous studies culminated in February, 2007 when a network of scientists formed by the United Nations, the Intergovernmental Panel on Climate Change, warned that temperatures will probably warm by between 3.5 and eight degrees in the future. The panel added that there was a 10 percent chance of a far greater warming. Scientists have said that is an unacceptable risk (IPCC, 2007).

Early suggestions that these increases were part of a natural variability have been discarded for findings that a build-up of gases in the upper atmosphere are the cause. These gases, including water vapor, carbon dioxide, methane, ozone and nitrous oxide, create what has been called the greenhouse effect, allowing the sun's radiant energy to warm the

Figure 1.2 The Mendenhall Glacier in Alaska could disappear in the coming years. Global warming is expected to be the world's biggest environmental challenge as well as the dominant story for environmental journalists (source: courtesy National Oceanic & Atmospheric Administration).

earth while slowing the escape of heat back into space. The major reason for the increase in climate temperature has been attributed to a rise in carbon dioxide created by industrial processes. In the 1750s carbon dioxide levels in the upper atmosphere were about 280 parts per million. By the 1990s they were 360 parts per million. Under current trends they would reach 500 parts per million by 2050 (Ward, 2003). A report in 2004 by the National Academy of Sciences stated that there was more carbon dioxide and methane in the earth's atmosphere than at anytime in the past 400,000 years (West *et al.*, 2003). What alarmed some atmospheric scientists was that carbon dioxide can last for about a century in the upper atmosphere. The February, 2007 IPCC report followed a three-year review of hundreds of studies including supercomputer simulations of how the earth would respond to a build-up of gases. It stressed that action needed to be taken immediately (IPCC, 2007).

Rising sea levels would threaten low-lying coastal regions and islands. Seas rose six to nine inches in the twentieth century and the IPCC has projected that the rise in the twenty-first century would be between seven and 23 inches. However, that trend could also continue for at least 1,000 years (IPCC, 2007). Increased temperatures would also affect agriculture, it could spread diseases now confined to warmer climates and it could produce more frequent and violent weather and storms. Growing seasons would lengthen for higher latitudes, while semi-arid and subtropical regions would be more susceptible to droughts. The changes would be great enough, say scientists, to adversely impact large populations, economies and infrastructures.

Around the world, political responses to climate change have varied. The IPCC was formed in 1989 and it issued its first of four reports in 1990. Political action has been slow to respond. The United Nations Framework Convention on Climate Change, composed of 181 nations including the United States, was created in 1992 as a means to negotiate international strategies on climate change. That effort resulted in the Kyoto Protocol in 1997 which called on 37 of the world's industrialized nations to reduce the extent of their greenhouse gases. While 120 nations ratified the agreement, President George W. Bush, in 2001, announced that the U.S. would not participate because the Kyoto treaty was too expensive to carry out and the science of global warming was too uncertain (West *et al.*, 2003). Since then, Bush has publicly acknowledged the existence of climate change but he warned that the U.S. would pay too high an economic penalty to carry out the Kyoto provisions.

Journalists have been accused of not understanding the science and of putting too much emphasis on stories about the uncertainties of global warming. News story standards call for fairness, which meant including comments from all sides of an issue. That practice allowed global warming skeptics to get what sometimes amounted to equal play in an issue that most mainstream scientists say was no longer a scientific issue of equal weight. The IPCC report short-circuited that argument. "We have high, very scientific, confidence in this work," said Richard B. Alley, a professor at Penn State University and an IPCC author. "This is real, this is real, this is real" (Rosenthal & Revkin, 2007, p. A-5).

Water

At the beginning of the twenty-first century, the U.S. was anticipating significant water shortages country-wide. In July, 2003 the U.S. General Accounting Office warned that 36 states anticipated water shortages in the next ten years. Some southeastern states were so worried that communities such as Tampa Bay, FL built desalination plants usually associated with drought-plagued developing nations. Even some seemingly water-rich midwestern and northeastern communities faced challenges from aging public water systems that will need billions of dollars to upgrade (Wyss, 2003b).

But the biggest problem was in the west where the agricultural interests that grow citrus and vegetables can use proportionally far more water than the thirsty new residents of booming cities such as Las Vegas and San Diego. Nowhere has the problem in the U.S. been greater than on the Colorado River. A 1920s compact governed water usage as the river passed through seven states and Mexico. In 2003 the federal government ordered southern California public agencies to cutback voluntarily on how much water they took from the Colorado and when that did not happen it reduced the public water share in the state by 17 percent. Yet ranchers and farmers in California's Imperial Valley were permitted to receive all the water they wanted (Wyss, 2003b).

Legal problems were also complicated by a prolonged drought in the west. While most observers believe that western water laws will have to be changed, it will not occur without a fight pitting ranchers and farmers against non-agricultural users.

Environmental justice

Over six weeks in 1982 police arrested 532 people who were protesting plans to build a landfill in Warren County, N.C. The site would store soil and waste laced with polychlorinated biphenyls (PCBs). Many of the protesters were black and they argued that Warren County had been selected for the dump primarily because it was predominately black, poor and had limited political clout. Despite the protests, the landfill was built. Later the non-partisan U.S. General Accounting Office produced a study that found that three out of the four commercial hazardous waste landfills in a portion of the Southeast were located in predominately African American communities even though blacks made up 20 percent of the area's population (Bullard, 1996–2006).

That was the beginning of what has been called the Environmental Justice movement. "People of color have known about and have been living with inequitable environmental quality for decades – most without the protection of federal, state and local governmental agencies," said Robert Bullard (1996–2006, p. 3) who has repeatedly written about the issue.

Minorities and poor people have had a well-documented history of greater health problems than the general public as well as shorter life spans. Research also showed that minorities and low-income residents were more likely to reside near environmental hazards. A 1987 report by the United Church of Christ Commission for Racial Justice found that communities with commercial hazardous waste facilities had significantly larger racial populations (West *et al.*, 2003). However, correlating a relationship between health problems and environmental hazards can be difficult and the research on such links is limited.

The EPA in 1990 began actively looking into the issue. In 1992 it created the Office of Environmental Justice. Two years later President Bill Clinton signed an executive order requiring federal agencies to develop environmental justice programs aimed at eliminating any disparities between health and environmental protection for minorities and the poor (West *et al.*, 2003).

David Pace of the Associated Press used that data collected by the EPA to report in news stories published in December, 2005 that blacks were 79 percent more likely than whites "to live in neighborhoods where industrial air pollution is suspected of causing the most health problems" (Pace, 2005). Pace also reported that places with the highest health risks from industrial emissions were usually the home of poorer, less educated and more unemployed people than the general population. The stories hit home, especially in the many communities around the nation that Pace named. Repeatedly local leaders said they had been unaware of the findings. Some disputed the results. Others vowed to make changes ("Reading Rack," 2006).

Population

In the 1960s and early 1970s population was one of the big environmental stories. Journalists reported that scientists, environmentalists and public policy officials were worried that the world's resources were going to be overwhelmed by too many people. As fertility rates declined, especially in the U.S., so did the story.

But just because the story died locally, it did not mean it was not an issue internationally. In 2000 the world had 6.1 billion people and that number was projected to rise to nine billion in the next 50 years before it might begin to stabilize. The biggest growth spurts have been in the most undeveloped portions of the world – Africa and Asia. On these two continents an estimated one billion people have not had enough food to eat. That trend has been accelerating. Overpopulation affected agriculture and food production but also water supplies, deforestation and urban infrastructures that are overwhelmed by demands. Increased urbanization affected the poor and placed strains on the energy needs and pollution by increasing the number of cars on the road and the number of industrial plants. Scientists were not certain how many people the earth and its environment could sustain (Population Reference Bureau, n.d.).

The U.S. population story in the early years of the twenty-first century was more complicated. The population was projected to grow from 292 million in 2000 to 422 million over the next 50 years. That 45 percent increase was not caused by an increase in births but by a large influx of immigrants. The U.S. is so wealthy and vast that it may be able to sustain such a large population increase with no noticeable impact on natural resources. However, Americans already consume far more resources than anyone else, including those in other developed countries. More Americans could disproportionately affect global resources (Wheeler, 2003).

Debates about immigration rates can quickly deteriorate into political and racial infighting. In early 2004 the Sierra Club's national board fought over the population issue. One group of candidates for the national board argued in favor of population control and immigration quotas as a tool to preserve environmental resources. A second faction responded that such controls and quotas were a form of racism. An analysis of news stories by the publication *Environment Writer* found that journalists seemed to center their stories on the accusations by each side while avoiding analysis of the environmental impact of population growth (Dawson, 2004).

Biodiversity

In April, 2005 researchers announced that they had found the long-lost ivory-billed woodpecker in the swamps of Arkansas. The woodpecker had not been sighted since the 1940s. The report created a sensation not just with ornithologists but with the general public. News of another lost species is far more common than reports that a species has been rediscovered. The joy of the discovery was later tempered by those who questioned the discovery (Schmid, 2006).

The world has been a rapidly changing biological environment. Over 3.5 billion years of evolution the world today hosts about 1.4 million known species. The estimated total may be as high as five million. But biologists say species have been lost at a far faster rate than at any time known in history. Between 1600 and 2000 more than 700 species vanished. More than half were vascular plants, 83 were mammals and 113 were species of birds. The number of species threatened with extinction has been far higher. A 1996 study by the World Conservation Union estimated that the numbers threatened were: 25 percent for mammals and amphibians; 11 percent for birds; 20 percent for reptiles and 34 percent for fish (Bryant, 2002).

In the last few hundred years the major threat to many species has been human-caused changes in habitat. For instance, the ivory-billed woodpecker once ranged across the southeastern U.S. and Cuba until logging and forest clearance gave way to farmland and drastically reduced the bird's habitat. That pattern began in Europe, spread to

(a)

(b)

(c)

Figure 1.3 Biodiversity will be one of the biggest reporting challenges for environmental reporters. Among the species that have been listed as either threatened or endangered are, the bald eagle (a), the Antioch Dune primrose (b), and the San Joaquin kit fox (c) (source: courtesy U.S. Fish & Wildlife Service).

North America and was now being repeated across Asia, Africa and South America. Tropical forests have given way to slash-and-burn agriculture and fertile river valleys have been supplanted by mega-dams and reservoirs that have fed the growing demand for electricity and water. In the U.S., about 80 percent of its citizens now reside in 20 percent of the land area, especially along the nation's coastlines. The Great Plains have been emptying while fragile beaches and estuaries for hundreds of miles along the ocean have been irrevocably changed (Wyss, 2003b).

As people leave the fields for the city there were also signs that humans were increasingly out of touch or did not understand nature. For example, people relished sighting a white-tailed deer and have taken steps to eliminate its predators. The result has been that in the U.S. there were more deer than ever before, perhaps 20 million, so many they were unavoidable. The National Safety Council reported in 2002 that 820,000 automobiles had collided with deer, causing 100 human deaths, 13,000 injuries and $1 billion in insurance claims (Wyss, 2003a).

What you will find

There are two ways to learn how to write about science and the environment. One would be to be shown the toolshed and invited to use the tools. The second option would be to list how every tool is used for every imaginable chore. This book uses the former.

Both journalists and scientists agree that they need more education and understanding helps to communicate about science and the environment. A study by the Knight Center for Environmental Journalism at Michigan State University found that only 12 percent of environmental journalists had degrees in scientific or environmental fields (Detjen *et al.*, 2000). It also found that four in ten had received formal training in those fields and 74 percent wanted to learn more. A separate study found that while scientists deplored the way many in the media were covering science and the environment, 81 percent said they would be willing to take a course or learn more skills on how to communicate (Hartz & Chappell, 1998).

It is a promising commitment. Each side needs each other to get their message out. Each side also needs to understand the other. Without that need to understand and communicate the world in the future will be a lesser place.

Study guide

1 The opening paragraph of a news story is called a news lead. It attempts to summarize the most important information in 35 words or less. Write a news lead on what happened in New Orleans when Hurricane Katrina arrived on Tuesday, August 30, 2005.

2 Carefully re-read the news lead and the beginning of Mark Schleifstein's story for Sunday, August 29, 2005. Rewrite the lead and if possible compare with what other students in the class have written.

3 What else do you believe Schleifstein of the *New Orleans Times-Picayune* could have written between 2002 and August, 2005 that would have better prepared New Orleans for Hurricane Katrina?

4 Go to www.NOLA.com and read about a typical day in New Orleans. Does the news today reflect any lasting effects of the hurricane?

5 Traffic on www.NOLA.com increased by 1,133 percent between August 27 and September 1, 2005. At the same time, radio station WWL-AM combined with other New Orleans radio stations to continue broadcasting live 24 hours. If you were responsible for

either or both of these two news organizations, how would you organize the content that they would disseminate?

6 Review the most recent Gallup Poll on the environment. Interview three students or colleagues about the findings and write a short news story.

7 Carefully read your local newspaper and a national newspaper for one week. Identify any news stories about climate change. Compare findings. Were you surprised by what you found?

8 For further reading, consider Elizabeth Kolbert's *Field Notes From a Catastrophe: Man, Nature and Climate Change* (2006), *The Reporter's Environmental Handbook* by Bernadette West, Peter Sandman and Michael Greenberg (2003), Barbara Kingsolver's *Prodigal Summer* (2000) and *The Path of Destruction* (2006) by John McQuaid and Mark Schleifstein.

Chapter 2

History of environmental communications

Rachel Carson's (1962) *Silent Spring* was to the twentieth century what Harriet Beecher Stowe's (1981) *Uncle Tom's Cabin* was to the nineteenth century and Thomas Paine's (1964) *Common Sense* to the eighteenth century. The modern environmental movement arose from the pages composed by this shy biologist turned writer. Carson's treatise affected millions. Her arrival was timely. Disgust was growing over the oil spills, toxic waste and foul air and water that had been tolerated in previous generations. The book's publication and its revelations about pesticides acted as the watershed moment in the U.S. and internationally for how society viewed both environment and technology. Carson's achievement was so powerful that it has overshadowed earlier environmentalists and environmental writers. Carson and the writers and journalists who followed owe a great deal to those early pioneers.

The early environmental messages

Civilized societies tampered with the environment, rarely for the better. Clearing the land and tilling the soil meant more crops, but it could lead to over-farming and erosion. Congregating in communities made life more secure from hunger and enemies but it spread waste and disease. Over time, civilizations such as those developed in China and Peru learned the value of conservation by terracing hillsides both to increase production as well as to prevent soil erosion. Sewer systems developed as early as 2500 BC in India, and Babylonian communities had strict rules about sanitation. Yet for every action there was an unanticipated reaction. Too often dust and wood smoke hung over communities. Streets reeked of garbage, sewage and fumes from smelters, tanners and other industries. Pollution and waste were not only tolerated but expected. A rare exception was recorded in 1306 when Edward I of England banned burning coal while Parliament was in session (Kovarik, 1997).

Early records of written or visual communication about the environment are scant. Art preceded the written word. Early cave paintings, which date back more than 40,000 years, depicted an environment of game and scenes of daily life. As civilizations developed, eastern artists favored landscapes and profiles of the environment more than western artists. Written testaments were also scarce until Europeans discovered moveable type. One of the first true books about the environment, Izaak Walton's *The Compleat Angler*, was published in 1640 (Kovarik, 1997).

Some of the first true writers of the environment may have been geographers or explorers who at the completion of their journeys described new lands. From the days of Homer to the late twentieth-century exploration of the planets, society has always wanted to know what was over the next hill. Detailed written accounts, followed by maps, illustrations, photographs and television images, depicted the new lands, often with great enthusiasm, to an eager audience. Christopher Columbus in a 1492 journal entry shortly after his arrival in what may have been Cuba described climbing a small mountain. He said the land "was so beautiful that his eyes would never tire of beholding so much beauty" (Shabecoff, 1993, p. 9). More than 300 years later when President Thomas Jefferson sent Captains Meriwether Lewis and William Clark up the Missouri River his command was not just to find a suitable passage to the Pacific Ocean. The expedition was ordered to compile a detailed accounting of the continent's natural resources. Lewis' and Clark's journals detailed what plants and animals they encountered, as well as the nature of the terrain and its availability for farming and mining. Accounts by Daniel Boone (Shabecoff, 1993) and John C. Fremont about the west were widely publicized; they strongly encouraged westward expansion by the new American republic.

America's nineteenth-century bounty inspired a new generation of American painters and writers who strived to portray this vast environment. John James Audubon shot, killed, mounted and then painted what was to become in 1826 his great folio, *The Birds of America*. George Catlin roamed the American west, painting Indians and the environment of the 1830s in what has become a priceless legacy. Catlin was one of the first to suggest that the federal government create a national park to preserve the Plains and its people (Shabecoff, 1993). Later, artists such as Thomas Cole and the Hudson River School strived to capture the scenic beauty of eastern rivers, gorges and seascapes. Sometimes the landscapes were under sunny, idyllic skies. Other times they were threatened by dark, looming thunderheads. The message was clear – nature was untamed and unpredictable. American writers too struggled to do justice describing this North American wild. James Fenimore Cooper's (1823/1959) Natty Bumppo in *The Pioneers* was trapped at the age of 71 by the restrictions of civilization after having spent a lifetime of freedom in the natural world. Cooper inspired

Figure 2.1 Yosemite in California's Sierra Nevada mountain range and other wonders of the western United States drew exploration and later settlers who inevitably changed the environment (source: courtesy National Parks Service).

Francis Parkman, who in 1849 wrote *The Oregon Trail* (1849/1943), which deplored the unrelenting changes society was making to the environment of the American west.

Henry David Thoreau emerged in the nineteenth century as a strong voice on behalf of nature and conservation. Born in 1817 in Concord, MA, Thoreau rarely ventured far from home even when he made some celebrated trips around New England. Thoreau joined another great Massachusetts writer and contemporary, Ralph Waldo Emerson, in writing in favor of nature and the importance of a natural life uncomplicated by the growing demands of industry and technology. The Industrial Age that would transform society and the environment was getting underway; yet it worried Thoreau. In his writings, many of which were only embraced years after his death, he argued for the concepts of preserving the natural order and of maintaining land as untrammeled as possible. He was in favor of animal rights and unafraid to protest or stop those who were harming natural resources. They were new ideas for the time, and nowhere were they spelled out as clearly as they were in his seminal masterpiece, *Walden*, completed in 1854. After spending two years in a rude cabin on Walden Pond, Thoreau wrote:

> I went into the woods because I wished to live deliberately, to confront only the essential facts of life, and see if I could not learn what it had to teach, and not, when I came to die, discover I had not lived. I did not wish to live what was not life, living is so dear; nor did I wish to practice resignation, unless it was quite necessary. I wanted to live deep and suck out all of the marrow of life, to live to sturdily and Spartan-like as to put to rout all that was not life, to cut a broad swath and a close shave, to drive life into a corner and reduce it to its lowest terms.
>
> (Thoreau, 1854/1930, p. 78)

Another New England native, George Perkins Marsh (Marsh, 1864/1965), built on Thoreau's treatise. Marsh's 1864 book *Man and Nature* argued that society was altering nature's balance of power. By harming the environment, he contended, mankind was ultimately damaging society. Both Thoreau and Marsh were ahead of their times. It would be decades before some of these concepts gained widespread credibility.

Journalism, muckraking and the rise of conservation

Some historians mark the birth of modern journalism as the 1830s when editor Benjamin Day began the *New York Sun* and the Penny Press era. For one cent the *Sun* offered easy to read stories that concentrated on crime news and political corruption. Imitators quickly followed, each trying to outdo the next. The stories featured sensationalism, violence and mayhem. Others were outright fabrication. Not everyone joined the fray. There has always been enough breadth in journalism to provide for both the sensationalists and the serious. Over the next two centuries this pattern would return in cycles. As technology changed the nature of journalism it evolved from newspapers to radio, to television and to the Internet. Disparity in defining what constitutes news is important when considering coverage of science and the environment. Sensationalists so often made a mockery of it. That legacy has continued to complicate the relationship between science and journalism. One of the first efforts by the *New York Sun* to report on science in 1835 turned out to be a hoax (Neuzil, 2005).

As New York newspapers became more popular their influence grew. William Cullen Bryant, editor of the *New York Evening Post*, in 1844 wrote an editorial urging the creation of a great new park in New York. That idea was the spark that led to the creation of Central Park in 1851. Bryant went on to write and praise such natural landmarks as the Palisades, the Delaware River Gap and the Catskills. He also was a

The moon hoax

Supermarket tabloid newspapers reveal the secrets of the universe, from the lives of Hollywood starlets to the aliens visiting the planet. Extraterrestrial life has been a staple of American journalism for nearly 200 years, a sordid history of why many scientists have become disenchanted with science and environmental reporting.

That history began in 1835 when Benjamin Day and the *New York Sun* printed dispatches under the byline of a noted scientist of the day, John Herschel, but in actuality they were written by reporter Richard Adams Locke. Over six days the *Sun* reported how Herschel had obtained funding for a powerful telescope that he set up near Cape Town, South Africa. The telescope was supposed to be strong enough to see objects on the moon as small as 18 inches in diameter. Peering through the telescope, Herschel reportedly identified meadows, forests, a lake, a beach and animal life. Next he purportedly spotted miniature bison, reindeer, elk, beaver, moose and horned bear. After several days Herschel had discovered people who had bat-like wings and who stood about four feet tall with copper-colored hair, yellow flesh and prominent beards (Neuzil, 2005).

The stories created a sensation. Crowds gathered outside the offices of the *Sun* waiting for that day's next edition, competitors of what was called the New York Penny Press were soon printing their own stories of the moon discoveries and the *Sun*'s circulation soared to a point where it had a greater circulation run than any other known newspaper in the world. Theologians discussed the prospects of missionary work on the moon while scientists from Yale College arrived at the *Sun*'s offices in New York seeking more information on Herschel's discoveries. Knowing when to quit, Locke ended the series on the sixth day by having the telescope burn up (Neuzil, 2005).

Journalism historian Mark Neuzil (2005) wrote that at first the scientist, Herschel, was amused by the series. "But people continued to pester him" wrote Neuzil and eventually Herschel issued a letter to the editor calling the stories "incoherent ravings" (Neuzil, 2005, p. 37). Locke later confessed to the hoax, although he called it a satire. The *Sun* never conceded that it had done anything wrong.

good friend of an editor at the *Brooklyn Eagle*, Walt Whitman, who sometimes wrote about nature in his later years when he became one of America's greatest poets (Frome, 1998).

As industrialization grew so did the concept of conservation. The era produced two great writers in behalf of preserving nature, George Bird Grinnell and John Muir. Grinnell joined the staff of *Field and Stream* in 1876 and later became owner and editor-in-chief. His editorial voice championed the establishment of both the national park system and the national forests. He closely allied himself with the nation's first conservation president, Theodore Roosevelt, and he helped organize a bird protection society which was called the Audubon Club (Shabecoff, 1993). Muir is known for his work in publicizing the beauty of the Sierra Nevadas and Yosemite. Muir and Robert Underwood Johnson, editor of *The Century Magazine*, led the campaign that created Yosemite National Park. Muir's books and journals argued strongly in favor of preserving the wilderness. "Thousands of tired, nerve-shaken, over-civilized people are beginning to find out that going to the mountains is going home; that the wilderness is a necessity; and that mountain parks and reservations are useful not only as fountains of time and irrigating rivers but as fountains of life," he wrote (S. Fox, 2004, p. 116). In 1892 Muir helped create one of the nation's early environmental organizations, the Sierra Club (Shabecoff, 1993).

The arrival of the twentieth century produced some of the finest and some of the worst examples of American journalism. The Penny Press was long gone, but a new era of sensationalism arrived with Yellow Journalism, William Randolph Hearst and Joseph Pulitzer. The two publishers competed daily to produce the most outrageous news in their respective newspapers. The competition could be fierce. In 1909 newspapers clashed over their respective sponsorship of who would reach the North Pole first, Frederick A. Cook or Robert E. Peary (Riffenburgh, 1993).

The sensationalism of Yellow Journalism was contrasted by the superb investigative journalism of the muckrakers. The greatest of these was Lincoln Steffens (1931), a reporter for newspapers in New York and later for *McClure's* and *American Magazine*, who specialized in exposing political bosses in his "Shame of the Cities" series. Among the graft and waste he uncovered was the timber frauds in the Pacific Northwest forests. Railroad and lumber companies cut fraudulent deals with public officials responsible for those resources. Frank Norris, another muckraker, wrote the book *The Octopus* (1901/1986), which exposed the greed of the railroad companies that were altering the environment of the west by opening vast tracts of land (McGrath, 2006).

Women would take an increasingly active role in the twentieth century and two pathfinders were Ida Tarbell and Alice Hamilton.

Tarbell was a muckraking journalist whose expose of the Standard Oil Company concentrated on John D. Rockefeller's ruthless business methods and the way his company transformed America and its environment (Tarbell, 1904). Hamilton was a physician who in 1910 began a series of on-site factory inspections for the U.S. Bureau of Labor who documented that lead at many factories was poisoning workers. Her reports shamed companies into cleanups and was the precursor to such occupational disease programs as the Public Health Service and the Occupational Safety and Health Administration (Opie, 1998).

One era led to another. The 1920s brought Tabloid Journalism, yet some journalists were finally beginning to take science more seriously. In 1924, a story in the *San Diego Sun* about a solar eclipse was awarded the nation's most important journalism award, the Pulitzer Prize (Snyder & Morris, 1962). Ten years later, 12 reporters created the National Association for Science Writers. Soon after, in 1937, the Pulitzer jury awarded prizes to five science writers (Burkett, 1973). Basic science and medical research dominated the awards and much of the coverage but some environmental reporting was getting noticed. Ecological disasters such as the dust storms of the Plains states demanded attention. Pollution also could not be ignored. In 1940 the *St. Louis Post-Dispatch* led a campaign against the industrial soot and smoke fouling the city. It won a Pulitzer Prize for that campaign (Hohenberg, 1974).

Aldo Leopold (1949/1966) became a powerful voice for the environment, although few would hear him until after his death in 1948. Leopold for years worked in the Forest Service and helped found the Wilderness Society. But his influence was especially felt in his book, *Sand County Almanac*, published posthumously in 1949 and called "one of environmentalism's sacred texts" (Shabecoff, 1993, p. 90). Leopold advanced the evolving philosophy of environmentalism, taking it further than Thoreau, Marsh, Muir and others. Leopold said that government had to go beyond just establishing parks by protecting undeveloped land and wilderness. He also wrote that humanity needed a new set of rules for dealing with nature, a set that was not based on the concept that mankind was the conqueror who held the power of life or death over ecosystems. He said it needed to be rooted in science, but at the same time predicated on the love and reverence for nature. Many of his arguments set the stage for the next act. Enter a shy biologist.

The silent spring of Rachel Carson

Dichlorodiphenyltrichloroethane, which became known as DDT, was first used as an insecticide in 1939. The white powder was extremely effective in wiping out colonies of mosquito larvae. During and after World War II the spraying of the insecticide was credited with wiping out malaria in the developed world and drastically reducing it globally. By 1970 it was estimated that DDT had saved 500 million lives. The chemist who invented it, Paul Muller, won the Nobel Prize in 1948 for his work (Watson, 2003).

DDT was so popular that in the 1950s American communities were using it to spray entire neighborhoods in order to kill unwanted pests, including gypsy moths that defoliated trees and beetles that carried Dutch elm disease. The problem was that it killed indiscriminately. In 1958, the *Boston Herald* published a letter to the editor from a resident who had found seven dead songbirds in her yard after the neighborhood had been sprayed. She wanted the poison spraying stopped (Watson, 2003).

Rachel Carson was a friend of the letter writer. When she read it she recalled a story proposal she had written in 1945 about DDT to *Reader's Digest*. At the time she was 28, had a master's degree in zoology, was a biologist for the U.S. Bureau of Fisheries and four years earlier had published her first book, *Under the Sea-Wind* (Carson, 1941). The book had sold fewer than 2,000 copies. The *Reader's Digest* editors rejected the DDT story idea. In the 13 years since Carson had written two more books, including *The Sea Around Us* (1951) which became a bestseller and won a National Book Award. Carson, as a scientist, was not opposed to DDT, but she did have concerns about its

Figure 2.2 Rachel Carson's 1962 book *Silent Spring* forced Americans to think differently about their environment. The shy biologist and author had no idea the book could have such an impact.

increased use without greater public awareness or knowledge of its full impact. She decided to write her next book about DDT and its ramifications. Her tentative title was *Man Against the Earth*.

She had expected the task to take several months. Instead it took more than four years. In 1960 she was diagnosed with breast cancer. She underwent a mastectomy and later radiation treatments sometimes left her nauseated and bedridden. Carrying the title *Silent Spring*, the book was published in June, 1962, after first appearing as a three-part serial in the *New Yorker* magazine.

In *Silent Spring* she called chemicals a sinister force that changes the nature of life. She went on to say:

> Among them are many that are used in man's war against nature. Since the mid-nineteen forties, over 200 basic chemicals have been created for use in killing insects, weeds, rodents and other organisms described in the modern vernacular as pests; and they are sold under several different brand names.
>
> The sprays, dusts and aerosols are now applied almost universally to farms, gardens, forests, and homes – nonselective chemicals that have the power to kill every insect, the good and the bad, to still the song of birds and the leaping of fish in the streams – to coat the leaves with a deadly film and to linger on in soil – all this, though intended target may be only a few weeds or insects. Can anyone believe it is possible to lay down such a barrage of poisons on the surface of the earth without making it unfit for all life? They should not be called "insecticides" but "biocides."
>
> (Carson, 1962, p. 7)

The chemical industry had prepared for months for the publication of *Silent Spring*. Even before the book's release it attacked the publication. Velsicol Corporation, a pesticide manufacturer, threatened to sue for libel and Monsanto published a brochure called "The Desolate Year," which described a world beset by famine, disease and insects because insecticides had wrongly been banned. The National Agricultural Chemicals Association launched a $250,000 campaign to refute the book's findings and it may have influenced at least some reviewers. *Life* magazine reported that Carson had "overstated her case" and *Time* called the book an "emotional and inaccurate outburst" (Watson, 2003, p. 251).

Some of Carson's prose was purposely emotional and hard-hitting, beginning with such chapter titles as Elixirs of Death, Needless Havoc, and No Birds Sing. Carson's research was not new. Based on years of scientific study, the book included detailed notes and references. In anticipation of attack, it had been read by a number of scientists. One of the first to publicly support the book, Supreme Court Justice William O. Douglas, called it "the most important chronicle of this century for the human race" (Watson, 2003, p. 251). Sales were brisk and by Christmas 1962, 100,000 copies had been sold. At the request of President John Kennedy, his Science Advisory Commission studied the issue of DDT and chemicals. In May, 1963 the commission reported that while pesticides could be useful and more research was needed, Carson's primary thesis was sound in saying that such chemicals should not be used indiscriminately. It criticized both the government and the chemical industry and it called for an orderly reduction in the use of pesticides. Nine years later DDT was banned. Yet society's reliance on pesticides remains unabated. In 1960 United States chemical companies produced about 32,000 tons of pesticides and 40 years later that number reached 615,000 tons. While pesticides today are far less toxic and break down faster, insects are continuing to develop chemical resistance to many of them (Watson, 2003).

The impact of Carson's *Silent Spring* cannot be measured solely by how it affected pesticides. Carson set the stage for a new era by encouraging readers to question, rather than to accept, what industry was doing to the environment and to human health. The publication came at a pivotal period of American history that would be marked by increased social and political protests of both government and society. Former Vice President Al Gore, in a foreword to a reprint of the book, questioned whether the environmental movement ever would have developed without the publication of *Silent Spring*. Carson's biographer, Linda Lear, said the public never quite looked at chemicals the same way after *Silent Spring*. "She changed the way we look at nature," Lear said. "We now know we are a part of nature, and we can't damage it without it coming back to bite us" (Watson, 2003, p. 253).

Carson missed witnessing what has since been called the rise of the modern environmental movement. By the fall of 1963 public support had clearly swung in her favor. The shy biologist who had once been "scared to death" when cajoled into accepting speaking engagements, now was sought after both to talk and to accept awards and praise. Her cancer was also progressing; soon she arrived at podiums in a wheelchair. She died in April, 1964. In her obituary the *New York Times* reported that some had compared Carson unfavorably with Carrie Nation, the hatchet-wielding temperance leader of an earlier time. Carson rejected the notion that she was a crusader, arguing that she was only a writer and scientist trying to present the facts so that the public could decide ("Rachel Carson," 1964). That approach set the model for the next generation of environmental journalists.

A toxic waste

In 1969 a Union Oil rig began to spill oil into the Santa Barbara Channel. Soon oil was washing onto California beaches. Day after day television and newspapers showed pictures and told stories of oil-stained birds caught in the muck and of the volunteers trying to save them. The accident shocked Americans who had already begun worrying about varying forms of pollution carrying names such as phosphates, PCBs, mercury and smog. Then flammable chemicals on the Cuyahoga River in Cleveland ignited. In April, 1970 the first Earth Day drew millions of participants around the country. People were demanding changes. The federal government under President Richard Nixon responded with a series of far-reaching environmental bills, including the creation of the Environmental Protection Agency. News organizations changed their focus, devoting new resources to the environment. *Time* and *Saturday Review* started regular sections on the environment, *Life* increased its coverage and *Look* and *National Geographic* produced special reports. Still, only "a handful" of reporters at daily newspapers were covering the beat, estimated Philip Shabecoff, who began writing about the environment in the 1970s for the *New York Times*. Even then he had to write out of the newspaper's Washington bureau about other domestic issues such as labor, consumer affairs and health policy (Shabecoff, 2004).

Jim Detjen (1991), an environmental reporter for the *Philadelphia Inquirer* and now the director of the Knight Center for Environmental Journalism at Michigan State University, remembered working in the 1970s with an environmental activist to discover how a manufacturer was dumping into a local river without the proper permits. There was no question the dumping was illegal and the company eventually pleaded guilty to violating federal pollution statutes. Detjen said it was a classic case of good guy vs. bad guy. The environment had been abused for so long that such stories were easy to find and had become the norm. By now, everyone was getting onto the environmental story. Pulitzer Prizes were awarded in 1967 to the *Louisville Courier-Journal* for its exposé about a Kentucky strip mine, to the *Milwaukee Journal* for its fight against water pollution in Wisconsin and in 1971 to the *Winston-Salem Journal and Sentinel* for stories about another strip mining operation in the Carolina hill country.

One of the biggest stories of the 1970s came out of Niagara Falls, NY when a local reporter, Michael Brown, wrote a story about how the Hooker Chemical Company had buried hazard chemicals beneath a residential neighborhood. The neighborhood, Love Canal, became the poster child for the hazards of toxic chemicals. It also led to the creation of the federal Superfund effort that spent billions of dollars clean-

The Nixon legacy

No one ever accused President Richard Nixon of being a tree-hugger, let alone an environmentalist. But midway through his first term in office he had a problem. The first Earth Day had just occurred, political polls showed strong voter support for the environment and his prospective opponent in 1972 was U.S. Senator Edmund Muskie, who many called Mr Environment.

Faced with that dilemma, Nixon and his administration allowed unprecedented environmental gains. The Environmental Protection Agency was established in 1970 and in a short period Congress also passed the Endangered Species Act, the Clean Air Act, the Clean Water Act, the Marine Mammal Protection Act, the Coastal Zone Management Act, while also banning DDT and dramatically expanding the national parks system. Nixon appointed several strong environmental advisors, including Russell Train, John Whitaker, and Walter Hickel. They helped mold the new EPA into a more powerful regulator than many expected (Flippen, 2000).

By 1972 Muskie was out of the race and Nixon began to question his policy to appease green voters. J. Brooks Flippen (2000), who wrote the book *Nixon and the Environment*, said that Nixon eventually concluded he could win without the environmentalists. In stump speeches he called them part of the "wacko fringe" and he went on to an overwhelming re-election victory that eventually was marred by the Watergate scandal and his resignation two years later (Flippen, 2000).

ing up old waste sites around the country. Love Canal catapulted to fame a 27-year-old homemaker named Lois Gibbs whose chief aim initially was to find out why her two children kept getting mysterious ailments. Soon she was a community organizer who helped initiate an unprecedented evacuation of the Love Canal neighborhood that cost $17 million. Eventually Gibbs moved to Washington, DC, and helped organize other local activists. Supporters said it gave credence to grass-roots efforts. Critics said it was an expression of social selfishness (Shabecoff, 1993).

Many stories in the 1970s and 1980s were often shaped by a white-hat–black-hat attitude. According to studies reporters seemed to be greatly relying on interviewing government officials, environmental activists and business groups (Sachsman *et al.*, 2006). There was far less reliance on science sources or even an understanding of the social, economic or science creating some of these stories. The derisive term eco-journalism was defined as "the practice of reporting ecological crises by ignoring, treating as unimportant, or mishandling the evidence on which the crises are based" (Friedman, 1991, p. 20). Another criticism was that local newspapers too often reported environmental problems in distant geographic areas as opposed to looking in their own communities.

There was also confusion about when a story was really environmentally oriented as opposed to politically driven. When President Ronald Reagan took office in 1981 and appointed Anne Gorsuch to head the EPA and James Watt as Interior Secretary the attention focused on how far the administration would attempt to curtail environmental policy. In some respects it was a classic Washington insider story.

Television tells the story

On March 30, 1979 Walter Cronkite faced the cameras for the 5:30 broadcast of the CBS Evening News and began: "Good Evening. The world has never known a day quite like today" (Stephens, 1980, p. 4). Over the next 19 minutes Cronkite described the developing story centering on the crippled Three Mile Island facility. He called it the worse nuclear accident of the atomic age and warned "the horror tonight is that it could get much worse" (Stephens, 1980, p. 4). Never before had CBS devoted so much time to a single story. In some respects, the story of a damaged nuclear reactor was not a good fit for television. This visual medium depends on pictures; there were few except for the concrete cooling towers that rose above the Pennsylvania countryside.

Television, and its predecessor radio, has always had a time advantage over its competitors in print. As the Three Mile Island story developed hour by hour it gave television an edge from the start. Television held it because the tale was so dramatic and the reports kept changing. One of the other major characteristics of the environmental story in the post-*Silent Spring* era was that such stories have often been tied to a disaster or emergency. That format can work well for television, at least in getting out basic details.

Some stories, even in the early days of television, were clearly visual. Edward R. Murrow in the 1950s ran the "See It Now" news program that looked at a wide variety of stories. In one segment Murrow and the television camera watched the Missouri River crest between Omaha and Council Bluff in what at the time was an historic flood. He also flew through the eye of Hurricane Edna aboard a U.S. Weather Service airplane and again the camera caught the immensity of what a giant storm looks like from the air. In a 1963 "CBS Reports," after Murrow had left the network, Rachel Carson appeared on camera to defend her work. This was a different visual image, but it could also be compelling. Viewers watched her and felt that she was both thoughtful and reserved. Hundreds wrote letters in support of Carson and to the federal government urging it to do something about DDT (Kendrick, 1969).

The 1984 chemical spill in Bhopal, India, the 1986 nuclear accident at Chernobyl and the 1989 oil spill by the tanker the *Exxon Valdez* in Alaska, were such dramatic environmental catastrophes that they drew extensive television coverage by U.S. television networks, despite obstacles of both distance and, in the case of the Russians, government hostility to the release of information.

By 1990 network television had reporters specializing in covering the environment and CNN was devoting a regular weekly news program about the environment. Environmental issues were also routinely covered in more entertainment-oriented programming such as *Nova*, *Nature*, *National Geographic* and Mutual of Omaha's *Wild Kingdom*. Local television stations also discovered the power of the beat. "Environmental reporting has tested very well from Portland, Maine to Toledo, Ohio," said Jim Will, a television consultant for the firm Audience Research & Development in 1991. "There is no one regional area that is more intense about it than other areas" (Brown, 1991, p. 56). In

Figure 2.3 Workers struggle to clean up oil spilled from the *Exxon Valdez* accident in 1989 in Alaska. The accident drew new attention to the consequences of a major oil spill (source: courtesy National Oceanic & Atmospheric Administration).

West Palm Beach, FL, a local station, WPEC-TV, said that it had made the environmental beat a significant part of its coverage. It had produced three 30-minute broadcasts on environmental issues, winning one local Emmy award, causing its two competitors to also upgrade their environmental coverage. Another station based in New Orleans, WDSU-TV, had a reporter who was producing five environmental stories a week as well as a topical series each month for the evening news (Brown, 1991).

The appreciation did not last. Television consultants and news executives got bored with the complexities and uncertainties of the environmental story. Many seemed ill-prepared by the early years of the 2000s to cover such stories as climate change.

Finding more complexity

In the summer of 1988 a severe heatwave hovered for weeks over the East Coast, a drought afflicted other parts of the U.S. and news stories began questioning whether global warming had arrived. The increased focus on the environment prompted *Time* magazine (1989) a few months later to call an endangered earth the "Planet of the Year." The coverage highlighted both the strengths and the weaknesses of the environmental beat. The problem was that once again the coverage was breaking down into simplistic storylines. The issue of climate change was real, but to cast it in the perspective of a weather pattern of a few months was at the very least naïve. Still, the coverage was extensive, the number of journalists reporting on the environment was still increasing, and as the 1990s moved into the twenty-first century at least some were grasping the realities of what was becoming an increasingly complex beat (Friedman, 2004).

Sharon Friedman of Lehigh University has followed the development of the environmental beat for over 30 years. In 1990, writing about the first 20 years, she had been fairly critical and wondered if the coverage would ever mature. Too many stories relied on too few sources, did not provide enough perspective, and coverage seemed rooted to transitory events, she complained (Friedman, 1991).

More than a decade later Friedman (2004) took another look and she was more encouraged. She said the development of a professional environmental news organization, better training, database resources and the Internet had helped better prepare environmental journalists. One reporter told her that many were realizing that the story was more than pollution and critters. Another said:

> The belching smokestacks and burning rivers of the 70s, that gave rise to the environmentalism of the 70s and 80s, had been cleaned

up. The obvious stories gave way to more complex issue:
ticulate air pollution, climate change, endocrine disrup
more non-point source water pollution. The challenge gre
the big stories, the big issues and to explain them thorough
space and time constraints.

(Friedman, 2004, p. 179)

A common complaint made during the first decade of the twenty-first century was that too many environmental reporters were being reassigned to other stories. They were having difficulty finding enough time to develop the most complex stories that made up the environment beat. They also reported that space both in newspapers and television was shrinking. This was a common lament for both the print and broadcast reporters, whether they were on general assignment or covered specialties. Environmental reporters also knew from the history of their beat that another big disaster or emergency story was never very far away. It might be another accident or a spill. One way or another they knew it would generate new interest and leave editors demanding more perspective. That meant that page one or the top of the daily newscast was always within reach (Ward, 2004).

Study guide

1 Write a lead reporting the *New York Sun* story about life on the moon is a hoax. The challenge here is to be concise, no more than 35 words, factual about the extent of the fraud without being opinionated.

2 Henry David Thoreau and Ralph Waldo Emerson were both proponents of transcendentalism, a nineteenth-century philosophical movement. Research transcendentalism and write a one-page essay on its major points and how it approached the issue of nature and the environment.

3 Based on the information in this chapter and other sources, write a concise 400-word profile of Rachel Carson.

4 Find a local environmental news story. Carefully examine the sources quoted. Why did the writer select the science, government, advocates or citizens? Is there one particular segment or voice missing that you think should have been consulted?

5 Many individuals have played a role in the history of the development of the environmental movement in the U.S. Who are Frederick Law Olmsted, Gifford Pinchot, Robert Marshall, Ansel Adams, David Brower, and Gaylord Nelson? Why are they important?

6 What is the biggest environmental story since Rachel Carson wrote *Silent Spring*? On what do you base this assessment?

7 For further reading, consider Rachel Carson's *Silent Spring* (1962), Henry David Thoreau's *Walden* (1930), John Opie's *Nature's Nation* (1998) and Philip Shabecoff's *A Fierce Green Fire* (1993).

Part II

Reporting the beat

Chapter 3

Understanding risk

In the early 1990s a group of parents in a fashionable suburban town became alarmed that their children were in danger from playing soccer twice a week on a local high school field. The parents were not worried that the kids might be hurt by falling, running into each other, or getting hit by the soccer ball. They also did not fear that older high school students might prey upon the younger children. Not even a lightning strike was their concern.

The parents were upset because one end of the field was traversed by high-powered electric transmission lines. They worried that their children might contract cancer.

For months the town had been battling plans to build a new electric transmission line corridor in a different part of the community. Residents near the proposed line were upset, because they would be able to see the unsightly lines from their homes and because recent research had suggested that the electromagnetic fields (EMFs) from the transmission lines could cause cancer. The EMFs were invisible but powerful enough that farmers living near power lines could describe how light bulbs mysteriously stayed on all night. A 1979 study suggested a link between the power lines and cases of childhood leukemia in Colorado (Taubes, 1994). Later, author Paul Brodeur (1989) wrote a well publicized book, *Currents of Death*, which suggested that the powerful electric utility industry had hidden the true dangers of EMFs. Parents in the suburban community realized that the power lines ran over a portion of the fields used by the town's youth soccer teams. Soon a clamor arose to either move the line from the field, or to move the field away from the line. Even if the research was not complete, said parents, wasn't it prudent to keep the teams away from the power lines?

We face risk daily. In this situation, running into another player or even being struck by lightning would appear to be more likely than getting cancer from EMFs. Research on EMFs showed that in virtually all cases the likelihood of a problem was based on prolonged exposure to the magnetic fields. People who lived near power lines or other sources of EMFs for many years were those most at risk. Their exposure would be anywhere from eight to 24 hours a day, almost every day of the year. Kids playing on a soccer field were going to be underneath the lines for no more than three or four hours a week at most for ten or 15 weeks in the year.

Why, then, were parents so upset? Perhaps they did not understand that the risk was based on a prolonged exposure. What they did know was that their children were being threatened by a force they could not see, that they could not control, and that it seemingly could cause a dreadful disease such as childhood cancer.

Another concern was that decisions had to be made with incomplete information. In 1999, after six years of research costing $60 million, the National Institute of Environmental Health Sciences announced that the evidence that EMFs caused cancer or other health problems was "weak." While the report has prompted some experts, including many in the electric utility industry, to maintain that EMFs are safe others maintain that society and individuals would be prudent to avoid unnecessary exposure. Even the NIEHS report urged utilities to alter large transmission lines and for electric codes to be adjusted to prevent household wiring that could produce a larger field than necessary (NIEHS, 1999).

Risk has dominated many environmental and public health issues. Yet, it has often been misunderstood. Researchers at the University of Michigan's Transportation Research Institute found a marked increase in motor vehicle fatalities between October and December 2001, in comparison to the same months the year before. Travelers were choosing to drive rather than fly after the September 11 terrorist attacks in the U.S. because they perceived flying to be more hazardous. The overwhelming evidence showed that this was not the case (Sivak & Flanagan, 2004). The key is to understand the level of risk. Douglas Hofstader (1985) described an invention that offered new conveniences with one liability – about every 18 years it would wipe out a population the size of San Francisco. The development was the automobile and the number of deaths was caused by the accidents they caused. Yet no one has suggested we ban cars and return transportation to the days of the horse and buggy (Cohn & Cope, 2001).

Identifying risk

The first step in understanding risk must be defining it. Researchers have broken down the definition into three parts:

- What was the hazard that might cause harm?
- How large a dose or quantity would it take before it became dangerous?

- How significant was the exposure that people could get? (Kamrin *et al.*, 1994)

Once those three concepts were understood, the level of the danger could be put into perspective. David Ropeik (2006b), former television journalist who specialized in risk communication at the Harvard School of Public Health, sometimes has posed this question: What risk would be greater, one that affected 76 million Americans each year or one that affected 7,000 each year? The response would seem obvious. It is not. Ropeik said that the 76 million is the amount of people who have suffered from food poisoning. One in four Americans contract it, and while the symptoms can be acute, they are usually temporary and rarely life threatening. In contrast, melanoma or skin cancer killed 7,000 Americans every year.

Hazard identification

The initial step of hazard identification attempts to assess whether a substance could cause harm. For instance, germs have been a part of our daily life. Some are harmful, some are harmless and some are actually beneficial. Rather than making a base assumption that all germs were hazardous, the priority should be identifying those germs that posed a danger. There are several ways to do this. One could observe

Figure 3.1 Scenes of workers dressed in hazardous waste suits became familiar beginning in the 1970s and caused Americans to label toxic waste as one of the bigger risks to the environment (source: courtesy Environmental Protection Agency).

people's reactions to certain substances. This was one of the ways that smoking was identified as a health hazard (Kamrin *et al.*, 1994). It was also how shipyard workers who came down with respiratory illnesses were identified to have been at risk from asbestos exposure (West *et al.*, 2003). But these epidemiological studies have had limitations because humans have been exposed over time to so many different substances. Another important way to identify hazard would be through studying animals, with the assumption that if the substance harmed an animal, it could likewise harm humans. Animal studies can be more carefully controlled and do not have to subject humans to any dangers. But animals have not been perfect indicators that humans would have the same problems and the laboratory conditions can be far different. Rats developed no adverse reactions when given a drug called thalidomide but pregnant human mothers had babies with serious birth defects, demonstrating that rodents were not always the best test subject. To put it another way, despite the best hopes for animal tests, a mouse is not a little human. Another complication has been that usually a select number of rats were exposed to large quantities of a substance over a relatively short period of time in an attempt to replicate human intake over a lifespan. In contrast, people have been exposed to small quantities of many substances over a long period (Cohn & Cope, 2001).

Exposure assessment

Even if a hazard can be identified, it would still not be a risk until one was exposed to it. This could be accomplished by measuring the amount of substance in the environment and calculating how much was taken in by individuals, either by inhaling, ingesting or absorbing it through the skin. For instance, a leak of benzene could be hazardous but it evaporates easily and breaks down quickly in the air. At the same time, it is soluble in water and does not easily absorb into soil. The risks vary significantly and the greatest would be a leak of a benzene substance that was poured onto the ground, got into the groundwater and reached humans through the water supply. Measurements could be made, both at the time of the leak and later to the water supply, although they might take time (Kamrin *et al.*, 1994). In reporting on a substance such as radiation, it is important to distinguish between actual human exposure and the compounding impact of the fallout to air, water, soil, crops and milk. The other factor that had to be included was duration of exposure and whether it was constant or intermittent. For instance, a plant explosion may sicken workers who inhaled fumes for only a few minutes. But those same fumes, in far lesser quantities over several years, might create even more serious health problems. The risk might be further complicated if the workers only used the chemicals periodically (Cohn & Cope, 2001).

Dose response

When calculating risk, the degree of the exposure or the dose also has to be considered. Many chemicals will vary in safety depending on quantities. Low amounts of chlorine safely purify water, which has made drinking water safe in systems around the world. High amounts of chlorine are extremely toxic. During World War I chlorine was the chief ingredient in deadly mustard gas. Often dose response relationships can be charted, with dose on one axis and response on the other. The curve or line would be drawn to show the relationship between dose and response. For example, a chart could show the risk of someone drowning while standing in a chamber higher than the person's head. When there was no water in the chamber, the risk of drowning was zero. As the water was added, the response remained flat until it got to the height of the mouth. Then the line suddenly would rise sharply upward and continue as it passed the nose and head, and then the ability to jump or float (West *et al.*, 2003). Another way to characterize this response rate would be in ratios. If test animals were fed a chemical and 25 of the 100 animals tested showed signs of getting a particular disease, the tests indicated that there was a one in four chance of developing the disease. However, another test with a different or higher dose might create a two out of three, or 66 percent, risk of getting a particular disease (Ropeik, 2006b).

Risk management

While science has established clear parameters to identify and measure risk, society has had greater difficulty in managing risk. Public policy managers have come up with systems such as risk management to consider the ramifications of what are acceptable and unacceptable risks. The public health field developed the concept of risk management in the twentieth century and it has spread to other fields including the environment. Risk managers in turn have developed tools such as risk assessment and risk benefit analysis to better measure the benefits and hazards. Risk analysis models look at the likelihood that a potential hazard would affect people. Cost-benefit analysis was based partly on economic models and was designed to show the cost of mitigating the problem.

Risk management has been harshly criticized at times by the very people who have been placed in charge of it. Former EPA Administrator William Ruckleshaus once said, "Risk administration data can be like a tortured spy. If you torture it long enough, it will tell you anything you want to know" (Cohn, 1989, p. 105). Added Vernon Houk of the Centers for Disease Control: "The difference between risk assessment and a five-year weather forecast is that at least with the weather forecast, if you wait five years you find out whether you were right" (Klaidman, 1991, p. 6).

The EPA in the 1980s made cleaning up hazardous waste sites a high priority even though both experts and risk analyses agreed that the comparative problem was far less serious than that posed by other risks. The assessed lifetime risk of cancer from hazardous waste ranged between one in 10,000 to one in 1,000,000, while cancer from radon in indoor air of many households was one in 100, smoking a pack of cigarettes or more a day ran a risk of eight in 100 and exposure to the sun leading to skin cancer was one in three. The EPA pressed on because its research also found that society was willing to spend $1 million mitigating environmental risk to prevent cancer in one person. This was occurring at the same time when the public was reluctant to spend $50,000 to sustain one person with a kidney dialysis machine. The public supported the Superfund clean up even though the EPA estimated it would cost $30 billion to tackle the 1,175 that were identified as the highest priority and up to $500 billion with the additional pollution sites authorities expected to find (Kunreuther & Patrick, 1991).

Unfinished business

In 1987 the EPA produced a study called "Unfinished Business, A Comparative Assessment of Environmental Problems" (Kunreuther & Patrick, 1991) which examined 31 environmental issues. Researchers consulted environmental managers at the agency and conducted public polling. It discovered a striking contrast in what each group felt were the highest priorities.

The public's concerns (ranked in order of importance)

- Active hazardous waste sites.
- Abandoned hazardous waste sites.
- Water pollution from industrial wastes.
- Occupational exposure to toxic chemicals.
- Oil spills.
- Destruction of the ozone layer.
- Nuclear power plant accidents.
- Industrial accidents releasing pollutants.
- Radiation from radioactive waste.

- Air pollution from factories.
- Leaking underground storage tanks.
- Coastal water contamination.
- Solid waste and litter.
- Pesticide risks to farm workers.
- Water pollution from agricultural run-off.
- Water pollution from sewage plants.
- Air pollution from vehicles.
- Pesticide residues in food.
- Greenhouse effect.
- Drinking water contamination.
- Destruction of wetlands.
- Acid rain.
- Water pollution from city run-off.
- Nonhazardous waste sites.
- Biotechnology.
- Indoor air pollution.
- Radiation from x-rays.
- Radon in homes.
- Radiation from microwave ovens.

EPA's 11 highest concerns (not ranked)

Ecological risks

- Global climate change.
- Stratospheric ozone depletion.
- Habitat alteration.
- Species extinction and biodiversity loss.

Health risks

- Criteria air pollution (e.g. smog).
- Toxic air pollution (e.g. benzene).
- Radon.
- Indoor air pollution.
- Drinking water contamination.
- Occupational exposure to chemicals.
- Application of pesticides.
- Stratospheric ozone depletion (Kunreuther & Patrick, 1991, p. 14).

The late Victor Cohn, who for many years was a science writer for the *Washington Post*, and Lewis Cope, a science writer for the *Minneapolis Star Tribune*, said that the problem with risk-based analysis was that it involved not only science but psychology, culture, ideology, economics, values and politics. He went on to ask:

> How do you put a cost on human life, or even on a pretty hilltop view? In deciding on the location for a waste disposal plant, how do we weigh the concerns of a small number of people who may live near the site with the much larger number of people whose wastes will fill the site?
>
> (Cohn & Cope, 2001)

In 2002 the administration of President George W. Bush was reminded of the fragility of economic-based risk assessments. John Graham, a risk analyst at Harvard University, had become head of the Office of Management and Budget. His office developed new regulations which directed EPA regulators to value the life of someone 70 or older at a level of only 63 percent as the life of someone younger (Borenstein, 2002). The principle behind the move was that it was fairer to count the years of life saved by a government regulation than the number of lives. The proposed regulation created such a furor that it was eventually withdrawn.

Journalists and risk

Journalists have also been accused of misunderstanding risk and one of the biggest critics has been John Graham, both at Harvard and OMB. He has complained that "what constitutes news is not necessarily what constitutes a significant public health problem." He said too often the press covered "the bizarre, the mysterious, that which people have difficulty imagining happening." He and others said that the press needed to focus on the greatest risks, such as smoking (Murray *et al.*, 2001, p. 116).

Reporters have been about equally divided on this issue of whether they understood risk sufficiently. "We have all been guilty, of course," said Christine Russell, former science writer with the *Washington Post* and *Washington Star*. She recalled how "reporters rushed from one environmental scare story to another and relentlessly provided readers with a weekly dose of worry" (Russell, 2006, p. 253). However, surveys of environmental reporters in the early 2000s found that an overwhelming number felt that they had not hyped or overstated risks (Sachsman *et al.*, 2006). James Bruggers, an environmental writer for the *Louisville Courier-Journal*, said he has not been afraid of using risk to alert the public of dangers in the environment. "I don't think there's anything wrong with scaring the public, as long as there's a good reason to do so," he said (McClure, 2003a, p. 5).

Part of this debate centered on a term many have long struggled to define – what was "news." One of the earliest stabs at a definition in the nineteenth century came from John B. Bogart, editor of the *New York Sun*, who said "When a dog bites a man that is not news, but when a man bites a dog that is news" (Morley, 1938, p. 677). Of course, if a rabid dog bit a man, that might be of interest. News that was negative, or that served as a warning or a threat, has been far more powerful than information that was viewed as positive or neutral. Some journalists believe that their colleagues too often veer to the extreme when reporting on risk issues. While balance was important, competitive pressure pushed both reporters and editors to the edge (Cohn & Cope, 2001).

A better way to understand the relationship between risk and journalism would be to review the traditional news criteria that have evolved in the profession from the days of Bogart's definition. Reviewing them clearly shows why some types of risk have warranted coverage while others have not. The criteria include:

- *Conflict* – news consumers have always been interested in disputes, whether they be personal or institutional, and the greater the degree of debate, tension or argument about the risk, the more likely it would be covered.
- *Human Interest* – news about people, that touched people emotionally, has been important. If the risk struck an emotional chord it was probably news.
- *Prominence* – well-known people and important recognizable issues revolving around risk have always been more important.
- *Proximity* – the closer the risk, the more it was newsworthy. Avian flu was a low risk when it began in Asia, but as the disease spread toward the U.S. it rose in importance to Americans.
- *Relevance* – news or risks that impacted people, or had the potential to affect them, have been important.
- *Timeliness* – up-to-date information about risks was prized. News that was occurring or had just occurred is far more likely to be pursued than something that has occurred over a long period of time (Itule & Anderson, 2007).

To get back to John Graham's criticism, the press has long been interested in the bizarre or mysterious. News consumers have been curious and want to learn more about the extraordinary.

Risk communications

Comparing these criteria to recent research into the field of risk communications also helped shed new light on risk coverage. Research indicated that there were both physical and psychological reasons for risk reactions. Much of the psychological research into risk perception was done by Paul Slovic of the University of Oregon and Baruch Fischhoff of Carnegie Mellon University. Additionally a risk consultant, Peter M. Sandman (1994), has conducted similar research and popularized it under the term outrage. "Outrage" described the reasons why people might judge risks emotionally as opposed to quantitatively. Some risk communicators believed that the term outrage was a poor word choice for identifying reactions to risk and that its connotations were too negative (Ropeik, 2006a).

The return of DDT?

In the 1960s the world nearly eradicated malaria. In the twenty-first century the number of cases was 350 million a year and still climbing (McNeil, 2006). About one million people a year have died of the disease, mostly children and pregnant women. The disease is especially widespread in the developing worlds of Africa, Asia and South America. In Uganda alone up to 100,000 fatalities occur annually. "It's like a jumbo jet crashing every day," said Dr. Andrew Collins, Deputy Director of the Malaria Consortium, an international group (Dugger, 2006, p. 2).

What happened? DDT was banned after Rachel Carson's *Silent Spring* (1962) demonstrated the immense environment damage it was causing. The problem has been that other control measures, from mosquito netting to insecticides to medicines to treat the disease, have been ineffective. Also, efforts to get these protections to the people most at risk have failed. Frustration has built in many countries and in international health communities and some have come to believe that using DDT again may be the solution. For years the United States had opposed such efforts but by 2006 it indicated it was changing its position (Dugger, 2006).

The risk issues were complicated by the fact that if DDT were deployed, the most efficient way it could be used would be to spray the pesticide over villages, including the living areas of residents (Rosenberg, 2004). While human health impacts so far have been minimal from DDT, the long-term effects remain a concern. The EPA has called DDT a probable carcinogen. There has also been some evidence that DDT can impair the infant's immunity system (Ropeik & Gray, 2002). Even when one understands all of the facts involving risk, making a decision can be daunting.

During the Great Depression, President Franklin Roosevelt tried to reassure Americans with the phrase "All we have to fear is fear itself" (Chapman, 2003, p. 17). Slovic and Fischhoff identified the reasons they believe people developed fear in this increasingly technological age. Among the factors:

- *Trust* – the less people trust those whom they look to protect them or who communicate risks, the more they have become afraid. The same applied to the people or companies who made the product or service that created the threat. The public was also far more likely to accept a risk statement from their physician than they would be from a source that they view more cynically, such as industry, government or the press.
- *Benefit* – the greater the perceived benefit, the less fearful people were of that risk. Fire has risks, but on a cold night when there were no other heating options its benefits became obvious.
- *Control* – people were less upset when they could manage the risk, as opposed to delegating it to someone else. The issue of control can relate to a direct action, such as sitting out in the sun and weighing the risks between using sunscreen, or getting a tan and being more susceptible to skin cancer. It can also be more direct, such as participating in a decision with others on siting an incinerator which would produce air pollution as opposed to watching business and government leaders make that determination.
- *Choice* – this was not a matter of controlling the risk but deciding whether to take it. With control, one weighed whether to use sunscreen or get a tan. With choice, the decision was whether or not to sit in the sun. There was less perceived risk if one could veto the potential hazard. People do not like to be forced to accept a risk such as a decision by a local community to build a nuclear power plant.
- *Natural* – the more a threat was part of nature, the less people feared it. The more it was made by humans, the higher the level of fear. People have become highly suspicious of radiation from a nuclear reactor generating electricity. They were far less alarmed about radon, a form of radiation that came naturally from the earth.
- *Dread* – the greater the degree of suffering from a threat, the greater the perceived risk. For instance, the U.S. spent far more on cancer research than on heart disease studies. In 2004 the National Cancer Institute had a budget of $4.7 billion to fight cancer compared to $1.8 billion for the National Heart, Lung and Blood Institute. Cancer annually killed about 550,000 Americans while nearly 700,000 died of heart disease. Cancer can be long and painful while a heart attack can be swift.
- *Catastrophic* – an airplane crash was a far bigger event than a

motor vehicle accident. That made the perceived risk of a plane crash greater than that of a car accident, even though most people are in motor vehicles far more often and autos cause far more deaths.

- *Uncertainty* – the less information about a risk, the more likely people will assume the worst. Uncertainty also applied to risks that people can not see, such as electromagnetic fields that occur from electric power lines or radiation.

- *Me vs. Them* – if the risk was one in a million, people would perceive that they were that one person in a million.

- *Familiar* – any material, chemical or event that was new, difficult to understand, or that even has a long, unusual scientific or technical name, was viewed as having greater risk. When stories first developed that cellular telephone use might cause brain cancer, the public was quick to assume the worst because at the time cell phones were relatively new to the market.

- *Vulnerable* – children in particular were seen as less able to cope for themselves so society has wanted to protect them. Any risk to children, therefore, was a heightened risk. The same applied to other vulnerable populations – the poor, the weak, or the handicapped.

- *Personification* – a risk made "real" by the story of someone who adversely experienced it was more frightening than a risk characterized by a statistic or by the hypothetical.

- *Awareness* – the more aware people were of a risk, the more concerned they would become. Awareness was often raised by the media, but could also be heightened through social or other contacts (Ropeik, in press).

Beyond these psychological factors affecting perceptions of risk, there have also physiological impacts. Neuroscientist Joseph LeDoux and his colleagues studied how the brain processed information that may appear threatening. They found that when an image or message was transmitted to the brain, the emotion of fear registered before more rational thought processes. Further, LeDoux suggested that the neural circuits leading to the portion of the brain where people feel fear essentially triggered a response, preparing the individual to either fight or flee. This response could be quite powerful emotionally in contrast to the reaction from the more rational portion of the brain (LeDoux, 1998).

How journalists can better report on risk issues

Obviously this task of trying to understand the relative hazards of various threats can be a risky business for both journalism and science. Once its nature and complexity were understood, it became easier to make decisions on what to focus on and what questions needed to be asked. The type of questions journalists should ask include:

- How great was the exposure of a hazard? Exposure of radiation from nuclear power plants can be widespread, but generally at levels far below natural sources. In contrast, research has shown that microscopic dust particles created from air pollution were widespread and when ingested did present a health hazard.
- What was the likelihood of the exposure and what safety measures were in place? Even though it can be difficult to measure the likelihood of a bioterrorist attack, the fact that an anthrax attack was carried out through the mail in the U.S. in 2001 was enough for the government to begin taking precautions.
- What was the legal standard for the substance? The standard for a pesticide such as DDT was essentially zero, because its production was banned in 1972.
- Was the source of the information reputable? Was it from one source, or multiple sources? Who funded the work? Much of the research on electromagnetic fields (EMFs) was financed by the electric industry. The industry had good reason to want answers and it

Figure 3.2 High-voltage electric transmission lines produce electromagnetic fields. In the 1980s they were considered a high risk because of concerns that the fields might cause cancer (source: courtesy Ania Beszterda).

also had deeper financial pockets than anyone else to get the work done. When much of that research showed that EMFs were not a significant health problem, the findings were tainted by charges that the industry had bought the results it wanted. That criticism quieted after the federal government completed its research in 1999.

- What were the benefits or trade-offs of the hazard? When airbags came on the market, the public was alarmed by the number of children who died after they were deployed. What was lost in the initial concerns was that airbags were still saving more lives than they were costing. In addition, as more information came to light, it was discovered that some of the deaths caused by airbags were complicated by motorists improperly wearing seat belts or incorrectly strapping infant car seats (Ropeik & Gray, 2002).

Another way to help understand risk would be to make comparisons, although risk researchers warn that this must be done carefully. One of the most common mistakes was to compare an involuntary risk with one that is voluntary. In the early 1990s a group that wanted to build trash incinerators in various communities argued that the emissions would be safer than eating peanut butter. They then produced studies that showed the amount of dioxins, a carcinogen in the emissions of incinerators, was less than aflatoxin, a naturally occurring carcinogen found in peanuts. Not surprisingly, the argument had little effect on opponents. Risks can also be compared to the potential benefits, to alternatives, to natural background levels and to regulatory standards.

Finally, journalists should use common sense and their natural reporting instincts. Dorothy Nelkin, who wrote extensively about the relationship between journalism and science, said that the biggest problem in risk reporting was the reluctance of reporters to challenge scientists (Cohn & Cope, 2001).

Study guide

1 Review the box that discusses how the EPA concluded that its risk assessment of various environmental issues differed significantly from the public's. Review the information with two or three other students or colleagues to gather quotes, and then write a story about the differences.

2 Based on the facts about DDT and malaria, write a news lead about the efforts to bring back the pesticide.

3 Review a news story about an environmental risk issue. How many of the traditional news criteria were involved that made this story

news? How many of the factors cited by Slovic and Fischhoff were in the story?

4 You have been assigned to do a story about attempts by the nuclear power industry to build a new, safer reactor. List the sources you would interview, the material you would review and the types of questions you would ask.

5 Taking the previous assignment a step further, besides making sure that the story fairly presents the risk issues, how would you work to make it readable?

6 Critics such as Peter Montague with the Environmental Research Foundation (Cohn & Cope, 2001) have worried about the flaws in risk assessments. He has suggested asking such questions as: who gave polluters the right to pollute? Where is the money from this project coming from? Who bears the risk and who benefits? Who decides what constitutes an acceptable risk? What do you think of these questions and would you use them in your reporting?

7 For further reading, consider Paul Brodeur's *Currents of Death* (1989), *Risk* by David Ropeik and George Gray (2002) and *A Field Guide for Science Writers* by Deborah Blum, Mary Knudson and Robin Morantz Henig (2006).

Chapter 4

Understanding science

For more than a decade Long Island, NY had lived in fear. Many residents were concerned that something in the island's environment was making them sick. After Rosalind Rubin was diagnosed with cancer she discovered that 15 of her neighbors in a four-block radius also had cancer. Other Long Island residents were also discovering what appeared to be cancer clusters. Activists had convinced Congress to appropriate $30 million to study cancer and the environment on Long Island (Fagin, 2002e).

Dan Fagin, formerly of *Newsday* and currently a journalism professor at New York University, had written many stories on the issue. In 2002 he produced a six-part series published in *Newsday* called "Tattered Hope" (Fagin, 2002a–f). It described how political pressures, inflated expectations and competing demands of activists had held up completion of the federally funded science studies. Worse, Fagin reported that none of the 12 studies would be able to answer the question of whether the environment was making people sick. In addition, New York's Health Department had been unable to ease the cancer cluster fears of Rubin and others. Fagin's stories also disclosed that health officials should have done a better job. *Newsday* retained a researcher who was able to produce a computer-assisted study indicating potential cancer clusters. The study was far more comprehensive than anything the Health Department had produced about Long Island.

Good environmental reporters understand science in order to explain and interpret it to readers. Some reporters have gone a step further by directing or doing scientific research. In recent years journalists have hired epidemiologists to find cancer clusters (Fagin, 2002f), conducted their own air tests for pollution (Cappiello, 2005a) and drawn their own blood to test it for the presence of potentially dangerous chemicals (Jones, 2001). The results have been startling. Some environmental writers have an extensive educational background in the sciences while others have picked it up on the job. The requirements are demanding since the stories range from marine science to nuclear physics to medi-

Figure 4.1 Scientists arrive at McMurdo Station, Ross Island, Antarctica, to begin field research. As concern about global warming has risen, scientists increasingly are focusing in areas such as the polar caps where the signs of change are most obvious (source: courtesy National Oceanic Atmospheric Administration).

cine. Journalists do not need to know the details of all disciplines but they should understand the basics of the scientific process.

Scientific process

The scientific process began many centuries ago with anecdotes which, while unreliable, were still provocative enough to get people thinking about the world around them. Anecdote evolved into observation, which was quite useful in watching the stars change and the tides ebb. Finally, around 1585, Galileo dropped some weights from a tower and introduced the idea of controlled experiments. Today the scientific method is well established and a basic taught in high school. A researcher must begin by developing a set of ideas and a hypothesis. He then conducts a test or procedure to see if the results match expectations. But doing the experiment can be easy in comparison to figuring out what it means and if it has been reliable (Cohn & Cope, 2001).

Clinical studies

A controlled, randomized clinical trial has been called the "gold standard" of scientific experiments. Such trials can be expensive and challenging. For every 100 scheduled trials only 20 on average produced any meaningful results. The most reliable were *parallel studies* that compared similar groups with different treatments or a treatment with one group and none with a second control group. In *crossover studies* the same patients received two or more treatments in succession and acted as their own controls. Another option would be to use historical controls where the comparison was made against old records or external controls where the comparison is with other studies. Clinical studies have worked for preventive measures, such as drugs, to combat a disease, but cannot be used to test the toxicity or danger of threats or hazards (Cohn & Cope, 2001).

Epidemiology studies

Epidemiology began with the search for the cause of diseases that often had environmental characteristics. One of the most famous was when John Snow in 1854 in London plotted cholera cases on a map and pinpointed the source to a drinking well because of the large cluster of cases surrounding the water source (S. Johnson, 2006). Basically epidemiology has been an observational study. It can be *descriptive*, such as describing the incidence and characteristics of a disease, *analytical*, where it seeks to analyze why a phenomena is occurring, or *ecological*, which seeks to look for a link between the environment and an illness (Cohn & Cope, 2001).

Epidemiology studies have been constructed as *case control studies*, *cross-sectional* or *prevalence studies* and *cohort studies*. In *case control studies* health history surveys are conducted on two groups, one with a disease and one without (Cohn & Cope, 2001). For example, in 1980 women who were diagnosed with toxic shock syndrome were interviewed along with women who did not have the disease. Researchers found that those with toxic shock were more likely than others to use a particular brand of tampon (Kamrin *et al.*, 1994). A *cohort study* is conducted to identify a group that differs on one or more characteristics and then that group is studied over time. A study begun in 1948 in Framingham, MA over time identified smokers as having a disproportionately high rate of lung cancer (Cohn & Cope, 2001). The *cross-sectional study* can be a quicker way for epidemiologists to identify a potential problem. It would involve interviewing a group about diseases and exposures to see if there were relationships. This method, while quick, usually has required further study to prove a cause and effect.

Many epidemiological studies have been *retrospective*, looking back in time at a person's medical records, vital statistics and recollections (Cohn & Cope, 2001). Most of the research in the Long Island, NY cancer studies was retrospective (Fagin, 2002c). Some researchers have questioned the reliability of data on environmental hazards in the community ten and 20 years prior. An alternative for epidemiologists would be to conduct *prospective studies* that worked into the future. That was how the Framingham study was conducted (Cohn & Cope, 2001). Because illnesses take years to develop, prospective studies can be expensive and time consuming.

Evaluating the results

Science would be far easier to understand if all the results reconciled. Over time, answers become clear but in its early stages science can be messy and its answers confusing and seemingly contradictory. Chlorine in drinking water has prevented cholera and other illnesses, yet at one point studies showed that the chemical might be linked to a higher incidence of bladder cancer (Kamrin *et al.*, 1994). Research beginning in the 1980s began to document rising upper atmosphere temperatures, yet other studies contradicted these results. Fortunately science has developed tools, both statistical and procedural, to help to interpret and untangle the confusion.

Probability

The first step in understanding a study would be to determine the possibility that its results were caused by chance. In laboratory studies especially, the most common cause of distortion would be through chance. Scientists attempt to answer such uncertainty by measuring probability. Called the p value or probability value, it can be an extremely valuable statistical measure that attempts to assess the possibility that the outcome was by chance and not due to the experiment. P values can range from 0 to 1 and the closer it is to zero, the more likely that there would be a real difference between these two samples. The generally accepted p value that is statistically significant is 0.05 or 5 percent, which means that in five times in 100 the observed difference could be caused by chance. An experiment with a p value of 0.01 is even more respected, because it means only one time in 100 could the observed difference be caused by chance. The p value of 0.05 is not a guarantee: it is just a measure of agreement and common sense between scientists and statisticians (Kamrin *et al.*, 1994).

Power of sample size

The p value is not infallible and the first reason it might be affected would be that the sample studied was too small. If the number studied was very small, just a few subtractions or additions would make the statistics change drastically. One of the biggest criticisms of cancer clusters, especially those suggested by non-scientists, has been that the sample size was too small to be conclusive. How large does the sample need to be in order to be credible? The answer will vary depending on what was being studied. A useful tool can be the concept of power, which means the probability of finding something if it is there. Cohn and Cope (2001, p. 25) gave this example of determining power: "Given that there is a true effect, say a difference between two medical treatments or an increase in cancer caused by a toxin in a group of workers, how likely are we to find it?" Power can be determined both by sample size and the accuracy of measurements. Tossing a coin and coming up with heads has a value of 50 percent chance. Researchers like to have a sample size large enough to have an 80 percent chance of finding something. Not all studies report power statements. In those cases researchers need to find out how many were in the sample and the number that were affected by the change. Coming up with these two numbers, the equivalent of the denominator and the numerator, allows the researcher to compute the power calculation (Cohn & Cope, 2001).

Bias and confounders

Bias can cause unreliable research data. An example was a scientist who theorized that baseball players who batted left-handed were among the game's elite because of hemispheric lateralization. What that meant was that the left side of the brain was superior. But another scientist pointed out that other variables could explain why the lefties fared so well. These included that they were already a step closer to first base than right-handed hitters and that most pitchers were right-handed and threw to right-handed hitters (Cohn & Cope, 2001). In most cases bias will not be intentional. In one study women who recalled drinking tap water while pregnant had four times the rate of miscarriage as women who recalled drinking only bottled water. But the survey was done at a time when publicity about such pollution was widespread and subsequent studies could not produce the same result. Researchers concluded that this was a case of recall bias, that the women with the miscarriages were more likely to remember the tap water as opposed to the bottled water because they associated the former with a health problem. Bias in a study simply can mean that there could be another explanation for the result (Kamrin et al., 1994).

Confounders, or confounding variables, are a form of bias that can occur when the researcher does not take into consideration all of the factors that might influence a study. One of the more famous examples of a confounder was a study in the 1970s of ten cities that had switched to water fluoridation. Significant increases in cancer had been experienced and the researchers thought it was caused by the fluoride. Follow-up investigators found that the study had not taken into consideration the significant urban demographic changes, which over the years had resulted in higher populations of elderly and minority residents in these cities. Both factors could increase the risk of cancer. When the confounding effects of age and race were factored in, the cancer rate fell. Other potential confounding influences can be gender, occupation, income and health status (Kamrin et al., 1994).

Reproducibility

On March 23, 1989 two scientists in Utah, Martin Fleischmann and B. Stanley Pons, shocked the scientific community by announcing that they had produced energy from a process called cold fusion. Producing energy from nuclear fission was well established, but clean power from fusion had never occurred before (Huizenga, 1993). Development of a commercial fusion process is highly desired because the raw materials involve readily available hydrogen and lithium as compared to the far more scarce uranium needed for fission. In addition, fusion does not produce the long-lived and highly radioactive waste that comes from contemporary nuclear fission processes (Hampel & Hawley, 1965). What was especially intriguing about the announcement by Pons and Fleischmann was that the way they described their accomplishment defied conventional nuclear physics. The news created a sensation, landing on the front pages of *Newsweek*, *Time*, and *Business Week*. Physicists rushed to replicate the results, to verify whether Fleischmann and Pons had achieved a new breakthrough. They could not do it. Some estimate that up to $100 million was spent trying and failing to produce cold fusion in a laboratory as Pons and Fleischmann maintained they had done. Only later was it learned that the two researchers had made their claim before actually observing any fusion process (Huizenga, 1993). Science depends on replication; it is the essence of what builds knowledge. Scientists call this the weight of the evidence. New research that conflicts with this weight of evidence may be important, but until it is replicated one must tread cautiously in evaluating it.

Peer review

The Pons and Fleischmann announcement succeeded in reaching the public partly because it was so astonishing but also because it bypassed

all conventional scientific safeguards. These included not only repro-
ducibility, but the peer review process. Research is considered more
valid and legitimate when it is both peer-reviewed and published in a
science or technical journal. When the research is completed, the
researcher will write it in the standard scientific style and submit it to an
appropriate journal for publication. The journal editors send the article
out to other scientists in the same field. The reviewers remain anonymous to both the writer of the article and to readers of the journal.
These reviewers critique the article, looking to see if it has conformed to
conventional research practices. They consider whether it offers something new to the field, and whether it demonstrates that the research
and analysis has been done correctly. Reviewers do not look for fraud
as much as they examine the paper to make sure that nothing has been
overlooked. They may also offer comments and corrections to
strengthen the paper. The author and editors then review the comments,
make adjustments as necessary, and then the editors decide whether to
publish the article (Siegfried, 2006).

In the Long Island cancer studies, the largest was an $8 million epi-
demiology project that attempted to link breast cancer to the environment. Marilie Gammons, an epidemiologist from the University of
North Carolina, led the project. Years behind schedule when she finally
completed the study, she submitted it to first one prestigious journal
and then another. In each case her paper was rejected. No explanation
was given, but other epidemiologists speculated it was because
Gammons' findings generally contradicted most other prevailing
research. Even when she found a less prestigious peer review journal
that would accept it, she needed to make numerous revisions before it
was accepted for publication (Fagin, 2006c).

Most research survives the peer review process but there are casual-
ties. The burden of proof rests with the researcher trying to get results
published. While the process is well established, it is not infallible.
Reviewers are only human and sometimes they concentrate more on the
researcher than on the research. In the Gammons' Long Island study
some reviewers were upset by the degree of publicity the study had
received, despite steps to curtail disclosures to the news media (Fagin,
2002c). When disputes arise between the researcher and the reviewers,
the journal editors ultimately will decide whether to publish.

Finding reliable information

Arsenic had been in the news. The Clinton Administration had proposed limiting the amount of arsenic in drinking water to ten parts per
billion, but the Bush Administration had decided to retain the current
standard, 50 parts per billion. Days after that announcement Seth

Asking the best questions

Victor Cohn and Lewis Cope (2001), veteran science writers at the *Washington Post* and *Minneapolis Star Tribune* respectively, compiled a list of what they called "golden questions" that reporters should use in examining scientific research. Cohn wrote that he was inspired to develop the questions after a conversation with Dr. Morris Fishbein, the longtime editor of the *Journal of the American Medical Association*. Cohn had asked how as a reporter he could tell whether a doctor was doing a good job of caring for his patients. Fishbein replied: "Ask him how often he has a patient take off his shirt" (Cohn & Cope, 2001, p. 59).

Here are the golden questions:

1 Was the study large enough to pass statistical muster? Are the findings unlikely to be due to chance alone?
2 Was the study designed well? Could unintentional bias have affected the results?
3 Did the study last long enough?
4 Are there other possible explanations for the findings? Are there any other reasons to question the conclusions?
5 Do the conclusions fit with other scientific evidence? If not, why?
6 Do I have the full picture?
7 Have the findings been checked by other experts?
8 What now? What's the potential from the research? What problems might pop up?

(Cohn & Cope, 2001, p. 180)

Borenstein, a science and environmental writer for Knight Ridder News Service in Washington, was scanning *Environmental Health Perspective*. One study in the peer-reviewed journal caught his attention. It suggested that the current level of arsenic in drinking water was high enough to cause cancer (Borenstein, 2002).

Normally Borenstein did not write about journal articles. But this, as he said later, "was a no-brainer." It was relevant to the recent and controversial policy decision that had been in the news, and also the results had been reported in a publication produced by the government's National Institute of Environmental Health Sciences (Borenstein, 2002).

Borenstein's decision illustrated a key point. The way science will be reported will vary. Sometimes a reporter's decision may be based less on the science than on other factors. Some critics complain that reporters have been too selective in their reporting of scientific research. "Of course we cherry pick, that is our job," responded Borenstein. "We find what is news. A month before, if I had seen this article, it would not have been news" (Borenstein, 2006).

When environmental journalists search for news from the science community, they often look first at peer-reviewed journals. After that, the reliability falls off rather rapidly. Journalists need to cautiously evaluate press conferences, press releases, reports on the Internet and even science conferences. Journals often are sent out in advance on an embargoed basis, with publication allowed on a set date. Sometimes the journal comes with press releases and other supplemental information. While the press release and other materials can be valuable, the best way for a journalist to accurately report is to read the entire article, with emphasis on the executive summary at the beginning and the conclusion. Getting articles in advance also gives reporters enough time to read other material to better understand the background issues, to interview researchers if possible and to talk to other experts in the field. Such interviews help gain a better perspective. Not all of this guidance necessarily comes in on-the-record interviews. Journalists must make their own determinations as to when it is important to take information on background or off-the-record.

Reporters also need to determine who provided the funding for the study. Usually the answer is benign. Funding sources gain more attention when they come from an environmental advocate such as the Natural Resources Defense Council or industry groups such as the petroleum-friendly Western Fuels Association. The funding source does not necessarily negate the results of the study. Journalists should still evaluate the research. The key is to report accurately and to not mislead the reader.

Balance

Getting both sides of a story, while generally desirable in journalism, does not always work in science and environmental coverage. Tom Siegfried, longtime science editor for the *Dallas Morning News*, said that balance in space stories would require that every story about satellites would require a comment from the Flat Earth Society (Siegfried, 2006, p. 15).

It has become incumbent on journalists to provide proper perspective. Nowhere has this become a bigger issue than in the coverage of climate change. Over the years a consensus has developed within the scientific community that greenhouse gases, primarily from human sources, have been contributing to heating the upper atmosphere and increasing the earth's temperature. The public policy steps that will be needed to solve this problem are costly and much of the burden will fall on the energy industry and the U.S., the largest consumer of energy. Not surprisingly, the energy sector for years has supported a small cadre of scientists who continue to question how much temperatures are rising and how much mankind is responsible. In 1998 the *New York Times* (Mooney, 2004) reported on an internal American Petroleum Institute memo calling for financing scientific views that questioned global warming. It also proposed training and recruiting scientists who shared that viewpoint to counter mainstream science on the issue. Such campaigns in the 1990s and early 2000s appeared to be succeeding. Research indicated that the concept of balanced reporting on climate change was still very common even in the most mainstream newspapers. A study of the *New York Times*, *Los Angeles Times*, *Wall Street Journal* and *Washington Post* between 1988 and 2002 found that 52.7 percent of the stories during that period gave equal attention to the scientific view that climate change was increasing and the industry-sponsored position that it was a natural fluctuation with no obvious tie to human activity. In contrast, only 35.3 percent of the articles emphasized the scientific consensus while downplaying the industrial view. The public has become the loser in such stories, because a balanced report is actually an imbalance of what science has been finding (Boykoff & Boykoff, 2004).

Sometimes the task of supplying balance and perspective can be more challenging. C. Richard Chappell, director of Science and Research Communications at Vanderbilt University, examined news stories about how farm-raised salmon was found to have high levels of polychlorinated biphenyls or PCBs. The initial report drew little coverage because it was an unpublished study by an environmental organization. Then a study was published in *Science* that found that "consumption of farmed Atlantic salmon might pose health risks that detracted from the beneficial effects of fish" (Chappell, 2004, p. 26). The study included a disclaimer from the authors which cautioned that the risks of eating salmon had not been well evaluated and that three previous studies were inconclusive. Chappell said that the resulting news stories did present both sides in a balanced way. But Chappell said that the most pertinent portion of the information may have been the disclaimer by the authors in the *Science* article and virtually no one used it in their story (Chappell, 2004).

Journalists doing science

The traditional way to cover the environment has been to report on what others have been finding – be it pollution, a health risk or a vanishing species. But some journalists have conducted their own tests or hired their own experts to document the extent of an environmental problem. They include:

- Bill Moyers in 2001 as part of a PBS television program about the chemical industry participated in a pilot study run by the Mount Sinai School of Medicine in New York. Moyers' blood and urine were analyzed and 84 chemicals were found. The results were not unusual, chemicals have become so widespread in the environment that trace amounts of many are not unusual (Jones, 2001).
- Julie Hauserman of the *St. Petersburg Times* in 2001 was working on a story about whether pressure-treated lumber was contaminating the environment. She was especially interested in whether playground equipment containing the lumber was causing arsenic to leach into the soil. The newspaper located one playground in each of the five counties in its circulation area and conducted soil tests. The tests were cheap, only $30 each, and when the results came in the arsenic levels were quite high. Rather than using a fairly standard parts per million figure, Hauserman learned what levels the state required for a neighborhood cleanup and reported the soil samples she had found were 13 times higher. There was nothing fancy about how the samples were taken and Hauserman said she was aided by the fact that Florida has very low background arsenic in its soil naturally. She said testing seemed to be the critical element in the story. "That made the difference between just a story about a possible threat and a story to show that it was actually happening, that we could show people," she said (Dunne, 2001, p. 22).
- When Dan Fagin was investigating cancer clusters on Long Island, NY, while at *Newsday* he asked a cluster analyst, Geoffrey Jacquez of TerraSeer Inc. in Michigan, to examine health and environmental data on the island. Jacquez searched for clusters of three of the most common cancers, lung, breast and colorectal. He found a number of clusters. While he found no strong correlation between environmental problems and breast and colorectal cancers, he did find an association between air pollution and lung cancer in several neighborhoods. The finding surprised Jacquez' who cautioned that it was only preliminary. Fagin used Jacquez' findings in his stories, but he did not lead with it or even stress the discovery. "I decided that while the results were interesting, that they were very preliminary and based only on statistics and not epidemiology work," he said. "I wanted to be conservative in how I dealt with it." Fagin said Jacquez was never paid for his work because the newspaper did not think that would be appropriate and Jacquez never asked to be paid. Jacquez did, however, later publish the research in a peer-reviewed journal (Fagin, 2006).

Understanding scale

Journalists sometimes have to describe how very small amounts of substances can affect the environment. Some substances are so toxic or powerful that they can affect anything from a pond to a building even in the most minute amounts. The most common of these measurements are parts per million and parts per billion, although some times they even get smaller, such as parts per trillion or parts per quadrillion. To place these substances in perspective, here are some analogies:

PPM

- A credit card lying in the middle of a football field.
- One pancake in a stack four mile high.
- A step in a trip of 568 miles or one inch in 16 miles.
- One minute in two years.
- One ounce in 32 tons.
- One cent in $10,000.

PPB

- One grain of salt in 110 pounds of mashed potatoes.
- One kernel of corn in a 45-foot high, 16-foot diameter silo.
- One drop of gin in 19,000 gallons of tonic.
- One sheet in a roll of toilet paper stretching from New York to London.
- One second of time in 32 years.

PPT

- One drop of detergent in dishwater that has filled each railroad tank car in a line ten miles long.

PPQ

- One mile on a journey of 170 light years.

(Kamrin *et al.*, 1994, p. 100)

Figure 4.2 Children play in Houston's Milby Park, one of the many places where the *Houston Chronicle* took air samplings. The tests showed dangerously high levels of 1,3-butadiene (source: courtesy *Houston Chronicle*).

One of the most ambitious testing programs was carried out by Dina Cappiello of the *Houston Chronicle* (Cappiello, 2005a–c). Houston is often mentioned as having among the worst air pollution in the nation. Cappiello said she would often talk to residents who lived near industrial plants who told horror stories about the foul air. But when she called the state she was told that their air monitors had never picked up any problems. "I strongly felt that we needed hard data to get the state's attention and the industry's attention," Cappiello said. "Without data, what was really going on would be lost in the anecdotal, as it had for years" (Dunne, 2005a, p. 22).

The newspaper set up 100 monitoring sites in the four counties of the *Chronicle*'s circulation area. The cost of the monitors and the analyst was $12,500 and neighborhood volunteers conducted the testing. Over a 24-hour period, the monitors were testing for 31 chemicals in the air. The samples were then sent to a laboratory for analysis. Maximum, minimum, median and average concentrations of each chemical were compiled in each monitored area. The results demonstrated in stark detail the level of toxic chemicals. It told of how an area along the Houston Ship Channel had air so foul that state employees no longer staffed a monitoring van. "It's either wear a respirator or leave it unmanned," said one state official (Cappiello, 2005b, p. 1).

Cappiello did the research to find the right testing equipment and to design the study's methodology. "My background in science also helped," she said. "In order to get my master's in environmental science I had to do a research project, so I knew how to set up a study that would answer the questions we had, which were: What pollutants are in neighborhoods near Houston's industry? And are the quantities enough to put people at risk?" (Dunne, 2005a, p. 17).

Study guide

1 Review an article in a prestigious journal. Consider such publications as *Science*, *Nature*, the *Proceedings of the National Academy of Science*, *Journal of the American Medical Association* and the *New England Journal of Medicine*. After reviewing, consider the following: identify the *p*-value. Does the sample size seem reasonable? Even if there are no known biases or confounders for this study, suggest hypothetical influences that could affect the study.

2 Write a news story on the basis of a journal article you have read. You may want to go to the Internet and see if a press release was issued along with the journal article. Also, consider interviewing a local authority in the field about the journal article.

3 Bill Moyers of PBS inserted himself into his story about the chemical industry by having his blood tested. Dina Cappiello and the *Houston Chronicle* paid for the air testing but asked volunteers to do the work. Julie Hauserman and the *St. Petersburg Times* paid for soil testing that found pressure-treated wood was contaminating playgrounds. *Newsday* did not pay a cancer cluster researcher who did extensive research for the newspaper because editors did not believe payment was appropriate. What are the journalistic ethical considerations in reporters getting involved in their stories either by having their blood tested or paying – or not paying – for lab work and research?

4 Write news leads based on the information you have on the tests by the *Houston Chronicle*, *St. Petersburg Times* and *Newsday*.

5 Julie Hauserman found an alternative to writing about parts per million in her story about pressure-treated wood. She said that no matter how creative you are, people's eyes start to glaze over when using ppm statistics. What would be some creative ways to describe the level of hazard or contamination without using ppm statistics?

6 For further reading, search newspaper archive files and read each of these series: "Tattered Hopes," *Newsday*, July 28–30 and Aug. 11–14 2002; "In Harm's Way," *Houston Chronicle*, Jan. 16–25 2004; "The Poison in your Backyard," *St. Petersburg Times*, March 11, 2001.

7 For additional reading, consider *News & Numbers* by Victor Cohn and Lewis Cope (2001), Lewis Thomas, *Life of a Cell* (1978), Phillip Meyer's *Precision Journalism* (1972), and Dorothy Nelkin's *Selling Science* (1987).

Chapter 5

Interviewing scientists

Roger Pielke Sr. was upset. The *New York Times* had reported that he was leaving a Presidential science advisory team and it said that the Colorado State University professor had "long disagreed with the dominant view that global warming stems mainly from human activity." Pielke, an atmospheric scientist, said that identification was wrong. Rather than just fret over the news article, Pielke wrote an explanation of his resignation and his views on climate change and then posted them on his climate blog on the Internet. The *Times* reporter, Andrew Revkin, learned of Pielke's comments and wrote a response explaining his story and offering to publish a correction if he had made an error. Pielke wrote a new blog item that said, in part:

> I very much appreciate your comment as this clears up our misunderstanding. I had come to respect you over 20 years of excellent coverage of climate science, so I was surprised by this one article. This clearly was an unfortunate aberration resulting from miscommunication between both of us.
>
> (Outing, 2005, p. 1)

Tales of miscommunication between journalists and scientists have been all too common. Perhaps the Internet and other tools will make it easier to reach out to each other in the future – assuming that the two sides will be as willing to communicate as Pielke and Revkin.

One great challenge in writing about the environment has been to deal with the distrust, wariness and at times hostility between journalists and scientists. In 1998 a journalist, Jim Hartz, and a scientist, Rick Chappell, spent a year studying this relationship. They wrote a report which they aptly titled *Worlds Apart* (Hartz & Chappell, 1998). They said: "The scientist sees the journalist as imprecise, mercurial and possibly dangerous – 'a man who knows the price of everything and the value of nothing,' to borrow Oscar Wilde's phrase. The journalist sees the scientist as narrowly focused, self-absorbed, cold-eyed and arrogant" (Hartz & Chappell, 1998, p. 13).

Understanding the nuances of the craft of interviewing can be particularly important in talking to scientists. It is important to work on the skills to conduct an interview. But first, it is important to explore and begin to understand why this divide exists between journalism and science.

The gulf

While Hartz & Chappell (1998) found that journalists and scientists did not get along, they also concluded that the two groups were remarkably similar in many ways. Both professions were highly educated and bright, dominated by the curious and motivated to search for answers to abstract and complex issues. They also had a commitment to communicate what they had found, knowing that such communication was essential for their profession but also for the public good.

There were a number of reasons they did not get along, especially because their communications were so different. Others have also looked at this gulf, including veteran environmental communicator Bud Ward, who in 2003 began gathering assemblies of scientists and journalists to talk about common problems and solutions ("Science Communications," 2003). There have been several reasons why the divide developed, which are discussed below.

Language

Even when both sides used English, their approaches differed. Scientists needed to be specific and precise. They have followed a rigid protocol in explaining how they have done their work and what they have found. They were careful not to overstate, their reports were also often highly qualified, seeking to include a number of conditions. Robert Oppenheimer, the scientist who helped usher in the atomic age, once said that words of science "can be more misleading than enlightening, more frustrating to understanding than recognizable technical jargon" (Hartz & Chappell, 1998, p. 15). The word "theory" may have one meaning to the general public, but a far more specific definition for the science community (Hartz & Chappell, 1998).

What scientists considered precise was often to journalists, and to the general public, jargon. Journalists were generalists; their role was to assess information and to communicate it to a broad audience in a quick, direct manner. They did not spend time on fine nuances that clarified what to them were minor points. Using excess words was clutter. An environmental writer's mission was further complicated by the

Figure 5.1 Scientists boat a group of reporters to an offshore site on Narragansett Bay in Rhode Island to demonstrate how they are working with eelgrass to help improve the quality of the bay's environment (source: courtesy National Oceanic & Atmospheric Administration).

degree of science knowledge among readers. "Science literacy in the U.S. is fairly low," said Steven S. Ross, an associate journalism professor at Columbia University (Giorgianni, 2004, p. 5). Studies have borne that out, showing that up to 70 percent of the American population did not understand the scientific process. Up to half of the American public gave the wrong answer when asked how long it took for the earth to orbit once around the sun. Other studies showed that the public would rather be entertained than be informed when it came to news of the environment. Broadcast journalists in particular said they needed to find a hook to get a story to compete, given the limited air time. Such a focus dismayed many scientists and discouraged them from working with journalists (Hartz & Chappell, 1998).

Timing

Science has worked slowly; journalists seem always on a deadline. The very nature of science has been to take enough time to adequately assess a concept, even if it took years or decades. Beyond gathering information, assessing it and coming to a conclusion, scientists must submit their findings to their peers and wait to publish in a journal. Gaining a consensus on an issue can take even longer. That pace has made the process for scientists clear (Hartz & Chappell, 1998).

The situation has been far murkier for journalists. When did the findings become newsworthy? When the conclusion was reached, when peers concurred, when it was finally published or when others replicated the results? If a journalist chose a time to make the report and the scientist did not agree with that timing, cooperation between the two sides might disintegrate. Publication in a journal might be the best point to go public for the scientist, but not for the journalist. Some journalism critics have called journal publications as meaningful as the period at the end of the sentence. Journalists want the information as quickly as possible and they prefer to report it exclusively. "When you wait for a peer-reviewed article," said Don Wall, a reporter for WFAA-TV in Dallas and Fort Worth, TX, "everybody gets the same story and there is no chance for a journalist to do something unique and individual" ("Science Communications," 2005, p. 5).

Hartz & Chappell (1998) said the divide was further stretched because the two professions held to different standards of evidence. Science had used a benchmark equivalent to what in legal terms would be a criminal standard – beyond a reasonable doubt. Journalism, pressed by deadline pressures, has used the more lenient level found in civil cases – a decision based on the preponderance of evidence.

Another aggravation for the science community was the tendency by many in the press to treat every new development as a major new breakthrough. Science works incrementally, building on previous work. But, that approach has made it hard for reporters to sell their stories, either in pitching it to their editors, or in conveying to readers why it is meaningful (Hartz & Chappell, 1998).

Balance

Journalists typically dealt with differences of opinion by making sure that all were represented. The dilemma in writing about science has been how to evaluate those differences. Did the preponderance of the evidence show that science was split 50/50 on an issue, or was it 75/25? If it was the latter, how did the story – and who it quoted – reflect that variation? The issue became extremely important, as was noted earlier, in such high-stake controversies as climate change. Scientists said that such journalistic practices showed just how naïve the press could be. At the same time, many were unwilling to work with journalists because they did not trust them to assess the complexity and uncertainty of many science and environmental issues. For journalists, this issue of balance was especially complex. Editors and many readers did not understand why the concept of balance was different for science-based stories. Plus, there was a danger in going too far even when a scientific consensus seemed firm. Some balance was necessary, especially to account for unusual situations, when a minority viewpoint in the science establishment eventually prevailed ("Science Communications," 2003).

Errors

The Society for Conservation Biology Media Committee had this to say about reporters: "At best (they) interrupt whatever you're doing. At worst, they misquote and misrepresent you" (Fleishman, 2002, p. 1451). Of all of the impediments in the relationship between journalists and scientists, errors may be the greatest. Too often scientists complained that journalists simply did not get it right. Sometimes that fear began with the way a reporter introduced the subject. A biologist at a major university described how, more than once, she returned to her office and retrieved a phone message. The reporter, who she did not know, described somewhat inaccurately a new development and posed a couple of question on the phone, both of which to the biologist were slightly off-base. The reporter was working on a deadline and asked the biologist to call back right away. What were the odds the biologist was going to make the call?

Journalists may not even know how inaccurate they have been, because some scientists say they have not sought corrections or clarifications when an error occurred. They said their expectations were so low that they feared even the corrections would not be accurate and that they rarely got as much attention or play as the original inaccurate report.

Professional reluctance

Many scientists have not liked show-offs. Call it what you want, from professional jealousy to shyness, but many have been critical of scientists who took a very public role in dealing with the press. Such professional pressure made it less likely that scientists would stick their necks out and agree to be quoted. Ira Flatow, host of Science Friday on National Public Radio, said that in over 25 years of covering the field he often found scientists were afraid to talk to him. "Over and over and over again it's been told to me, 'I can't speak to you because I won't be able to walk the hallway the next day without people coming up to me and saying, "How dare you talk to the press?"'" (Hartz & Chappell, 1998, p. 22).

Carl Sagan, an astronomer whose skill at talking about space science led to lucrative public speaking appearances, television programs and

Making corrections

Journalists need to make corrections when they make an error. Most news organizations have a policy about willingly correcting mistakes. Usually such corrections have been published in a specific place in a publication. Corrections by electronic journalists also occur, but not as frequently.

Critics say journalists make too many errors and are too defensive. Jerry Ceppos, a former editor of the *San Jose Mercury News*, believed that journalists did not publish nearly as many corrections as they should. In a speech to other journalists he said "In a newspaper of 25 or 50 or 100 pages, we must make hundreds of errors. But I've not seen a single newspaper run even a dozen corrections a day" (Ceppos, 2000, p. 3).

Ceppos had suggestions for making corrections. Editors should:

- Tell the staff that they expect all mistakes to be corrected.
- Decriminalize corrections. Don't complain that there are too many, complain that there are not enough.
- Use corrections as a teaching tool, to educate the public about how difficult it is in daily journalism to get all the facts correct.
- Work on mindset within a newsroom. When readers call complaining about a perceived error, do not get defensive (Ceppos, 2000).

book contracts, was criticized by his peers for spending more time talking to the public than in working on research. He was denied membership to the National Academy of Sciences in part because members complained he was too popular and too well-known. Sagan maintained he was the victim of professional jealousy (Hartz & Chappell, 1998).

Finding sources

Despite all of these barriers, a journalist interested in talking to scientists should relax and not get too worried about this gulf. Ultimately the rules of journalism will not be that much different than they have been in covering other fields. "Too often reporters assigned to cover scientific stories react as if they are allergic to science," said Janet Raloff, senior editor of *Science News*.

Some people, when they hear scientific terms, freeze up. They think I don't understand. It is beyond my ability to understand. Most of science reporting is going in cold, not understanding it either. You ask people what the science is. What are they finding? Why is it important?

(Dunne, 2002c, p. 1)

But who should be asked? Where are the right sources? A starting point would be universities or research institutes. Public information officers at these institutions are paid to assist. Another option would be professional organizations that represent virtually every scientific discipline. The organization may not have a staff, but it has officers who are usually very knowledgeable. Many have websites on the Internet, including lists of organization officers and members.

Information services have also developed over the years, such as Media Resource Service (Media Resource, 2005), formerly Scientists' Institute for Public Information, and ProfNet (ProfNet, 1995–2005), both of which can also be found on the Internet. These organizations were designed to assist journalists in tracking down experts in a particular field. ProfNet was originally a network of information officers at universities around the nation, although after it was acquired by PR Newswire it circulated to corporate information officers as well. It advertised that it had a database of 16,000 experts (ProfNet, 1995–2005). Media Resource, which was begun by the research society Sigma Xi, said it could contact up to 30,000 experts (Media Resource, 2005). Names could also be gathered by reading research into a particular discipline and becoming familiar with who was writing. Good journalists also collected names. They interviewed one scientist and asked whom else they should talk to. In the early stages of gathering information, such steps can be extremely valuable.

Another potential resource would be the Science Citation Index or the ISI Web of Knowledge. They provide information not only about potential sources but their specific research. The Science Citation Index has bibliographic information, author abstracts and references from 3,700 science and technical journals. The Index can be found at research libraries and on DVD (Science citation index, 2007). ISI Web of Knowledge has comparable information and it can be found online. Thomson Company, which produces both services, said that the Web of Knowledge has information from 22,000 journals, 5,500 Internet sites and 5,000 books (ISI Web of Knowledge, 2007). Both sources allow reporters to find scientists who have published in a field by geography and also to find out how a scientist has been cited in a particular subject.

Having the names can be helpful, but reporters must determine the reliability of their sources. Scientists with alliances, either overtly or subtly, to business or environment organizations need special attention. But even someone working at Harvard or at the Scripps Research Institute should be probed about their background. Journalists should ask gentle questions about any university or institute affiliations, specialties and financial sources of income. Many science and environmental research projects have been financed by sources outside of the researcher's university or institute. Much of this money came from government grants, but even more was financed by industry, especially in such areas as medical and health, where pharmaceutical research funds were quite common. Public information officers at universities can be extremely helpful, but no one can be an expert in everything, and their referrals need to be double-checked. Increasingly we live in a global society where experts can be reached by phone or the Internet. Still, don't neglect the value of local specialists. Getting to know local experts can help you evaluate who is reliable. Some journalists also ask scientists to name those who disagree with their findings but who they consider reputable. If they cannot name anyone, they drop down on the reporter's list of credible sources ("Science Communications," 2004b).

Figure 5.2 EPA Administrator William Ruckleshaus holds a press conference when he ran the agency in the 1970s. While a press conference can be helpful especially for deadline stories, it is not as preferable as a personal interview (source: courtesy Environmental Protection Agency).

Sometimes the best sources were not necessarily the people quoted by name. Trust has been built by how accurate a journalist was with a story. Experts quickly learned who they could count on for accurate reports. Most information traded between journalists and their sources was on-the-record, meaning it could be freely reported. Yet off-the-record information, material that could not be freely quoted or used, could also be valuable. Such sources were especially helpful for journalists in trying to gauge the reliability of sources who were discussing complex or technical environmental or science issues. Veteran journalists developed a group of experts they could go to, where there was mutual trust, and they could freely discuss what they had found. The goal of the discussion was not to get quotes from the source, indeed such a practice would be forbidden under the off-the-record ground rules, but to make sure the journalist understood the issue correctly and was not being led astray. There were also dangers in such a practice. Journalists should handle off-the-record relationships with care. Novice journalists would be wise to seek advice from either their editor or a veteran journalist before they begin to make such arrangements with news sources.

Bridging this gap between scientists and journalists may be formidable, but it can be accomplished. Sometimes the best way to do it was simply for journalists and scientists to get together. Revkin of the *New York Times* said:

> The more scientists and journalists talk outside the pressures of a daily news deadline, the more likely it is that the public – through the media – will appreciate what science can and cannot offer to the debate over difficult questions about how to invest scarce resources or change personal behavior.
>
> (Revkin, 2006, p. 228)

The interview

Building trust is paramount. In approaching any news source, but especially one from the science community, a reporter should begin by providing clear identification, explaining the purpose of the interview and the plans for the story. Unless evidence is obvious that the source has often been in the news, do not assume they have been interviewed or that they understand the rules. Explain them. Clarify fine points, such as that on-the-record means that a source cannot retract a comment or place it off-the-record after it has been stated. News stories, unlike science journal articles and press releases, are not reviewed by the news source prior to publication. Other science sources who have been interviewed may be wary, they have been burned in the past by a reporter who did not understand them or printed an inaccuracy. It is important to not rush into an interview, even if it has to occur by telephone and the journalist is on deadline. Sometimes news sources want to know more about the reporter's background or the types of questions that will be asked in the interview. Journalists should not be afraid to respond to such queries, even if it means supplying a list of sample questions or providing previously published stories that the journalist has produced on similar issues. Again, building trust is paramount.

When possible, always try to interview sources in person on the turf where they are most comfortable. That can be the office, their lab, out in the field or in their home. Take the time to get to know them and their work: one story might lead to others. Telephone interviews have become an unfortunate necessity in deadline situations, but avoid them when possible. Once a relationship has been established, phone conversations and interviews become easier. Keep away from email interviews unless there is absolutely no other way of obtaining the information.

To tape or not to tape

The technology of tape recorders has consistently improved from reel-to-reel to eight-track to small portable recorders to digital. Yet the debate among writers about whether or not to tape has never ceased.

Journalists who take notes try to take copious, detailed notes. They listen for quotes. Few know shorthand, but most have their own system which includes leaving out some words, abbreviating others and using symbols or other marks to designate something important or something to follow up. Once the interview is completed, they review notes immediately. Often gaps are clearly obvious and need to be filled in and abbreviations and symbols need to be clarified while the interview is still fresh in the writer's mind.

Tape-recorded interviews make stories better. The tape does better than the mind in filling in missing gaps and listening to an interview a second time produces additional insights into what the speaker was saying. Those who have used tapes say that when they compared their notes they were surprised by how much they had left out and in some situations not captured correctly.

There can be problems with tapes. They can be less than helpful in deadline situations. They take time to listen to and even more time to transcribe. No technology has yet been developed to resolve the transcription process, which must be done manually. Tape recorders are also machines and they can malfunction, the batteries can go dead, the volume may be left too low or the speaker is too far away, or the tape breaks. Sometimes sources become intimidated by the presence of a tape, creating an artificial intrusion into what should be a conversation. Hiding the recorder and secretly taping a source is illegal in some states and raises ethical concerns across the profession.

Is there a solution? Consider both taking notes and using a tape recorder. The key is not to rely on the tape, but to use it as a back-up source. Note good quotes in your notebook but find them and verify their accuracy on the tape. Even writers on deadline can use this technique, if their notes are complete enough. While tape recorders can be intrusive, part of the skill in establishing a rapport with a source is getting them to forget that they are talking to a reporter or that a tape recorder is even in the room. Usually the skill of the questioner and the unobtrusiveness of the tape will solve that problem (Rosenbaum, 2005).

Always go in to an interview as well prepared as possible. Read at least summaries or abstracts of what the scientist has written and other research in the field. If a particular interview is especially key, interviews with others in the field should be done first. Do not neglect other published articles including newspaper stories, magazine profiles and press releases. Talking to other journalists who have covered the field or the scientist can be helpful. While such talks are often handled on a background or off-the-record basis – journalists are not going to want to be quoted in your story – they often try to be helpful.

Establishing rapport can help get an interview started. Sometimes establishing a connection is less important, depending upon the type of interview and how news-savvy the source is. A sports reporter was assigned to interview a middle-weight boxing champion. The writer knew that the boxer had been interviewed many times over the years. The boxer always heard the same questions, he was known to give the same pat answers. Realizing that the boxer was bored in most interviews, the sports writer tried something different. He began by asking a series of very technical questions about boxing. The boxer was surprised and a little caught off guard, but willingly answered. As he did, he began to warm to the subject and to the writer. Soon the sports writer and boxer were deep into the interview and the journalist was getting answers to the more general questions that he knew his readers would appreciate. Much of the information from the first questions was never used, but it helped establish a bond. The completed interview, and story, sparkled in comparison to the tired quotes in other stories.

This is only one example of how to establish a rapport. Less experienced news sources may be nervous and as a result their answers may be stilted or unnatural. In this situation the source needs to forget that a journalist is in the room. The aim is to make the conversation as natural as possible. Usually this is handled the way many conversations begin, with small talk. At this stage, many reporters do not even have their notebook, pen or tape recorder out. It is only after a few minutes, when they begin easing the source into the conversation, that the tools of the trade appear. Even then, it might be wise to take notes sparingly. There is no sure way to advise how much work needs to be devoted to establishing rapport, it could vary with every interview.

Ask short questions. Expect long answers. Try to not interrupt. Quotes may be less than sterling, researchers are used to stating their views in qualified terms. Jargon may be common. Do not be intimidated and if you do not understand the comment, ask for an explanation. Ask repeatedly. Irene Wielawski, a medical writer for the *Los Angeles Times*, told of once interviewing a doctor and having what she later described as a failure of nerve. They had been discussing a catheter. It was not until she got back into the office that she realized that there were a number of different types of catheters and that she should have asked the physician to define what he was talking about at the time. Robin Mejia, a freelance environmental journalist, says that earlier on in her relationship with an ecologist she had to stop him when he kept talking about "trophic cascades." At first, the researcher was confused. He assumed everyone knew what the term meant. The last thing either a journalist or a source wants is for the reporter to be sitting down to write and realizing he is not clear what something means (Mejia, 2003).

Repeat back comments. The reporter's version may be more general than what the scientist said, but usually an understanding can be reached. This is especially important in dealing with numbers. There is a major difference between one part per million and one part per billion.

Ask open-ended questions. Do not try and fill silences. Sometimes a source will finish what they intended to say and there will be a silence while the journalist takes notes. Don't ask the next question until you are ready. Sometimes the source will try and fill that space, offering information they had not intended or you had not considered. It is also extremely important to listen and to observe. Eric Nalder, an investigative reporter for the *San Jose Mercury News*, said: "Use your ears. We talk too much during interviews. Let the other person do the talking. Listen with an open mind" (McClure, 2003b, p. 10).

Plan the interview and the questions. Often journalists bring a set list of questions and make sure they have covered them before they leave. In these situations, do not be afraid to follow-up on something unexpected. Allow the interview to go in unanticipated directions, but try and manage the flow. It is important to remain in control. If a source is taking an alarmingly long time to answer the first questions, remind them of the purpose and that you only have limited time with them.

"Get paper," said Tom Meersman, an environmental reporter with the *Minneapolis Star Tribune*. "During an interview, always ask about letters, emails, reports, lawsuits or anything else in the paper trail" (McClure, 2003b, p. 10).

Christy George, who covers the environment as a documentary producer for Oregon Public Broadcasting, believes that the best questions in an interview are the first and the last. "The first question is when the subject spits out everything he or she has pre-rehearsed. The last question is important because I keep going until I get something that really pleases me" (McClure, 2003b, p. 10). The last question – and answer – may also come after you have put your notepad down. Carol McCabe, who was a veteran reporter for many years for the *Providence Journal*, recalled how she would be getting ready to leave. The source would relax and become more conversational, more open. McCabe could see it in the source's posture, in their appearance. McCabe could see they were thinking something like "Oh thank God, they're leaving. I've survived" (McCabe, 2006). Sometimes what was said at that moment would be a gem that McCabe would remember until she could get outside and madly scribble it down. Generally in interviewing scientists there are not very many questions that would be considered "tough" or would get them upset. Journalists wait to ask their toughest questions at the end, when they are confident that rapport has built and they will still have something on their pads or in their camera if a source gets upset.

Follow-up

Rarely does a journalist gather everything needed in one interview. In a deadline situation, reporters must cope with the limitations imposed by the interview but in most other situations journalists expect to follow-up, either in phone or even in person, with the source. They tell scientists during the interview that this is likely. This raises one of the most vexing issues between journalists and scientists, whether to allow sources to review the notes or the finished story.

Scientists are used to peer review. They expect to be able to review a work before publication, often several times. It eliminates errors, eliminates inconsistencies and generally makes an article more specific. Given that background, it has been difficult for them to understand or accept one of the cardinal rules of journalism: that a finished story, or even notes, are not shown to sources. Providing sources with this opportunity may open the door for them not only to make corrections, to make self-serving additions or add inaccuracies to the story. Allowing sources to review or edit work can result in censorship. There are exceptions and the situation is difficult when a journalist has a trusted relationship with a science source. The key in most news organizations is that these decisions are usually not made by the reporter. Instead, policies set by editors and news organizations may prohibit any disclosure prior to publication.

While the divide on this point seems broad, it can be bridged. Both sides should start even before the interview ends. Journalists need to work hard to make sure they understand important concepts during the interview, but scientists should also share in that effort. Reporters should anticipate that sources may ask them to repeat back the main points of the interview. They should not ask for direct quotes. But scientists should be able to probe the journalist to make sure the reporter has a thorough understanding of the main points. "It's a teaching trick," explained one journalist in a conversation with environmental scientists. "You go 'Did you understand?' And the student says 'Yes.' And you say, 'Good, explain it'" ("Science Communications," 2004a, p. 9).

Continue this dialog both in follow-up questions and when the journalist is writing or editing the story. The most important questions deal with accuracy. Various reporters have different techniques. Some will say something like, "Is this a good analogy?" or "Have I got this right or did I really screw it up?" Others might go so far as to read phrases, sentences or even paragraphs from their story. In such cases the material being submitted to the source should only be a technical review. Rarely are quotes even offered and even less rarely do journalists turn over an entire story to a source.

Importance of persistence

Janet Raloff of *Science News* has written about a range of issues including a form of pollution that for years was not recognized. It had to do with hormones, pharmaceutical residues and other "micropollutants" sometimes found in concentrations nearly too weak to detect that were getting into the environment and potentially effecting human health. Raloff first began hearing about the issue in 1993 when she went to a meeting in New York of the Vice President's Council on Breast Cancer. She said the underlying theme of the meeting was that the pollutants once they were ingested were acting like estrogen. That led her to Theo Colborn, a zoologist who had done work in the area and co-wrote a book *Our Stolen Future* (Colborn *et al.*, 1997). Colborn said that the correct term for these problems was "endrocrin disruption" but Raloff was turned off by the phrase. "I told her I didn't think it is something reporters can relate to, it's kind of a jargon term" (Dunne, 2002c, p. 22). She was also not convinced when Colborn told her the most important effect of the substances was that they affected a second generation. Raloff decided to concentrate on what she had heard in New York, where the focus had been on how these micropollutants might cause breast cancer. Several months later Raloff heard that Colborn was doing new research. Colborn told her: "You really made a mistake in the first story by focusing on the breast cancer thing, because cancer is not the issue. It is the second generation effect" (Dunne, 2002c, p. 22). Raloff was intrigued and asked for more information. That eventually led Raloff to write a two-part series on the concept of environmental hormones and how they could affect reproduction (Dunne, 2002c).

Journalists and scientists need to continue to talk. Scientists should reach out to journalists even when they believe that reporters have made an error in judgment. Journalists should keep an open mind in talking to scientists. Science is complex and it is not getting any easier to understand.

Study guide

1 Find and interview two science professors at your local university or college about whether there is a gulf in understanding between science and journalism. Write a story, incorporating information provided earlier in this chapter.

2 Conduct an interview with a friend or another student. Ask the source to choose a subject they are very familiar with, their job, their family, their education and vocational plans. Keep the interview short, no longer than ten minutes. You should both stand during the interview. Write up your notes and then ask the source to review them for accuracy. Or, tape record the interview but don't listen to the tape until after you have written up your notes. Compare the accuracy of your notes to what is on the tape.

3 Good journalists know that interviewing is a skill that always needs to be honed. Some journalists go to courtrooms and listen to good lawyers cross-examine witnesses to pick up tips asking questions. Consider going to a local court house. What other sources might be good for learning how to ask questions?

4 Televised presidential press conferences and political debates where journalists ask questions are often not a good place to learn interviewing skills. Watch one. What problems can you find?

5 How far would you go in checking facts with a science source before writing your story? Are there any circumstances in which you could see turning your story over to these sources for their review prior to publication?

6 The Poynter Institute has been publishing award-winning stories along with interviews with the writers in an annual series called *Best Newspaper Writing* since 1977. The interviews are in a question-and-answer format. Examine how the questions are worded. What questions worked? Which did not?

7 For further reading, consider John Brady's *The Craft of Interviewing* (1977), *World's Apart* (1998) by Jim Hartz and Rick Chappell, *Our Stolen Futures* by Theo Colborn, Diane Dumanoski and John Peter Meyers (1997). For something a little bit different, consider how author William Least Heat Moon interviewed people as he drove around the country in his book *Blue Highways* (1983).

Chapter 6

The regulators

Massey Energy already owned a 168-foot-high silo that contained up to 10,000 tons of coal in Raleigh County, WV near the Marsh Fork Elementary School. In the summer of 2005, the company wanted to build another one. Federal law prohibited the construction of such energy facilities within 300 feet of a school and both would be within that perimeter. Over the objections of residents, the West Virginia Department of Environmental Protection granted a permit to build the second silo. Environmental regulators said that years before the current restrictions were enacted a permit had been issued and since the new silo was within the perimeter of that older approval there was nothing they could do. That permit, they said, took priority over federal law (Ward, 2005a).

Ken Ward Jr. of the *Charleston Gazette* wondered how the state had ever allowed a school to be so close to an active coal operation. He decided to look at the permitting records of DEP, especially the maps that showed the boundary where Massey was allowed to build. The department's reading room was adjacent to where its records were stored and Ward was a regular visitor. He asked the clerks, who he knew by their first names, for the files on the Massey Energy project. "I pulled the most recent map and then pulled the earliest permit boundary map that I could find and compared the two," he said. "It was obvious that something was amiss, that the boundaries had changed. That process took 10 minutes" (Ward, 2006). But it took hours and hours to figure out how the boundary had changed. Eventually Ward discovered that an engineer had moved it on a map drawn after the permit had been issued. The redrawn map allowed the company to build closer to the school, much closer than the original permit.

Ward told DEP what he had found and began preparing a story for the Sunday newspaper. He wanted DEP to explain what happened, but for days officials cancelled appointments. "They stalled and stalled," said Ward (Ward, 2006). Finally on Friday afternoon they gave him a press release. It said that the department had discovered the proposed

Figure 6.1 A survey crew for the state of West Virginia begins trying to figure out whether two new coal silos are too close to the Marsh Fork Elementary School in Raleigh County, WV (source: courtesy Lawrence Pierce, *Charleston Gazette*).

coal silo was outside of its permit area and that permission to build was being revoked. It was only months later that a DEP official acknowledged, in a sworn statement, that it had been Ward who had found the error (Ward, 2006). Still, the story did get out and residents whose children lived in the shadow of the silo were grateful. "Once again the coalfield residents were left to fend for their communities," said Bo Webb of the Coal River Mountain Watch. "We were abandoned years ago by the DEP" (Ward, 2005c, p. 1).

Ward, considered one of the nation's foremost environmental reporters covering the mining industry, sees himself as a watchdog. "Many reporters like to tell stories of how people around here are fighting the coal companies," he said. "I find that rather mundane. I see my job as looking at how the mining companies are being regulated. The job of the press is to give information to the public to make government more responsive" (Ward, 2006).

In this case, what bothered him the most was that for years DEP officials had maintained that the permits had been checked and clearly showed they could not prevent the coal company from building its silos. "It boggles my mind that no one at DEP went back and looked at the original permit," he said. "But DEP is both underfunded and understaffed. Many judge DEP only by how fast it processes permit applications, not by how well it processes them" (Ward, 2006).

In the United States, there is no single governmental agency responsible for protecting the environment. The U.S. Environmental Protection Agency (EPA) is the first to come to mind. While it is the key federal environmental regulator, there are a number of other federal agencies and the EPA has delegated some of its responsibilities to state environmental departments. There are numerous local and state agencies that work to keep the water and air clean, to regulate the use of land, to dispose of waste and to develop parks and other resources that bring the environment closer to people. Plus there are even more regional authorities within states and across state lines. Finally, international efforts to protect the environment are increasing and can only grow as society and the economy become more global. Journalists need to understand this complex web of bureaucracy.

A beat primer

Starting a beat such as the environment is not that much different than getting ready for an interview. Both begin with preparation. Reading this book and others listed in the study guides at the end of each chapter would be a good beginning. Read news clippings, or clips as they are called, of what has been in the news about the environment both locally and nationally. Begin to develop names of potential sources and visit them. Phone conversations are a poor substitute for meeting someone in their office, home or where they are most comfortable. Government regulators at all levels, from local water districts to international commissions, are important sources. Begin making the rounds of these sources' offices. Introduce yourself, explain your mission, and start to ask questions about what they are working on. Begin developing calendars and dates of important meetings, hearings and deadlines of particular issues. Work to understand environmental laws and regulations and how they are administered by environmental agencies. Detailed paperwork is common with governmental environmental regulators, and reporters quickly learn to begin asking about and looking at records. Check for permits, inspection reports, notices of violations and other documents (Detjen, 2003). Ward was assured by West Virginia officials that the silo could be built close to the school but he was not willing to just take their word for it. He checked the records and found they were wrong.

Jim Detjen, a longtime environmental writer and currently the director of the Knight Center for Environmental Journalism at Michigan

State University, said he has found it important to cultivate government officials.

> Many state and federal environmental agencies are filled with altruistic people who genuinely care about improving the environment. You may discover inspectors or enforcement officials who are disgusted with politics in their agency and who are even eager to talk to you about the political pressures they see and experience.
>
> (Detjen, 2003, p. 22)

Not all staff employees at a government regulatory agency want to be quoted. Sometimes these employees are under significant political pressure. A good reporter will learn who to quote and who it is best to talk to on a "background basis." Conversely, political appointees and elected officials usually relish the opportunity to get their names in print.

A good beat reporter will talk to others besides the environmental inspector. These could be employees and managers of an industrial plant suspected of polluting the environment, to neighbors who have the opportunity because of their presence to see, hear or smell what is happening, or others. A number of reporters covering climate change issues have visited the Arctic, to personally observe the changes occurring. They interviewed everybody from the natives who were finding changes in the herds they hunt to the charter air pilots who saw changes every day in the terrain they traverse (Revkin, 2004a–c). Added Detjen: "I've sometimes found it useful to interview anglers, swimmers, or water skiers who utilize the river to get their views on the situation. When I have written about air pollution, I've interviewed window washers, city foresters and pilots" (Detjen, 2003, p. 23).

Start locally

Tom Philp, an editorial writer for the *Sacramento Bee*, decided to report and focus attention on the Sacramento Suburban Water District. Nothing sounded more boring. The district was responsible for supplying water to residents north of Sacramento, one of more than 400 major water districts and departments within California. But when Philp began examining financial records he found expense accounts so padded that his investigation eventually led to the federal indictment of two water district employees. Then he began looking at other water authorities in the state. He found a water district director who had "lunch" at a casino where his expenses were $180. Water customers were paying for perks such as having employees play rounds of golf at Pebble Beach and four-figure dinners at Disneyland (Philp, 2004h).

Often obscure agencies such as a water district can be researched for good stories because they have been ignored for so long by other journalists, but also by the public officials and regulatory watchdogs. Local agencies provide the vital basic necessities of life. Water departments supply drinking water; sewer districts handle waste water; household waste is hauled away and disposed of either by local agencies or by private firms who have been hired to perform the job. A former speaker of the U.S. House of Representatives, Tip O'Neill, said that all politics is local (O'Neill, 1994). In many respects, the same can be said for coverage of the environment.

One of the first lessons students learned in many environmental classes was where did such basic necessities come from including water, sewage and waste disposal. Depending on the size of the community, water can be obtained either by private wells or through a public water system. The source of that water may be a nearby reservoir, well, aquifer, river or lake, or it may be piped in from hundreds of miles away. In areas such as the northeast, water supply is a local issue. In the arid west and rapidly expanding southeast, it is often a regional issue that can cross state lines. Wastewater is usually disposed of privately, through an individual septic system, or publicly, through a sewer system. State and federal governments in the 1970s and 1980s helped pay for billions of dollars in improvements to sewage treatment systems, but by the beginning of the twenty-first century most of that money had dried up. Increasingly improvements have needed to be financed locally, usually through borrowing. Few residents or businesses have the option of disposing of any solid waste on their property. The issue of waste disposal exploded in the 1980s when communities across the country worried that they were running out of places or ways to dispose of their trash. Much of the concern was a result of sharp government regulatory crackdowns on landfills, causing many to close because they did not meet new tougher standards. This inspired new efforts both to build waste incinerators and to increase recycling. While the worry has subsided, the cost of waste disposal and recycling has remained a concern.

Water, sewage and waste have been managed locally but regulated by county, regional, state or federal agencies. Reading old stories about these systems may not be enough to get a full understanding. Talk to the regulators who oversee these facilities and read the reports and files. Grassroots and neighborhood organizations may also be helpful resources.

Another local authority that has impacted the environment have been local planning and zoning agencies and boards. Their role has been vital, especially in areas of high-growth such as the western and southeastern U.S. Planning and zoning can be the responsibility of a municipality, a county or a regional authority. An example of the latter is the Southern California Association of Governments, called by its unfortunate acronym of SCAG. It has advised 160 communities in the sprawling counties of Imperial, Los Angeles, Orange, Riverside, San Bernardino and Ventura on transportation, air quality, aviation and housing issues. Like many other advisory agencies, its recommendations have often been ignored (Kelley, 2005). High growth communities have been beset by many pressures, most noticeably their rising population bases which demand all the basics of modern living, from adequate water supply to efficient transportation systems to good schools. Good planning dictates that a community needs such features as adequate open space, the preservation of important local ecological features, and plentiful recreational opportunities. In many cases, these are some of the reasons new residents have been attracted to an area. But they sometimes can become less of a priority than housing, highways and schools for local officials beset by fierce political and economic pressures.

While government, developers or residents cannot ignore zoning, they have found loopholes to sometimes evade it. Planning establishes ideals for future development. Zoning has been more restrictive, setting restrictions on geographic subsections of a community, dictating what residential, business, industrial, rural, public or other allowable uses can occur. Sometimes those restrictions have been minimal, such as in an industrial or rural area of a county. Other times they can be more rigid, such as the distance between a liquor establishment and a church or school. When requests for changes or variances in the zoning laws are requested, they are usually considered by a zoning board or commission. Hearings are called on the zoning request, and they can be long and tedious, centering on discussions of setbacks and other arcane issues. Zoning boards can have a powerful impact over time both in changing a community's planning and zoning rules, in the area's overall values and environment. Also, while the vast numbers of citizens who sit on such boards are motivated by a sense of public duty, the pressures and conflict create openings for a range of misbehaviors from cronyism to corruption (Schulte & Dufresne, 1994).

From an environmental standpoint, pollution has been the most significant local problem. It can be confined to a couple of city blocks, such as when gasoline from a local service station leaks into the groundwater. Or it can sprawl across an entire metropolitan basin, such as when cars and industry spew pollution into the air. Talking to local people at the municipal or county level about a specific incident can be helpful, but the people empowered to solve the issue of gasoline leaks or air pollution are more likely to be state and federal environmental regulators.

EPA

The Environmental Protection Agency was created in 1970 as a pollution control agency, a federal regulator assigned to administer the various environmental laws passed by Congress. Federal departments such as Agriculture and Interior retained their jurisdictions over the management of such areas as national forests and parks (Kraft & Vig, 1994). The EPA has been called the largest environmental regulator in the world (Rosenbaum, 1994). Its projected 2007 budget was $7.3 billion with more than 17,500 full-time employees (EPA, 2006a). Administrators who have run the EPA have ranged from high-profile politicians such as former New Jersey Governor Christine Whitman, who headed the agency between 2001 and 2003, to Stephen L. Johnson, a career scientist at the agency appointed to the top post in 2005 (Janofsky, 2005).

From an organization standpoint, the EPA has been composed of a series of program offices responsible for a particular aspect of the environment, such as air, water, toxics and pesticides. Usually these divisions correspond with major environmental laws (see pp. 92–93). All of these acts have had a profound impact on the nation's environmental policy, but two early laws stand out: the Clean Air Act and the Clean Water Act (Kraft & Vig, 1994).

Originally called the Federal Water Pollution Control Act Amendments of 1972, the law was amended to the Clean Water Act in 1977 and established authority to regulate all wastewater discharges. Pollution was coming from municipal sewage plants and manufacturers. Both sectors have had to upgrade their facilities and sharply reduce the amount of pollutants they had been dumping into waterways. The act has been amended and reauthorized over the years with increasing attention being paid to pollution problems in the Great Lakes and with so-called non-point pollution, contaminants that seep into the waterways from roads, farms and even lawns (EPA, 2006b).

The Clean Air Act gave similar authority to regulate the nation's air pollution with EPA limiting the amounts of particular pollutants. States then established State Implementation Plans (SIPs) to indicate how they would comply with limiting those pollutants in their jurisdiction over time. Much of the early work centered on controlling emissions from industrial smoke stacks. Some states have also tried to limit vehicle emissions (EPA, 2006d).

While the EPA's headquarters has been in Washington, DC, much of the local activity has taken place within EPA's ten regional offices. Each is headed by a local administrator who has had latitude in dealing with a multitude of issues within a region. In many cases journalists are more likely to deal with their respective regional offices than with the

Major environmental laws

More than a dozen major statutes or laws form the legal basis for the programs of the Environmental Protection Agency.

National Environmental Policy Act of 1969 (NEPA)

NEPA was the basic national charter for protection of the environment. It established policy, set goals, and provided the means for carrying out the policy.

The Clean Air Act (CAA)

Required EPA to regulate and set standards for air emissions including mobile sources such as vehicles, ambient air standards and hazardous air emissions. It also directed EPA to focus on geographic areas that do not meet certain standards.

The Clean Water Act (CWA)

Established sewage treatment construction grants programs and a regulatory and enforcement program for discharges into U.S. waters. Focused on both stationary and mobile emissions.

Comprehensive Environmental Response, Compensation, and Liability Act (CERCLA or Superfund)

Established a fee-based system to clean up the nation's most serious hazardous waste sites.

Emergency Planning and Community Right-To-Know Act (EPCRA)

Designed to help local communities protect public health, safety, and the environment from chemical hazards. Created a database detailing both inventories and emissions of toxic chemicals.

The Endangered Species Act (ESA)

Established a program for the conservation of threatened and endangered plants and animals and the habitats in which they were found.

Federal Insecticide, Fungicide and Rodenticide Act (FIFRA)

Provided for federal control of pesticide distribution, sale, and use. EPA was given authority to study the consequences of pesticide usage but also to require users to register when purchasing pesticides.

The Oil Pollution Act of 1990 (OPA)

Strengthened EPA's ability to prevent and respond to catastrophic oil spills. A trust fund financed by a tax on oil was created to clean up spills when the responsible party is incapable or unwilling to do so.

The Pollution Prevention Act (PPA)

Focused industry, government, and public attention on reducing the amount of pollution through cost-effective changes in production, operation, and raw materials use.

The Resource Conservation and Recovery Act (RCRA)

Provided for cradle-to-grave regulations for hazardous substances and waste.

The Safe Drinking Water Act (SDWA)

Established primary drinking water standards, regulated underground injection practices and established a groundwater control program.

The Superfund Amendments and Reauthorization Act (SARA)

Amended CERCLA in 1986 and established revised standards for cleaning up hazardous waste sites.

The Toxic Substances Control Act (TSCA)

Required the testing and regulation of chemicals and their use.

(EPA, 2006c)

Figure 6.2 Then-EPA Administrator Lee Thomas tours the Love Canal neighborhood of Western New York after concerns arose that toxic chemicals were harming residents. EPA is the nation's primary environmental regulator (source: courtesy Environmental Protection Agency).

program offices in Washington (Cooper, 2002). EPA also has research laboratories around the country.

While obvious responsibilities center on the substance of carrying out laws on air, water, toxics and waste, the agency has other administrative responsibilities that are spread across the divisions and regional offices. These include rule making, enforcement, cleanup, education and research.

Rule-making

Federal law gave the EPA wide latitude to establish specific requirements. For instance, under the Safe Drinking Water Act the EPA can determine how much arsenic is permissible in drinking water. The Clinton Administration lowered that standard from 50 parts per billion down to ten parts per billion. When the new Bush administration arrived, the standard was rolled back to the old level (Borenstein,

2002). Rarely have issues been decided so rapidly. One criticism of the rule-making function has been that it was wrapped in layers of red tape. "A multitude of different bureaucratic, professional, geographic and political interests must be included in the agency's decision-making," wrote Political Scientist Walter A. Rosenbaum (1994, p. 127). The EPA has taken years to adopt some rules.

EPA's regional offices

Region 1, Boston – Connecticut, Maine, Massachusetts, New Hampshire, Rhode Island and Vermont.

Region 2, New York – New Jersey, New York, Puerto Rico and U.S. Virgin Islands.

Region 3, Philadelphia – Delaware, Maryland, Pennsylvania, Virginia, West Virginia and the District of Columbia.

Region 4, Atlanta – Alabama, Florida, Georgia, Kentucky, Mississippi, North Carolina, South Carolina and Tennessee.

Region 5, Chicago – Illinois, Indiana, Michigan, Minnesota, Ohio and Wisconsin.

Region 6, Dallas – Arkansas, Louisiana, New Mexico, Oklahoma and Texas.

Region 7, Kansas City – Iowa, Kansas, Missouri and Nebraska.

Region 8, Denver – Colorado, Montana, North Dakota, South Dakota, Utah and Wyoming.

Region 9, San Francisco – Arizona, California, Hawaii, Nevada, Guam and the American Samoa.

Region 10, Seattle – Alaska, Idaho, Oregon and Washington.

(Cooper, 2002)

Enforcement

The EPA regulates a range of activities. It is responsible for monitoring how much companies can pollute the air and water, how many pesticides a farmer can use, and how pure drinking water must be. Truckers need to carry a manifest detailing how much hazardous waste or chemicals they have been carrying. A manufacturer must seek a permit authorizing the firm to discharge a certain volume of pollutants. The company must install monitoring equipment and periodically renew its permit. Often the permit levels are tied to what is technologically feasible to achieve in limiting pollution. A permit holder does not have to upgrade its equipment each time the technology improves. However, if that firm does make a significant capital improvement to the facility, under EPA's rules it might be required to buy the latest pollution control technology and cut its emissions

Cleanup

One of the EPA's most expensive and controversial roles has involved the cleanup of hazardous waste sites. The program has been called Superfund because of its vast scale. Usually, the EPA has not physically removed the waste and cleaned the site. More often it hired a contractor and supervised the effort. It also often paid the bill and then tracked down the responsible parties so that it could be reimbursed. Finding who was responsible has been controversial and time consuming. Also, cleanups have been increasingly complex. In 2006 there were more than 1,200 sites listed on the National Priorities List and only 270 had been cleaned up over the previous 20 years (Luechtefeld, 2004). A significant portion of the EPA budget, about $1.27 billion in 2007, was projected to go toward cleanups (EPA, 2006a). Another 10,000 hazardous waste sites have been identified (Janofsky, 2005). In the past the EPA has also helped finance improvements such as upgrades to municipal sewage facilities.

Research and education

Over the years the EPA has become a major repository of information about the environment and more specifically about sources of pollution and toxics. One of the most significant has been the Toxics Release Inventory which has compiled data reported annually from industrial facilities on releases and transfers of toxic chemicals. The data has been made available to the public online (Luechtefeld, 2004). EPA has also engaged in research from ocean dumping to pesticides. It has also actively promoted educational programs aimed at large companies and households, which could engage in more recycling and reduce their volume of solid waste (Rosenbaum, 1994).

Other federal players

Environmental policy has been a shared role. Congress often has initiated legislation and the courts, including the Supreme Court, have weighed in on environmental issues. Still, the primary role has been administrative, with the responsibility falling to a myriad of agencies beyond the EPA. Some of the key players, listed in their level of responsibilities in managing the environment, are discussed below.

Figure 6.3 The rock formations at Bryce Canyon National Park in Utah annually draw thousands of visitors. The federal government is a major landowner in the western U.S. (source: courtesy National Parks Service).

Interior

The department has been the closest to the nation's land resources agency. It has managed recreational facilities primarily through the National Parks Service, which runs the "crown jewels," the great national parks and also national monuments, historic sites, and natural and cultural preserves. The department has also managed much of the federal government's property, which amounts to nearly 20 percent of the land in the country. In the west, its Bureau of Land Management has been responsible for that task. Another branch, Fish and Wildlife Service, has managed 540 wildlife refuges, protected endangered species and worked on invasive species issues. The Bureau of Reclamation has been responsible for dams and reservoirs in the western states and the U.S. Geological Survey monitored ground and surface water (Luechtefeld, 2004).

Agriculture

From an environmental standpoint, its chief responsibilities have centered on managing the National Forest Service and the National Resources Conservation Service. While the U.S. forests have been run primarily as a timber crop, they have a significant impact preserving open space and providing recreation. The NRCS maintains a national resources inventory and programs to preserve wetlands (Luechtefeld, 2004).

Nuclear Regulatory Commission

The Commission has been charged with overseeing civilian use of nuclear materials and with regulating nuclear reactors, materials and waste. It was responsible for licensing the first generation of nuclear reactors and for overseeing the retirement of some of the earlier models. If the nuclear industry can overcome public concerns about safety, it would be responsible for regulating a new, second generation of plants (Luechtefeld, 2004).

Army Corps of Engineers

While part of the Defense Department, the Corps has been involved in numerous civil works projects that affected both small, local environmental sites and several of the nation's important natural resources. It was the Corps that built levees and dredged the Mississippi. Such major public works projects significantly altered the ecology of the Louisiana bayous and coast (Luechtefeld, 2004).

National Oceanic and Atmospheric Administration

NOAA could be a key player in the future on developments linked to climate change. The agency has had responsibility for both the National Weather Service as well as climate programs that predict hurricanes and measure droughts (Luechtefeld, 2004).

Energy

The department has had a significant impact on the environment in its researching of fossil energy prospects and in managing such hydroelectric complexes as the Bonneville Power Authority in the Pacific Northwest. The department has also had a responsibility for managing some nuclear materials including cleaning up waste from defense and civilian uses of nuclear material. It has played a key role in developing the Yucca Mountain Waste Depository in Nevada for commercial nuclear waste (Luechtefeld, 2004).

States

Most state environmental departments have been natural resources agencies, responsible for both managing public lands as well as regulating the environment. The EPA and state environmental departments have worked together on many regulatory issues. Over the years the EPA has delegated much of its direct regulatory oversight to local state governments, especially in such areas as managing air and water discharge permits. Of the EPA's $7.3 billion 2007 budget, more than $1 billion went to the states, territories and Indian tribes to carry out EPA responsibilities (EPA, 2006a). Organizational structure will vary by state although most of these departments have been headed by a director appointed by the governor. Department responsibilities have usually been split among such divisions as air, water, waste, and natural resources.

Research has indicated that the states can be strikingly different in how they manage and regulate environmental initiatives. A study in the early 1990s by the Institute for Southern Studies found that such states as California, Maine, Minnesota, Oregon and Vermont were the leaders in environmental protection, both in how they administered current laws and how they developed new and innovative programs. That study labeled Texas, Mississippi, Arkansas, Louisiana and Alabama as the states that were least committed to environmental protection. Other studies have looked at both total expenditures and per capita spending on environmental protection and found wide disparities between states (Lester, 1994).

When political scientists first began looking at variations between states, some assumed that the range was based on the severity of environmental problems. They believed that a state with concentrated population growth, extensive industrialization, and a steady rate of consumption of goods would create more environmental problems and a stronger public demand for environmental protection. A case in point would be California, where air pollution was so severe that the Clean Air Act gave special authority to the state beyond the national commitment. Because of its size, California has had a significant impact in the development of products that cause air pollution. For instance, California air concerns helped force auto-makers to develop the hybrid automobile. But environmental problems in Texas would argue against this theory. Texas has had a huge petrochemical complex in the highly populated Houston and Gulf Coast region, yet it lags behind almost every state in its commitment to the environment, according to the research (Lester, 1994).

A better case could be made for finding greater environmental protection in states with stronger socioeconomic resources and with greater fiscal resources. Researchers have also suggested that there may be a partisan split on environmental issues, with states where the Democratic Party held control exhibiting a stronger commitment than in states where the Republican Party was in the majority. Or, the difference may have been simpler. It could be that states that recently reorganized their environmental bureaucracies and eliminated jurisdictional overlaps, were better equipped to manage environmental policies than more entrenched administrations. Whatever the reason, even the most progressive states have encountered problems at times in dealing with environmental issues. Some environmental problems, such as toxic waste, need enormous amounts of money and a highly trained staff. Many states have been hamstrung by inadequate resources, especially if staffs were inexperienced and had high turnover rates. Also, some problems transcend state boundaries and sometimes even national boundaries (Lester, 1994).

Regional approaches

The five Great Lakes sprawl across eight states from Minnesota to New York. For decades they have been affected and fouled by sewage spills, pockets of toxic sediments on lake bottoms and the arrival of invasive plant and marine species. Between 1992 and 2001 dozens of state and federal agencies spent $1.7 billion towards restoring the health of the lakes. Yet, there was little coordination in these efforts. Realizing that such disparate actions were not in their best interests, the states began meeting with U.S. and Canadian governments. In 2004 the Great Lakes Interagency Task Force was created to streamline cleanup efforts. Officials have estimated that the total cost of the cleanup could be $20 billion and take at least 15 years to accomplish (Egan, 2005).

Such regional efforts are not unusual. Watersheds far smaller than the Great Lakes often sprawl across state lines, air pollution can travel thousands of miles and by necessity electric transmission lines are not usually contained within individual states. In response, regional authorities have been created to deal with these issues. Their range of authority has varied significantly. Some have been merely advisory, devoted to compiling research to help guide states. Others have used the information they have collected to actively work towards public policy changes. Few are very well known. Many states have created cooperatives to deal with vexing issues such as the disposal of low-level radioactive waste or have signed agreements to work together fighting forest fires. A number also have regional organizations devoted to preserving fisheries, such as the Connecticut River Atlantic Salmon Compact and the Gulf State Marine Fisheries Compact. Some are reserved for planning and development, such as the Columbia River Gorge Compact, which advises

Oregon and Washington about growth along the Columbia (Council of State Governments, 2001).

Some regional authorities, while largely invisible to the average resident, can exert significant power. The Northeast States for Coordinated Air Use Management, or NESCAUM, has dealt with air pollution issues in the northeast. It has a board of directors consisting of the state air directors in the six New England states as well as New York and New Jersey. Its staff of 30 has worked on regional air pollution issues, such as ground-level ozone or smog that can affect the region on hot days. It has had no statutory authority but it has been effective in convincing governors within its region to ratchet up air emission standards. It has also coordinated lawsuits by states in the region contesting the federal government or states in neighboring regions over air regulations that it considered too lax (NESCAUM, 2004–2006).

A different kind of political muscle has been flexed in the Ohio River Valley Water Sanitation Commission, or ORSANCO, which has handled water pollution issues in the Ohio River basin. Commissioners represent states along the watershed from New York to Illinois as well as federal representatives. Besides conducting research and education about the Ohio River, it has the ability to set standards and monitor the levels of waste water discharged into the river and its tributaries (ORSANCO, n.d.).

International efforts

While environmental problems may become clear at the local level, sometimes they reach global proportions. Consider population growth, food supplies and famine, water resources and scarcity, agrarian reform and desertification, climate and energy. Beginning in the 1970s, the United Nations explored such global issues. Part of its work was concentrated in the United Nations Environment Program, or UNEP, which was established in 1972 and is based in Nairobi, Kenya. The UNEP coordinated such programs as monitoring the upper atmosphere ozone level to assisting in protection programs for the great apes. The U.N.'s most significant international work on the environment has occurred diplomatically through global conferences and treaties (Soroos, 1994). Three stand out: a 1972 conference in Stockholm; a second gathering in 1992 in Rio de Janeiro; and a 1997 treaty negotiated in Kyoto.

The landmark Stockholm assembly was called the Conference on Human Environment. It focused on global environmental issues and created a set of 26 principles, called the Declaration of the Stockholm Conference. The principles established ideals on a variety of environmental issues that were so far-reaching that some have proved unreasonable to meet. One key principle reinforced the right of a nation to exploit its resources, but not at the cost of harming the environment. Another called on countries to develop international law on liability and compensation for environmental damage (Soroos, 1994).

Twenty years later delegates met in Rio and examined a range of environmental issues. Two stood out – tropical deforestation and climate change. The Soviet power bloc had collapsed, the Cold War was over, and expectations were high that a new consensus could be forged. Instead, new lines of conflict over environmental issues began to emerge between developing and industrialized nations. The schism was the strongest over how to reduce carbon dioxide emissions that were believed to be causing climate change. Industrialized nations, which use the bulk of the earth's resources and correspondingly created the greatest air pollution, balked at how much they would have to cut their emissions. Developing nations could not agree to forego their use of global resources, and their volume of emissions, without compensation. After the conference the conflict sharpened further as such massive nations as India and China increased their rapid rate of industrialization. Another complication has been the intransigence of the United States – in comparison to other industrial nations such as those in the European community – either to recognize the severity of the problem or to make concessions (Soroos, 1994).

Despite the clash, international delegates met in 1997 in Kyoto and negotiated a new climate change treaty. The agreement called for industrialized nations to reduce greenhouse gases by 5.2 percent, using 1990 as a standard base year. Since economies and production increases over time, so would emissions. By 2010 that anticipated reduction on average would be 29 percent. Under the terms of the treaty, the amount specific nations would have to reduce emissions varied. It went into effect in February, 2005, after at least 55 countries ratified the agreement. The U.S. was a signatory to the treaty, which was largely a symbolic gesture. The Bush Administration consistently opposed ratification. While action to reduce greenhouse gases remained controversial and its success was still uncertain, efforts by the international community to compile information and to educate the world have significantly contributed to the debate (UNFCCC, n.d.).

Not all environmental issues are as divisive or impossible to resolve. In 1973 two scientists reported that chlorofluorocarbons (CFCs), used in a number of consumer products and industrial processes, were migrating to the upper atmosphere and damaging the earth's protective ozone layer. By the 1980s the public was alarmed about CFCs. Scientists had documented that these chemicals were likely responsible for the seasonal holes developing in the ozone layer over the polar regions. In this situation the international community reacted rapidly. Delegates met in Vienna in 1985 and negotiated a general agreement to cut CFC production. Two years later they created the Montreal Protocol, with firmer requirements that called for reductions of between 20 to 50 percent of CFCs. In June, 1990 a third agreement in London called for the phase-out of all ozone-depleting chemicals (Soroos, 1994). Nations, including the United States, were more willing to act against the ozone threat because they believed that the scientific evidence was overwhelming and the threat was evident.

Public information officers

Journalists working with government agencies may have the opportunity to interview a range of officials. The foremost person many will deal with will be the agency's public information officer, or PIO. A PIO can be the best friend or the worst enemy of a reporter. A PIO can be extremely helpful in guiding a journalist through the complex maze of federal bureaucracy, cutting red tape when necessary and finding the key sources. A PIO can be just as effective in placing a wall between a reporter and the information or sources needed. Large agencies, such as the EPA, have PIOs assigned to the Washington headquarters and to the ten EPA regions. Policies will vary among public information offices. From a journalistic standpoint, the best policy is one where the PIO provides general information and a list of knowledgeable sources at the agency who can supply more detailed replies. Or, a policy where reporters are free to talk directly to officials and employees. In 2002 the Society of Environmental Journalists surveyed the press policies of the ten EPA regional offices and found a wide variation. At least three regions, New England, the upper Midwest from Ohio to Minnesota, and the Pacific Northwest including Alaska, allowed EPA staff members to answer reporters' questions without first getting clearance from the press office. Others, such as New York–New Jersey and the southwestern region that included California, encouraged reporters to first contact the press office to get clearance. The degree to which PIOs sat in on interviews would vary. Regions in the central U.S. from Texas to Iowa required that almost all questions be answered by a PIO. In the rare cases when EPA staff were allowed to do interviews, a press officer had to sit in (Grimaldi, 2002).

Peyton Fleming, who was the press officer in EPA's Region 1 in Boston from 1994 to 2003, said as a former reporter he always tried to make staff people available. "Reporters need to feel that they are getting the information from the people who are developing the policy," he said. "I always felt that transparency was the best policy at the department" (Fleming, 2006). Fleming said there were rare cases when he did step in and handle questions, but they were only with reporters who had limited knowledge of the issues or who had made mistakes in the past. He said he left the EPA after the Bush Administration imposed a far more restrictive policy on press access. Environmental reporters generally concurred that access had become more difficult since the 2002 SEJ survey. Those who have supported a more centralized approach to press information say a single source is able to present a more accurate viewpoint of the department's policy or position. They also argue that press specialists better understand what information is within public jurisdiction and what is restricted. Fleming disagreed. He said that as a PIO he worried at times about sending reporters to talk to staff people, but he felt the risks were worth it. "More times than not, (the restrictive policy) is going to hurt you," he said (Fleming, 2006).

The human element

Writing about government and regulation can be challenging. Candace Page of the *Burlington Free Press* faced that task when she needed to write about Vermont's Act 250, a one-stop permitting system that regulated all new development. "Environmental protection is so much about process and it is so difficult to get people to read about process and understand process," she said (Page, 2006).

Figure 6.4 John Lambert, a 26-year-old auto mechanic, in his garage in Vermont. Lambert's frustration with Vermont's land regulations helped illustrate how difficult it is to find land uses that everyone supports (source: courtesy *Burlington Free Press*).

Readers can, however, relate to people and to conflicts. Page focused on several regulatory disputes to highlight what was good and bad about the current system in Vermont. One dispute involved a proposal to use 22 acres in rural Vermont to store, crush and sell scrapped cars. John Lambert, a 26-year-old mechanic, wanted to start the business. Eleven months and $9,000 in lawyers' fees later, Lambert's project was dead. Would he do it again someday? Page asked him. "No," he said, "I couldn't put myself and my family through that again" (Page, 2003, p. 3).

Page then interviewed the opponents, 29 neighbors upset about the prospect of a junkyard being established in their rural community. Kristina Lutes and her husband had only just moved into their old farmhouse when they learned of Lambert's plan. She wrote to her neighbors: "There is great concern that if this goes through that Mr. John Lambert's operation will be an eyesore. We all know how sound travels here. The beauty and peacefulness of our properties will be diminished as well as our property value" (Page, 2003, p. 3).

These kinds of conflicts were the reason Vermont legislators wanted to change Act 250. Page's stories showed that land disputes occurred for many reasons and that some were inevitable. "There were well-meaning people on both sides of such development projects, but their goals and values were so different that you couldn't resolve what they both wanted through the regulatory process," she said. "Their aims were so divergent that one is going to win and one is going to lose" (Page, 2006). Readers told her that they liked the stories and they were learning about the complications in amending Act 250. "They'd say, 'Oh yeah, I get it'," she said. "I got people to read about the issue, I felt really good about that" (Page, 2006).

Study guide

1 Examine your community. Where do such basic necessities come from such as your drinking water, sewage treatment, and waste disposal? Write a story about one of these issues, focusing on the quality of the environmental service and if and when change will be needed.

2 If you were to develop a local environmental beat, who are the people you would need to contact? Compile a list that includes each person's full name, job title, affiliation, address, phone number and email.

3 Research how much your state spends on its environmental protection department and how that has changed over the last five years. If there is a change, how do officials explain it? Is there enough information here to write a story?

4 What is the current status of the Kyoto Protocol? Examine how the U.S. position has changed since 1997. What are the prospects at this point for a reduction in greenhouse gas emissions either globally or in the U.S.?

5 Practice writing some news leads both from the information about Ken Ward Jr.'s stories about the coal silo and Candace Page's story about the conflict over the Vermont junkyard.

6 For further reading consider *The Investigative Reporter's Handbook* by Brant Houston, Len Bruzzese and Steve Weinberg (2002), Daniel Yergin's *The Prize* (1991) and *Theodore Rex* (2001) by Edmund Morris.

Chapter 7

The advocates

The land baron, whose initials were N.C., was wealthy. N.C. was worth $3 billion and had annual revenue of over $950 million. Most of N.C.'s wealth was in land. The land baron owned more than two million acres around the world and managed another seven million acres. N.C. directed that empire out of a gleaming $28 million, eight-story headquarters in Arlington, VA. But with 3,200 employees, N.C. had them spread around 528 offices in every state as well as 30 countries. N.C. was a devoted environmentalist. Yet at times N.C. hung around with some shady characters. Some of N.C.'s partners had repeatedly gotten into scraps with environmental regulators and some had paid millions in environmental fines. N.C. had also cut some corners at times. N.C. had logged forests, engineered a $64 million development that allowed for construction of lavish homes on fragile grasslands and drilled for natural gas under the last breeding area of an endangered bird species (Ottaway & Stephens, 2003a).

N.C. was not a person – it was the environmental group the Nature Conservancy. The *Washington Post*, in a three-part series in 2003, labeled the Conservancy "Big Green." It called the organization the richest and most powerful non-profit environmental organization. The investigative series by Joe Stephens and David Ottaway described how the Nature Conservancy grew from modest beginnings in 1951 by eschewing the confrontational approach so common in the environmental movement. Instead, it acquired vast tracts of environmentally sensitive land by relying on donations, first from individuals and later from corporate sponsors, to build what became its "bucks and acres" strategy. It's refusal to criticize polluters paid off, and by the time of the *Post* series the Conservancy had 1,900 corporate sponsors and was receiving up to $225 million in donations (Ottaway & Stephens, 2003a–c).

Stephens said that the *Post* was drawn to the story because of the Nature Conservancy's sizeable assets and the fact that it was involved in some unusual situations for an environmental organization. Some endangered birds died after drilling began for natural gas on the Texas

Gulf Coast and the Conservancy inadvertently sold natural gas that was owned by someone else. In New York, the Conservancy bought environmentally sensitive property for $2.1 million, then sold it for $500,000 to a former chairman of a regional chapter. Stephens cautioned that "We do not consider the Conservancy to be a good guy or a bad guy. We approached the Conservancy as we would any organization" (Dunne, 2003, p. 24).

It is important to not make assumptions when dealing with environmental advocates. Understand that politics plays just as important a role in environmental issues as do science or government. When Rachel Carson wrote *Silent Spring* (1962) she never intended it to be an objective examination of the role of pesticides. It was designed to be a polemic, a wake-up call to arouse America to examine more closely what chemicals were doing to the environment and especially to wildlife. Even before publication, it generated a massive public relations campaign by the chemical industry designed to counteract her main points. Society, including journalism, has depended on a free flow of ideas. The danger lies in not understanding the perspective, or political viewpoint, of a particular actor in the debate.

That was what made the "Big Green" series (Ottaway & Stephens, 2003a) about the Nature Conservancy so powerful. The fact that the organization was so deeply tied to large corporations and questionable development projects surprised many readers. In dealing with advocates journalists must understand their motives and tactics, and use the tools available to report fairly on what they say and do.

The big ten

The ten largest environmental groups, by annual expenses reported, were:

Organization	Expenses
Nature Conservancy	$569,529,901
Wildlife Conservation Society	$139,510,005
Zoological Society of San Diego	$134,647,847
Ducks Unlimited	$129,495,365
The Trust for Public Land	$109,632,976
National Wildlife Federation	$105,693,844
World Wildlife Fund	$94,106,425
Conservation International Foundation	$83,701,035
National Audubon Society	$71,997,904
Humane Society of the United States	$69,548,619
	(NCCS, 2006)

Sometimes the consequences can be surprising. The Nature Conservancy, defensive and at times combative while the *Post* reporters were working on the story, afterwards agreed that changes needed to be made. Conservancy President Steven McCormick, on a radio talk show shortly after the series, said the *Post* may have done his organization a favor. "This could be good for us," McCormick reportedly told a caller. "This is an opportunity for us and other organizations to take a hard look at our activities. Non-profit organizations are held to a higher standard, and they should be" (Dunne, 2003, p. 25).

The big boys

The Nature Conservancy has been by far the largest environmental organization in terms of financial support, but others are more visible and well known. Advocating and working to protect the environment today is a big-money proposition. The National Center for Charitable Statistics (NCCS) reported in January 2006 that according to federal tax records there were 14,651 organizations that identified themselves as non-profit environmental groups. Annual gross receipts were $6.79 billion (NCCS, 2006).

Some of these organizations would be recognizable and some would not. Some have had a single purpose, such as Ducks Unlimited, which has confined its efforts primarily to support of one wildlife species. Others such as the World Wildlife Fund have a far broader mission. The two most recognizable would be the Humane Society, which has a limited role in environmental issues, and the National Audubon Society. Audubon began as an activist organization in 1905 that worked to prevent the widespread killing of birds that was occurring at the time. The birds were sought for their feathers, which were highly fashionable at the time as ornaments on women's hats (Knudson, 2001c).

Environmental groups such as Audubon and the Sierra Club began as small grassroots organizations that have evolved into major political players. But size can divert attention from priorities. In 2001 Tom Knudson of the *Sacramento Bee* wrote a series titled "Environment, Inc." (Knudson, 2001a), reporting that the nation's largest environmental organizations had grown distant from their grassroots origins. He said that they were now characterized by high-rise offices, ritzy conferences, rising executive salaries, fat Wall Street portfolios and costly fundraising consultants. While they had made some valuable improvements to the environment through legislation, litigation and land preservation, they were also spending sizeable amounts of money on bureaucratic overheads and fundraising. Audubon at times has struggled as its membership has grown to over 500,000 in more than 500 local chapters. Chapter members at times have accused the headquarters staff of being out of touch and of working too hard to appease corporate sponsors (Knudson, 2001c). The Sierra Club has also been shaken by membership revolts, including one in 2004 over whether proposed immigration controls in the U.S. merited the organization's attention (Dawson, 2004).

Large environmental organizations believe they have to build staffs and budgets to compete with corporate critics. Many now have teams of scientific, technical, legal and public relations experts. Groups issue detailed reports and press releases, they lobby in Congress and at State Houses for stronger environmental legislation and they go to court when they think current laws are not being properly enforced. Janet Raloff, senior editor of *Science News*, said that many environmental groups can be extremely helpful in analyzing new research, crunching databases, and getting their views expressed. But she said they also too often can't see both sides of some issues. "If they are anti-nuclear, for instance, they turn a blind eye to the fact that coal mining and its emissions are anything but benign," she said (Bruggers, 1998, p. 17).

The better-known groups blend political lobbying with public relations campaigns. One of the most effective in getting a response from the public was the effort by the relatively unknown group Natural Resources Defense Council to impose pesticide controls on apple production. Such tactics have drawn criticism. Some of the harshest critics have been scientists who said that too often environmental groups twist facts into fantasy. Knudson (2001a) cited a 1999 report by the U.S. General Accounting Office which identified 39 million acres of Western forest that were "at high risk of catastrophic fire" (Knudson, 2001a, p. 2). He contrasted that with the opposition of several environmental groups to selective thinning efforts that could reduce fire risk. Jerry Franklin, a University of Washington professor of forest ecology and ecosystem systems, said: "A lot of environmental messages are simply not accurate. But that's the way we sell messages in this society. We use hype. And we use those pieces of information that sustain our position. I guess all organizations do that" (Knudson, 2001a, p. 2).

In 1999 Paul Rogers (1999), a reporter with the *San Jose Mercury News*, conducted a very informal survey of 35 environmental journalists, asking them who they thought were the most credible and reliable environmental organizations. The leader of the 15 groups he selected was the Nature Conservancy and the Environmental Defense Fund. Taken several years before the *Post* series about the Conservancy, Rogers said the group rated high because of its ability to build coalitions and consensus. The New York-based EDF was known for its litigation record and its support for economic incentives to solve environmental problems such as emission trading, an economic and regulatory device to control air pollution and toxic chemical releases.

The Apple scare

The television program was titled "A is for Apple" and the first image on the screen depicted a large red apple plastered with a skull and crossbones. It was being featured February 26, 1989 on the CBS News program *60 Minutes* and it began with host Ed Bradley saying, "The most potent cancer-causing chemical in our food supply is a pesticide sprayed on apples to keep them on the trees longer and make them look better" (Arnold, 1990, p. 61). The EPA's acting administrator, Dr Jack Moore, acknowledged that the EPA has known about the cancer risk for 16 years.

On the program Bradley turned to Moore and said, "A lot of these chemicals got on the market when we didn't know that they were cancer-causing agents, and they're on the market now, and we know that they do cause cancer."

"Correct," responded Moore.

Replied Bradley, "But you say that we can't take them off because they're already on the market, they went on the market and we didn't know that they caused cancer."

"That's the paradox of the situation," said Moore.

"It's crazy!" exclaimed Bradley (Arnold, 1990, p. 61).

The chemical they were referring to went by the trade name Alar. In production since the 1960s, it had been used as a plant growth regulator in apples and other fruits to keep them on the tree longer and to prevent spoilage. Beginning in the 1970s studies began to show Alar might be a carcinogen. By the time of the *60 Minutes* broadcast the EPA had been reviewing whether to take it off the market, and environmental groups had been campaigning to have it removed (Arnold, 1990).

The story that apples might be tainted with a chemical poison hit a nerve with the American public. *Newsweek* and *Time* responded with cover stories about the safety of the food industry and the story was picked up by such major news organizations as *USA Today*, NBC's *Today Show*, the *Phil Donahue Show*, *Woman's Day*, *Family Circle* and *People* magazine. The Natural Resources Defense Council held a press conference the day after the *60 Minutes* broadcast that drew 70 journalists and 12 camera crews while it also coordinated local news conferences in 12 other cities. Less than two weeks later actor Meryl Streep held a related press conference to announce the creation of a new organization, Mothers and Others for Pesticide Limits. People stopped buying apples and soon school systems were banning apples. The American apple industry estimated it lost $75 million in reduced sales.

Apple growers struck back, hiring the public relations firm of Hill and Knowlton for $700,000. Soon new stories were appearing reporting that the levels of Alar were below federal standards and that the press had exaggerated the story (Arnold, 1990).

It also became clear that the *60 Minutes* story was part of an NRDC public relations campaign to alert the public to the dangers of Alar, a campaign that had been wildly successful. The environmental organization until then had generally taken a low profile and devoted its efforts to legislative lobbying and litigation tactics. In October, 1988 it hired a young publicist, David Fenton, to mount the public relations campaign to get its message about Alar to the average American consumer. NRDC had produced a report called "Intolerable Risk" about Alar, and Fenton reached an agreement with CBS permitting *60 Minutes* to have an exclusive in breaking the story of the report (Arnold, 1990).

Claims that news reports, including that of the *60 Minutes* broadcast, were false were tossed out of court. A federal judge in 1993 dismissed a lawsuit by Washington apple growers, saying that CBS accurately reported the science and the controversy ("Judge Dismisses," 1993). The U.S. Supreme Court refused to consider an appeal ("Court Denies," 1996). The Alar story created new debate about the use of pesticides and helped hasten the withdrawal of Alar. Still, it also raised troubling questions for the press. While it generated significant attention to the issue, the public was left to flounder between competing claims made by the environmental community and industry. Only a fraction of the stories, estimated at about 15 percent, contained any risk analysis which attempted to place the hazard in perspective (Friedman, 1991). Perhaps even most troubling was the failure by CBS and *60 Minutes* to engage in its own thorough investigation. While it did some research, its primary mission seemed aimed at breaking a story that had been prepared by an environmental agency and its public relations firm. The Alar campaign generated numerous articles and even a book about how environmental advocates used the press (Arnold, 1990).

Other credible groups according to the survey included the Natural Resources Defense Council, League of Conservation Voters and World Wildlife Fund.

Of the 15 organizations selected by Rogers, the least credible were the environmental groups that may be best known because they use the strongest, most theatrical and colorful confrontational tactics. These

Figure 7.1 Greenpeace activists demonstrate against a facility that raises tuna in Cartagena, Spain. The international environmental organization has earned a reputation for staging protests designed to draw attention to environmental problems (source: courtesy Pedro Armestre, Greenpeace).

organizations were Earth First! and Greenpeace. Earth First! gained attention in such places as the old growth forests of California where it spiked trees to prevent timber operations even though that jeopardized the safety of lumber employees. Greenpeace chartered ships to prevent native tribes in the Arctic from killing seal pups. The tactics have drawn attention to the cause, but they have also angered opponents and alienated would-be supporters. Rogers found reporters complaining that the groups were inaccurate, tended to exaggerate, were emotion-based, acted without data, and had a holier-than-thou attitude. One writer complained to Rogers that the groups had a "tendency to characterize some journalists as biased because the journalist doesn't completely embrace their viewpoint (which really isn't our job)" (Rogers, 1999, p. 9).

The corporate perspective

In 1929, a troop of New York debutantes marched in the city's Easter Parade, each conspicuously lighting and smoking a cigarette. The march was organized by Edward Bernays, the founder of the modern public relations industry, and it was financed by the American Tobacco Company. Called the Torches of Liberty, the campaign was extremely successful in breaking the taboo against women smoking in public. Sales of Lucky Strikes soared in the months after the parade and Bernays was hailed as a public relations genius (Stauber & Rampton, 1995).

As environmental activism rose in the mid-twentieth century and businesses were forced to spend more time and money on environmental regulation and compliance an adversarial relationship developed. Many business and industries maintain that they support a clean environment. However, their records often tell a different story. Often they have argued that the price and efforts demanded by environmental activists, and at times by scientists and government, have been too costly and counterproductive. To change opinions and policies corporate public relations campaigns were launched. Some were designed to counter a short-term objective, such as the publication of *Silent Spring* (1962). Others were long-term, such as elements of the energy sector that have worked for more than two decades to resurrect the long moribund nuclear energy industry. While numbers are readily available for quantifying how much non-profit environmental organizations spend, it is much more difficult to figure how much business and industry spend on environmental public relations issues and lobbying campaigns. Authors John Stauber and Sheldon Rampton, who wrote the anti-public relations book *Toxic Sludge is Good for You*, estimated in 1995 that U.S. businesses were spending $1 billion a year on the services of professionals hired to fight environmental organizations. The figure was only a guess, based on interviews with public relations professionals (Stauber & Rampton, 1995).

Public relations consultants call such environmental campaigns "green p.r." while critics use the phrase "greenwashing." One of the pioneers in this field was E. Bruce Harrison (1993), who helped lead the campaign against Carson's *Silent Spring* and later wrote a book, *Going Green: How to Communicate Your Company's Environmental Commitment* (Harrison, 1993). Harrison's advice in *Going Green* was that the environmental activism of the 1960s was dead and that the large environmental organizations were so intent on maintaining their budgets and bureaucracies that they were open to being co-opted by business. Such alliances have almost always been controversial. One of the more famous in the 1990s occurred in a partnership between the Environmental Defense Fund and McDonald's. It was designed to cut the amount of waste generated by the fast-food restaurant chain that at the time was under attack for generating tremendous waste. After several months the groups announced that they had dramatically reduced plastic foam containers and also promoted recycling and waste reduction efforts. Yet critics maintained it was more show than substance and was primarily designed to win EDF's endorsement so that McDonald's could sell more hamburgers (Stauber & Rampton, 1995).

The public relations profession has a code of ethics, but over the years some campaigns and professionals have been found doing everything from spying on environmental organizations to issuing fake press releases designed to sabotage environmental campaigns or organizations. Perhaps the best documented practice is the use of creating organizations with misleading names that sometimes hide the real sponsors. In the environmental arena the list of front organizations would be too long to detail but it would include:

- The National Wetlands Coalition, whose members included oil companies and homebuilders opposed to U.S. wetlands policies (Hebert, 2003).
- The Sea Lion Defense Fund which lobbied against limits on the harvesting of pollock on the argument that the fish was a staple of sea lions. The campaign was financed by the Alaskan fishing industry (Hebert, 2003).
- The Foundation for Clean Air Progress, supported by the American Highways Users Alliance, designed to show that the U.S. made significant progress already in combating air pollution (Hebert, 2003).

Another interesting organization has been the Greening Earth Society, which garnered significant press attention for its argument that global warming was a myth and that there was not a scientific consensus on climate change. The organization with the lush, verdant name was created by the Western Fuels Association, a consortium of coal mining companies and utilities based in the western U.S. (Hebert, 2003). In publications such as *World Climate Report* it criticized scientific suggestions that the planet's temperatures might be rising and that any build-up of carbon dioxide was caused by humans (Michaels, 2005).

Grassroots

Lois Gibbs, who was first mentioned in Chapter 2, said she considered herself a homemaker and mother until she began to learn that toxic chemicals might be poisoning her family and her neighbors in Love Canal, NY. Gibbs and her neighbors began a campaign which drew national attention to the chemical dumping in her community and made the term Love Canal the poster child for environmental activism in the 1980s. Gibbs eventually moved to Washington, DC and created the Center for Health, Environment and Justice (formerly the National

Clearinghouse on Hazardous Waste). Unlike the Sierra Club or Audubon, it was not a national organization but a network of grass-roots groups run by volunteers often on a shoestring budgets. Local groups operated autonomously. Sometimes they embraced a set of environmental objectives. Other times they centered their attack on a specific problem or issue in the community. It was locally based and it would run high on emotion. The groups were often accused of unchecked or hysterical NIMBYism, the Not-In-My-Back-Yard Syndrome. The work was direct and personal. Gibbs said that grassroots campaigns caught on because the large environmental organizations were no longer connecting with the average citizen, their work was too abstract. "They don't know what it is like to live in a community and have everything you've ever worked for – your home – become worthless overnight," she said. "It's a different emotional sense that drives people like me. For people like me, the environmental movement is about survival" (Bosso, 1994, p. 44).

The range of local groups has been as varied as the issues they have confronted. Consider the following three organizations:

Kentuckians for the Commonwealth (KFTC)

The group was begun in 1981 by two women fighting against a local coal company's efforts to control mineral rights beneath residents' properties. The group, comprised of moderate-income residents with modest educational backgrounds, mounted an aggressive campaign, which resulted in a 1988 referendum that revised the state's mining laws. The group went on to fight other campaigns, including efforts to block garbage from being imported into the state (Cheves, 2004).

Mothers of East Los Angeles

Low-income Spanish-speaking residents originally created the organization in 1984 to fight a proposed prison for the neighborhood but it was best known for its battles against waste incinerators and oil pipelines. Signature protests featured mothers carrying white kerchiefs and wheeling babies in strollers ("Mothers Group," 1989).

Shovel Brigade

A group of Nevada ranchers and fishermen created the brigade after federal officials refused to rebuild a washed-out road near Jarbidge, NV, along a stream that was home to the threatened bull trout. The group, beginning in 1997, began battling the U.S. Forestry Service and U.S. Fish and Wildlife service for access to the remote area. In 2002 it built a symbolic shovel with a 12-foot blade and hauled it on a trailer on a 3,000-mile trip to Florida to build support for its cause (Sonner, 2002).

Members of the Shovel Brigade were part of the Wise Use movement, a network of individuals and groups organized around property rights issues and generally opposed to government interference. Sometimes called the Sagebrush Rebellion in the western states, many of these groups sought to open federal lands in the west to greater use at a time when some federal agencies were already under attack from environmentalists for allowing overgrazing and other exploitations of the region's natural resources (Stauber & Rampton, 1995).

The aims of the Wise Use movement at times have paralleled the goals of some business and industrial groups, and there have been suggestions that some of these organizations were also fronts for major energy, agriculture or development companies. Stauber and Rampton cited the strong corporate sponsorship of national Wise Use conferences, including Chevron, Exxon, Shell Oil and Georgia Pacific. *Consumer Reports* examined membership rolls and found they were dominated by employees of regulated industries, antigovernment ideologues, and recruiters who had been paid $500 for every citizen they could recruit. However, to characterize all Wise Use groups as fronts for corporate interests would be an oversimplification. The Wise Use movement has been dominated by politically active individuals who were politically conservative and who preferred the least degree of government oversight, whether it involved their gun, how they hunted, or what they did with their ranch, farm or property (Stauber & Rampton, 1995).

The extent of corporate involvement in the grassroots movement reached the point where certain terms have been coined. A synthetic grassroots effort has been called Astroturf lobbying or "democracy for hire" and such movements have sometimes been led by hired guns called "grassroots grannies." The best grannies, according to Pamela Whitney who headed the firm of National Grassroots and Communications, were local women. They had been active in local affairs, as head of the local PTA or other organizations, or recently retired with time on their hands. Whitney's firm advertised its services in such publications as *Campaigns & Elections* magazine which was read by public relations professionals. A full-page ad on the back cover of one issue had a headline that screamed "Real Grass Roots – Not Astroturf" (Stauber & Rampton 1995, p. 79).

Identifying points of view

The goal of an advocate is to spin the message in a way that is beneficial to a particular cause or purpose. For journalists to detect the spin, they must first understand the motivation of the advocate or the organization. There are a number of tools that can help in this process.

Federal tax records can assist. Most environmental groups are not-for-profit and enjoy tax-exempt status through the Internal Revenue Code Section 501(c). In 2000 the IRS reported that there were 1.35 million tax-exempt organizations recognized under Section 501(c) whose assets were $1.2 trillion, with annual revenues of $720 billion (General Accounting Office, 2002).

A 501(c) organization must make an initial application for non-profit status, a form 1023, as well as annual filing if its revenue is more than $25,000 a year, which is a form 990. The 990s can provide a wealth of information including: an organization's identity and tax status; its income including specific revenue sources; its expenses and breakdown between program, management and fundraising; its net assets; the types of programs it runs; its board members and salaries of top staff; any new activities or changes in programs; whether the organization is a private foundation and if it lobbies. Federal law requires nonprofits to make available for public inspection their 990s for the previous three years and examining at least a three-year history that provides a more complete picture of an organization's finances (Swords et al., 2003). However, the U.S. General Accounting Office in 2002 warned that there may be reporting errors in the 990s. It reported that IRS oversight had not kept pace in recent years with the growth in the charitable section and that the rate at which the IRS reviewed form 990s had fallen from less than 1 percent, or 0.73 percent, in 1998 to only 0.43 percent in 2001. State officials, who have their own monitoring requirements of charitable activities, have also complained that the filing data was incomplete (General Accounting Office, 2002).

The 990s must be read carefully, as Knudson (2001a) of the *Sacramento Bee* discovered when he did his series on the major environmental organizations. Knudson found that some groups had tried to disguise their fundraising efforts by labeling them as conservation activities. He said they were labeling many of their direct-mail material as education, so that they could tell their donors that a large percentage of their money would go directly to conservation. While technically correct, Knudson felt it was wrong for them to fail to mention that this "conservation" included millions of dollars of costs for mail solicitation. The 990s proved to be a wealth of information in providing such other tidbits such as the average top salary of the ten largest environmental organizations in 1999 was $235,918. That compared to $62,843 at Habitat for Humanity International which built homes for the poor and $69,570 for the president of Mothers Against Drunk Driving (Knudson, 2001a).

While many 501(c) groups will voluntarily supply their form 990s, there are other ways to access them. GuideStar (2006), which calls itself a searchable database of more than 640,000 nonprofits in the United States, can be found online at www.guidestar.org. Another source for tracking contributions to organizations is The Foundation Directory Online (2002), which is at www.fconline.fdncenter.org. While GuideStar has offerings that are free along with others that require a fee to be accessed. Foundation Directory Online had prices that can average $20 to $30 a month. A third group that tracks form 990s is ActivistCash.com (2006), located at http://activistcash.com. According to its Internet site, ActivistCash "is committed to providing detailed and up-to-date information about the funding source of radical anti-consumer organizations and activists." It is particularly concerned about advocates who promote "false science, scare campaigns, inflated public health causes, and sometimes even violent anti-consumer direct actions" (Activistcash.com, 2006, p. 1).

Other watchdog organizations may not necessarily track federal tax records but may have revealing information about a particular group, a study, or a researcher. While they may reflect a particular perspective, the information they provide might be a helpful starting point. One is the Integrity in Science Project (CSPI, n.d.) run by the Center for Science in the Public Interest, a subscription-based advocate for health and nutrition, that can be found at www.cspinet.org/integrity. The purpose of the site is to provide information about the commercialization of science, especially illuminating financial support by business or industry groups to scientists or researchers. Another site is Undue Influence (Center for the Defense of Free Enterprise, 2005–2006), at www.undue-influence.com, which said it tracked "the environmental movement's money, power and harm." Finally, Stauber and Rampton, who wrote *Toxic Sludge* (1995), discuss front groups and what they call "disinfo-pedia" at their site called PR Watch, which is at www.prwatch.org. (prwatch, n.d.)

An even more direct source for information is the organization itself. Examine the literature it produces about itself, both written and online, including its mission, board members and staff, membership, press statements and studies, annual reports and sources of financing. What organizations is it linked to and what do the biographies say about key staff or board members? Talk to members of the organization about what they are doing, and also question critics on the other side.

Most environmental advocates depend upon research to back their claims. In Chapter 4 guidance was provided to help examine a scientific study. In recent years, advocates have complicated the situation by either funding or running their own studies, or attacking their opponents for undertaking those tactics. Knowing who sponsors a study is important, both for the journalist and for the reader. A significant amount of scientific research is funded by private sources; even government-funded studies may contain biases. Ultimately the science in the study may be sound, no matter who pays for it, but the funding source still remains important. It can be helpful to talk to both the researcher and to anyone on the other side of the issue to better understand the study. Consider also looking at other studies the researcher has undertaken. Some journals publish what they consider potential financial conflicts, including *Lancet* and the *New England Journal of Medicine*. In addition, some science conferences require speakers to provide conflict-of-interest statements, which are either provided or published, as part of the conference report (Luechtefeld, 2004).

Deciphering messages

When the environmental group Earth First! in the late 1990s was trying to prevent the last major privately owned and unprotected stand of old growth redwoods from being cut down, it chose a publicity stunt as a way to draw attention to the issue. Several members of the group, along with actor Woody Harrelson, climbed San Francisco's Golden Gate Bridge. Their efforts caused traffic to be backed up for miles in both directions. James Bruggers, who was then a reporter with the *Contra Costa Times* in California, interviewed motorists who stewed for hours waiting for authorities to get the climbers down. They were furious, and the article disclosed how the stunt may have done more harm than good to the cause (Bruggers, 1998). Advocates like to use the press and it is a tactic journalists resent. From a journalistic viewpoint, the key is to get the best story. That does not mean looking for the counter story from what the activists intended, but it does mean getting as close to the truth by digging deeply. That's what Bruggers accomplished. As a side note, some environmental organizations like to use celebrities as a way of drawing even more attention to their cause or issue. Names do make news, but they may also overshadow the primary issue.

Press releases are far more common than stunts. Some environmental organizations and their messages are more credible than others. But no matter the source, press releases must be closely scrutinized, researched and rewritten. Problems can vary from arcane jargon to absolute falsehoods. Begin by deciding if the issue highlighted in the press release actually is news. Is it simply publicity for the group or will readers care about the information? If it is news, then the next step is to examine whether the issue can be verified. Is it factual, or simply opinion? Decide how far to take the story. Does the release only address a single, basic issue, or is there more at stake here? How many sources, how many facts, need to be addressed?

Setting the agenda

Some environmental reporters say they get so many press releases daily from environmental advocates that they could virtually spend all of their time reporting on what advocates were saying. Journalists must determine what is news. They cannot delegate what should be on the public agenda to any one group, be it science, government or political and environmental advocates. No matter how frenzied the agenda, journalists must report on what they consider the most important issues in their beat. Over time reporters who know their beats become just as great an expert as any of the sources they quote in their stories.

Journalists should also take care in seeking comments from environmental advocates and avoid using particular sources as a crutch. Sometimes such sources can offer quick, predictable, and valuable insights that a reporter also believes but is hesitant to write without attribution. But at the very least journalists should not keep returning to the same sources. In reporting on an obvious hazard, such as pollution, the voice of outrage or concern may be just as powerful coming from members of the public as it would be from an environmental group. A person living near a facility spewing chemicals into the air may be upset about the pollution, but he may also be concerned about the number of jobs at that plant and the economic welfare of the community if the business were to shut down. Calling the same sources repeatedly is not only lazy, but it can mislead readers (Detjen, 1991).

When Scott Streater was working on a series for the *Pensacola News-Journal* about the volume of toxic chemicals being released in Escambia County in Florida, he decided to exclude the voice of environmental activists in the series. "There were not going to be advocates (in the story) making cheap shots at anyone," he said (Luechtefeld, 2004, p. 97). Nor would there be voices of industry responding to unfounded accusations. Stories sometimes thrive on conflict, but the strongest investigative stories document problems in detail. They are far more powerful than stories that quote two or more sides to a dispute without giving any guidance to the reader as to who is more believable.

Study guide

1 Find a local environmental organization or activist in your community. Conduct interviews and write a profile, presenting a balanced but representative look at the group or person.
2 See if the environmental organization or activist you are writing about has posted a form 990, or ask the group for copies of their 990s. Examine it and use any appropriate information.

3 If you had to write a story about Alar what are the risk issues you would want to examine? Why did the public respond so emotionally to the message presented by the NRDC and the *60 Minutes* broadcast?

4 The Greening Earth Society has a website at http://greeningearthsociety.org. Examine its position and compare it with the Pew Center on Global Climate Change, which can be found at www.pewclimate.org. Find a press release from each organization, research and write a story.

5 What is the ethical line for a public relations advocate preparing a campaign? How important is it for these advocates to disclose their purpose and their funding sources?

6 Who are the ten environmental organizations listed near the beginning of the chapter that have the highest in annual expenses? Prepare a summary of each and possible stories that could be written about individual organizations or similar groups.

7 For further reading, consider *Toxic Sludge is Good for You, Lies, Damn Lies and the Public Relations Industry* by John Stauber and Sheldon Rampton (1995), *It Ain't Necessarily So, How Media Make and Unmake the Scientific Picture of Reality* by David Murray, Joel Schwartz and S. Robert Lichter (2001), and *The Skeptical Environmentalist* by Bjorn Lomborg (2001).

Chapter 8

Reporting tools

Ron Nixon was reporting for the *Roanoke Times* in 1998 about the practice of clear-cut logging in the Virginia mountains. State forestry officials told Nixon that 90 percent of the companies operating complied with the department's logging guidelines, assuring that logged areas would be less susceptible to landslides, erosion and flooding. Nixon then learned that the Virginia Department of Forestry had audited logging sites. Using the state's open record law, he obtained the computer data that was the basis for the audits and discovered that 92 percent of logging sites audited at random in 1997 failed at least one of the department's "best management" guidelines (O'Donnell, 2004).

Journalists use many tools. Two of the most important are first, the federal and state laws allowing them access to government information and second, the ability to analyze government data usually in computer form to find trends and results. Seth Borenstein of Knight-Ridder News Service in Washington, DC said, "With numbers you don't have the he-said, she-said spin of giving both sides. This is a city (Washington) of spin, but numbers give you a sense of trust that rhetoric doesn't. After I spend a lot of time with numbers, I feel more comfortable that I know what I'm talking about" (Dunne, 2004, p. 19).

Freedom of information

The federal government and virtually every state have sunshine laws designed to allow public access to government meetings and records. Local and state laws vary. The law that applies to federal agencies and records is the U.S. Freedom of Information Act, often called FOIA. The federal law only addresses records, not meetings. Many state sunshine laws cover both meetings and records. Generally, meetings of government agencies and boards are open to the public except for discussions about employees or a pending legal case, or if the gathering is considered a staff meeting or caucus. Public record exceptions can range from certain law-enforcement reports, some personnel data, testing scores and so-called preliminary drafts. Sometimes a verbal request to see a record is all that is needed, but journalists should be prepared to file formal, written requests and to appeal rulings denying access to records (Schulte & Dufresne, 1994).

The range of information available is only as limited as one's imagination. Government agencies produce mounds of data. Environmental records are available on who is polluting the air and waterways, the quality of drinking water, how hazardous waste is being handled and where it is being disposed and the volume of toxic chemicals released into the environment. While they may be slightly more difficult to obtain, public records also detail how effective government agencies and officials are in enforcing current laws and pursuing polluters. Veteran environmental reporters say to get that kind of information they sometimes have to be creative in their requests. For instance, most email is a public record and has to be made available if requested. Another potential source is the agency visitor log that is compiled daily, detailing exactly who is visiting, who they are seeing, and sometimes why they are meeting. Other documents that should be public are calendars, correspondence, inspection reports, audits and budgets. Sometimes reporters have had documents leaked to them and then filed a FOIA request for the very same document. The reason is that they want to protect whoever provided the information. They have sent requests to related agencies in the hope of turning up more information (Ward *et al.*, 2005). Ken Ward Jr. of the *Charleston Gazette* said that he feels a little bit less than whole if he has not filed a records request in a week. "You will never set yourself apart as an enterprising reporter, an 'investigative reporter,' if you don't independently seek documents and data," said Michael Mansur (2005, p. 1) of the *Kansas City Star*.

The spirit of the federal FOIA, passed in 1966 and amended several times, is designed to open up access to government unless it jeopardizes such issues as personal privacy, a law-enforcement investigation, or national security (Schulte & Dufresne, 1994). The administration of the law does not always comply with the spirit. A month after the September 11 terrorist assaults in New York and Washington, then-Attorney General John Ashcroft wrote a memo offering new advice on what records should be released. For decades federal policy had been to release any information unless there were substantial legal reasons to retain it. Ashcroft changed that standard, urging federal agencies not to disclose information if they could find any legal reasoning. In the years after that ruling numerous documents once in the public domain were removed from Internet sites and denied to the public (Davis, 2005).

FOIA is famous for other obstacles. Even though a federal agency is required to respond within 20 days and usually assigns a specific employee to be the designated FOIA officer, waiting for a response sometimes takes weeks, months or even years. Other pitfalls include an excessive amount of information blacked out, or redacted, and surly or passive-aggressive FOIA officers (Mansur, 2005). Efforts just in the period of 2004 and 2005 to keep documents or information away from the public included:

- About 50 U.S. mayors wrote the Department of Homeland Security complaining they needed more information about hazardous materials shipped by rail through their communities. They were especially concerned because a chlorine tank car had spilled in South Carolina, killing nine people. It was not their first attempt to get the information. They said they had been asking for it for four years and it had been repeatedly denied (Davis, 2005).
- The Bush Administration pushed Congress to adopt the Data Quality Act, which critics said had provisions for "keeping the public in the dark about environmental health threats" (Davis, 2005, p. 20). The Salt Institute tried to use the law's provisions to suppress a government study that said a lower salt intake resulted in reduced blood pressure.
- The Federal Energy Regulatory Commission removed public records about dams, power plants and transmission lines which it said could be used by terrorists. The information included environmental and safety studies about liquefied natural gas terminals that residents in some communities were opposing on the grounds that they should not be built in large urban areas (Davis, 2005).

Some journalists and First Amendment experts suggest that journalists should look first for some other way to obtain information before filing an FOIA request. A significant amount of information is now on the Internet and it is surprising how much information officials and other interested parties acquire (Ward *et al.*, 2005). Others say it is never too early to file a FOIA request. Ken Ward Jr. said that FOIA should not be seen as a last resort. He said he often tries to talk staff into releasing information, but he usually files a FOIA request at the same time. "I have heard plenty of stories about reporters who tried to work sources and negotiate, hoping to avoid filing a FOIA request – only to be caught near deadline with needing to file anyway, and not having enough time to get a response back," said Ward (2007).

Over the years working reporters have come up with a number of techniques for using FOIA. Perhaps the most important is to plan out what documents are needed, figure out the easiest way to obtain them and identify the most appropriate agency (Mansur, 2005). Many federal departments and offices have FOIA reading rooms, in Washington and elsewhere around the country where documents are available. Many of these reading rooms also post the most-requested documents. Sometimes it pays to travel to the location where the records are stored. Sam Roe of the *Toledo Blade* was working on a story about how government and industry officials had allowed thousands of workers to be exposed to toxic beryllium at levels far in excess of safety limits. During the investigation he learned that the U.S. Energy Department had declassified thousands of documents involving the Cold War build-up of weapons, which had used beryllium in their production. He learned the records were available at federal repositories and spent several days at one in Oak Ridge, TN. While he was there two more boxes of beryllium documents were formally declassified. Roe said he did not even spend time reviewing the documents, he simply copied them while he was at Oak Ridge and shipped them home (Roe, 2000).

Often a fee is charged both for having officials compile the information and for copies of documents. However, reporters are eligible for fee waivers. Journalists seek the fee waiver when they make their initial request. It helps to point out that the information is in the public interest. Sometimes agencies do charge after the first 100 pages of material (Wilson, 2002). Some reporters bring their own portable copying machines, others bring computer scanners.

The initial letter spells out the specific scope of what is wanted and what is not. Some reporters have had FOIA officers call them to clarify what is being sought. Reporters have found it is best to stick with what the letter said. Some FOIA officers try to negotiate down the volume of documents, and work, that they will have to do (Ward *et al.*, 2005). If part of a record is exempt from disclosure, the agency must still supply the document with appropriate sections blacked out or redacted. Veteran journalists say they insist on getting the redacted document, because it at least gives them a starting point on the issue (Wilson, 2002).

Trying to collect information or records from government agencies can be demanding, time-consuming and exasperating. It is important to develop strategies on what is the best way to obtain the information. There may be various ways, and they each should at least be considered. Rejection is not unusual, but if there are multiple strategies it does not mean an end of the quest. It is important not to become discouraged and to keep filing FOIA requests. "Use this option or the future may mean you won't have it," said Mansur (2005, p. 21).

FOIA case studies

What can one find by trolling government records? The range of examples is broader than the news. Below are three. One demonstrates how a reporter, even when faced with years of obstacles, used even a limited number of public records to uncover information that the government and a group of scientists had tried to hide for decades. A second shows how reporters can acquire troves of documents, from both government and private corporations, which can be used to demonstrate environmental malfeasance. The third example suggests how to think of records in unusual and innovative ways to track news leads, sources and information that corporations and their lawyers also tried to hide from the public.

In 1987 Eileen Welsome was a reporter for the *Albuquerque Tribune* working on a story about a radioactive waste dump. She was going through declassified documents about the dump, which had been at an Air Force base, when she learned the waste site contained irradiated animal remains. Then she saw a footnote on the document mentioning that 18 people had been injected with significant amounts of bomb-grade plutonium. She told her editors about it. She recalled, "They said 'that's quite a story, but you're the neighborhood reporter'" (Puchalla, 1994, p. 4). She began working on the story quietly, on the side, between other assignments. She reviewed publicly available documents at the University of New Mexico library and at government agencies. Eventually she came across a report released by U.S. Rep. Edward Markey which confirmed that radiation experiments had been carried out on human subjects. The story had only received cursory press attention. In 1989 she filed her first FOIA requests with the Energy Department and received only three brief documents. The newspaper appealed to no avail and Welsome left the paper for a fellowship at Stanford University. When she returned in 1991 she began again. She wanted to know who these 18 people were and what had happened to them. New FOIA requests produced very little information. The documents only identified the subjects by code letters and numbers, but there were enough clues so that she could resort to old-fashioned reporting. She found the widow of a deceased man from Texas and also tracked down the family descendants of a woman only identified as "Charlton-died 198?" Eventually she had enough for a three-part series which ran in November, 1993. One was about how doctors in the 1940s injected plutonium into the leg of Elmer Allen, a black railroad porter, and never told him what they had done. Allen always suspected that the government had made him into a human guinea-pig; no one would believe him. The story was picked up by the wire services, but only got minimal attention until Energy Secretary Hazel O'Leary mentioned the experiments during a press conference on December 7, 1993. Eventually the government disclosed that thousands of people had been subjected unknowingly to radiation experiments. The following spring Welsome won the Pulitzer Prize (Puchalla, 1994).

Welsome's story shows how reporters can construct a powerful story with minimal documents. Sometimes reporters find more records than they would expect. Robert McClure and Andrew Schneider of the *Seattle Post-Intelligencer* wanted to investigate an 1872 federal mining law and its impact on the American west. They knew that the nineteenth-century law had opened the door to a range of mining abuses on the environment and their task was to document what had happened. Soon they had a spare desk in the newsroom that they were calling the "mining annex" covered with thick documents. Many of them were Security and Exchange Commission documents, quarterly and annual reports from mining companies. McClure said that while the documents were written for stockholders, by reading them closely they clearly revealed details of the companies and their mines. "You could read through these and see, 'Oh, wow, they started running into trouble in 1992' because they had done some sort of bizarre note" (Dunne, 2002a, p. 18). Other government reports came from the U.S. Geological Survey and the EPA. The documents were the foundation for a 2001 story reporting that private mining companies had mined ore from public lands that was worth $11 billion. The federal government not only did not share in those proceeds, but Congress had also granted to these private mining companies tax breaks over a ten-year period of $823 million (Dunne, 2002a).

In the summer of 1997 Susan Stranahan and Larry King of the *Philadelphia Inquirer* were working on the story of the after-effects of a spectacular fire that had occurred nearly 20 years before. About three million gallons of industrial refuse had blown up at a waste recycling plant in Chester, PA, and about 200 fire and other emergency workers had responded. The February 2, 1978 fire and cleanup had been big news but over time it had faded from public memory. Now the reporters were hearing that the toxic fumes may have caused many of those emergency workers to die prematurely. The challenge was to find those firefighters, police and paramedics two decades later and to document their health status. Some of the survivors gave the reporters a sketchy list of fire veterans they believed were dead and the journalists compared that list with probate records of wills and estates. Some of those court records included an inventory of assets, including cash amounts from a settlement in a little-known court case. A group of emergency workers had sued companies such as Boeing, DuPont, Scott Paper, SmithKline, Texaco and Wyeth that had brought material to the waste plant. Modest settlements had been paid to 20 of them, however, the records had been sealed. Widows provided some of the settlement documents and a source offered a portion of the case file. The writers also found a former *Inquirer* reporter who had covered the case years before. Surprisingly, she had picked up many of the court records before they were sealed and she still had them in a box upstairs in her attic. The last remaining question, the total amount of the settlement, was found by searching through records in state labor department files. A long-dead Chester fire captain had itemized the settlement amounts. The story reported that 39 workers, or about 20 percent of the workers called to the scene, had been stricken prematurely with a range of cancers, many of them fatal. Epidemiologists hired by the newspaper said that the rate of cancers was five times greater than what should have been expected and the odds of these numbers occurring by chance was less than 5 percent. The median amount of the settlement made to the 20 plaintiffs was $31,500 apiece (King, 2000).

Computer-assisted reporting

Sometimes examining paper documents and records is not enough. Many journalists are demanding the data and the numbers that back up scientific analysis and public policy. An increasing amount of this information is being made available electronically on the Internet. The EPA and other federal and state environmental agencies provide a series of databases about water, air and waste pollution sources online to the general public. The data allows anyone who examines it to find patterns or examples of either improvements or increasing problems in the environment in areas as small as a neighborhood to as broad as the entire nation. Ron Nixon, the reporter who wrote about the clear-cut timber problems in Virginia, said that environmental data is particularly rich, with state agencies often providing numbers supplementing federal sources (O'Donnell, 2004). Such work does not come easily. One needs to be familiar with computers, spreadsheets and data software used to manipulate the data and make comparisons. Like all other information, computer databases have potential pitfalls. Anyone working with a database should understand how the data has been compiled and whether it is complete or has errors.

Computer-assisted reporting has been around for a select number of journalists since the days of huge mainframe computers that used key-punch cards. One of the first to popularize it was a journalist named Philip Meyer who in 1972 published the book *Precision Journalism* (1972) urging reporters to adopt and understand basic research methodology. The advent of personal computers and software pro-grams, including Microsoft's Excel and Access, led more journalists to data-crunching.

Access to the government databases will vary. Some government databases are posted on the Internet and are regularly updated. Other online databases are maintained by environmental organizations or self-proclaimed watchdog groups. In addition, there are numerous data-bases that government officials never designed for public access, but which meet the legal definition of a public record. As these databases

---

FOIA and CAR help

Wrestling public records or analyzing databases is never easy. Fortunately there are many resources available by telephone or online.

For help with records, the FOI Center at the University of Missouri can be reached by phone at (573) 882–4856 or online at http://foi.missouri.edu. Other helpful sites include the National FOI Coalition, www.nfoic.org, Citizen Access Project, www.citizenaccess.org, Reporters Committee for Freedom of the Press, www.rcfp.org. (Freedom of Information Center, 2005), and SEJ First Amendment page at www.sej.org/foia/index1.htm.

For computer-assisted reporting, the Investigative Reporters and Editors (IRE) and the University of Missouri School of Journalism jointly run one resource, the National Institute for Computer Assisted Reporting. It can be found online at www.nicar.org. NICAR runs week-long "CAR Boot Camps" at Missouri's Columbia campus and also sponsors shorter training sessions on a regular basis at various locations around the country. In addition, the Poynter Institute for Media Studies in St. Petersburg, FL. has many CAR resources at its Internet site, www.poynter.org. ("National Institute," 2005).

---

proliferated and reporters began requesting them, they often met stiff resistance. Some of that may have eased but easy access is never assured. Journalists should expect to have to file a FOIA request to obtain these databases. It is helpful in making the request to know as much as possible about the database, especially its record layout, which contains a list of various fields, or categories of information (Luechtefeld, 2004).

One of the richest, deepest environmental databases is the Toxic Release Inventory, which is managed by the EPA. Created by Congress in 1986 following a chemical accident in Bhopal, India, the index contains data on releases and transfers of about 650 toxic chemicals from industrial facilities. It covers toxic pollution releases directly into the air, water and land as well as the disposal of toxic chemicals in landfills, deep-injection wells and the transfer or disposal of waste at treatment facilities. Reports have been filed since 1987 and are available online. Information can be broken down by category and geographically, so that comparisons can be made between communities or at a particular facility, over time. However, the data at times can be as much as two years old (Luechtefeld, 2004). Handling such data can be tricky. Using

Figure 8.1 Air emissions remain a major concern: pollution and the chemicals coming from stacks such as these have to be reported in the Toxic Release Inventory (source: courtesy U.S. Environmental Protection Agency).

the TRI data, Scott Streater of the *Pensacola News Journal* discovered that the amount of chemicals local industries were releasing was huge. It took further analysis to find that his county, Escambia, was among the 25 highest in the nation in releases into the environment. Even then, to place the figures in perspective, he gathered medical statistics showing that emissions had links to birth defects and behavioral disorders (Luechtefeld, 2004). The TRI data is helpful not only for comprehensive investigations such as Streater's, but also for daily reporting. When a fire occurs in a plant or when a chemical truck overturns, such an incident can be placed in perspective using TRI records. Even what appears to be a minor accident provides additional insight if the records show that the company has had a history of significant releases or a patchy enforcement record with regulators.

The Toxic Release Inventory was designed to be a comprehensive source for telling the public how man-made chemicals were being released into the air, water and land. There are more detailed databases maintained by EPA that provide information more specific to each of those ecosystems. For instance, information about industries regulated by the Clean Air Act, including their compliance with permit levels, can be found under the Amerometric Information Retrieval System and

AIRS Facility Subsystem. The online information allows one to examine trends and to access information on a particular company and to obtain more complete details about a specific facility (Luechtefeld, 2004). Similar online information is available both about water polluters and regulated suppliers of drinking water. In 1998 *USA Today* was able to use computer databases and online resources to report that thousands of water systems each year were violating safe drinking water laws, causing hundreds of thousands of people to get sick. Reporters used EPA's online Safe Drinking Water Information System (SDWIS) database. The site also helped document how lax the EPA was in enforcing drinking laws. Another significant source of EPA online data deals with hazardous waste. EPA's Office of Solid Waste manages a database called RCRAInfo which provides information about regulated waste handlers including their compliance history. It also tracks hazardous waste generation, storage and destruction (Luechtefeld, 2004).

CAR case studies

In computer-assisted reporting, obtaining the data is only the first of several reporting steps. In the following examples journalists faced several other obstacles. One needed to interpret the data so that it made sense to the reader. In the second, reporters dealt with the frustrations of working with ten databases. In the third case, they used the data in new and unorthodox ways.

At first James Bruggers of the *Louisville Courier-Journal* thought he was going to receive an exclusive draft report about the quality of the air in his Kentucky city. When that did not happen he filed a FOIA request for air sampling data that he knew had been collected in the draft report. He was surprised when the information was emailed to him within a week, already in a Microsoft Excel format. Bruggers' review discovered a problem. "I realized that despite my experience covering the environment, I had stepped into a foreign country that used a different language than I, my editors and most of the *Courier-Journal*'s readers did," he said (Bruggers, 2003, p. 17). The air monitors had detected more than 100 chemicals and compounds known to be hazardous, but federal officials had never established nationally recognized standards for safety levels. Instead, Bruggers had to search for what risk standards had been set in various regions of the country. Even then, he discovered that these levels varied. Ultimately he compared the results in Louisville to threshold risk standards set by environmental officials on the East and West coasts as well as the Southeast U.S. The work led to some startling findings. Bruggers was able to report that people in portions of Louisville were breathing air containing 18 toxic chemicals whose concentrations were up to 2,400 times higher than

Figure 8.2 Fishing boats find a refuge in Puget Sound in Western Washington. The Sound is an active resource for fishing, commercial shipping and recreational uses although a study by the *Seattle Post-Intelligencer* found that pollution remains a concern (source: courtesy National Oceanic Atmospheric Administration).

what had been considered safe elsewhere in the nation. Some of the higher readings had been taken at an elementary school. Still, they were his assumptions, based on the evidence he had gathered. Even though he had thoroughly checked the results and findings with numerous officials, he said he did not sleep well the night before the story ran. However, if anything, the story underplayed the level of risk. A week after his 2003 story the consultants to the draft report about toxic air contamination in Louisville released their findings that were even more damning (Bruggers, 2003).

The task at the *Seattle Post-Intelligencer* in 2003 was to report on the state of pollution in Washington's Puget Sound 30 years after passage of the Clean Water Act. Reporters Lise Olsen, Robert McClure and Lisa Stiffler tapped into ten different state and federal databases. One of the first challenges was to obtain a list of who was permitted to dump pollution into the bay. Surprisingly, there was no single list or database that could supply this. Olsen said data had to be compiled from several agencies of the Washington Department of Ecology. "That means that just to figure out who had Puget Sound discharge permits, we analyzed six tables in all; three with address information and three with monitoring data," said Olsen. "Luckily the address tables included the watershed and gave latitude and longitude information" (Olsen, 2003, p. 8). Even then the list seemed to lack some of the state's major industries. Reporters asked state officials, who explained that they maintained a separate database for major industries which included the state's biggest refineries and paper mills. They had failed to provide that list earlier. Some of the results were surprising, especially the number of firms that were allowed to dump into the sound. Reporters were able to answer one important question – who was the biggest violator of a permit to dump into the sound? That was easy. The polluter was a primitive treatment plant on an isolated island in the sound. But identifying how much was being dumped into Puget Sound 30 years after the landmark Clean Water Act was enacted proved to be impossible, despite all the data available. Permits for some of the major polluters were based on concentrations rather than exact quantities, making it impossible to come up with exact figures (Olsen, 2003).

Craig Pittman and Matt Waite faced a similar problem in 2005 at the *St. Petersburg Times*. Pittman had read a National Academy of Sciences report describing how the nation's wetlands were being destroyed and it included an indictment of the role of the U.S. Army Corps of Engineers. He knew that the Corps had issued more wetlands permits in Florida than anywhere else in the country and eventually he obtained a

EPA databases

The EPA has a number of environmental databases that are available online.

Basic information about the Toxic Release Inventory can be found online at the EPA website, www.epa.gov. The actual database is called EPA TRI Explorer and it can be found at www.epa.gov/triexplorer/chemical.htm. In addition, Scorecard.org, which is a project of the advocacy organization Environmental Defense, provides a state-by-state analysis of TRI release reports. That site is www.scorecard.org/env-releases/us-map.tcl (Luechtefeld, 2004).

For other EPA databases, try www.epa.gov/epahome/data.html. In addition, the EPA also has an Internet site called Envirofacts which includes a search option so that all environmental data pertaining to a specific geographic area can be examined. It also allows for more structured queries based on the subject matter and allows the user to pick various databases. That site is www.epa.gov/enviro (Luechtefeld, 2004).

database of those permits. He and Waite discovered it was nearly worthless. Some data fields had never been filled in and many geographic reference points were wrong, with locations ranging from the Atlantic Ocean to Pennsylvania for permits granted in Florida. A National Wetlands Inventory and Florida's database of permits contained just as many problems. That was when Waite, who is one of the paper's computer-assisted reporting experts, suggested using satellite imagery analysis to calculate how many wetlands had been lost to development in Florida. That simple idea quickly became a very complex solution. To accomplish the task, Waite took two college courses to learn about satellite imagery. He also convinced the newspaper to buy $4,000 of software and a computer upgrade in order to do the analysis. Waite compared satellite images of Florida 15 years apart and his initial analysis indicated that there had been a huge loss in total acres, far larger than what the two reporters had anticipated. They studied the data and noticed that much of the loss had occurred along the coast. Looking closer, they found that in one image the tide had been out and in the other that the tide had been in. To resolve that problem, they looked at areas that had been converted to urban use, because such changes were both permanent and more obvious to detect. Waite and Pittman said they probably would have been better off if they had concentrated on a smaller geographic area than Florida. The key, Waite believed, was to learn more about Geographic Information Systems, which is a digital database keyed to geographically oriented information. "I believe GIS is the most useful computer-assisted reporting tool journalists can use," said Waite. "Readers get maps. Editors get maps. More and more government data is being mapped. And environmental data is by far the most common data available in maps" (Dunne, 2005c, p. 19). Their resulting series was quite powerful. Called "Vanishing Wetlands," it reported that Florida has lost 84,000 acres of wetlands in 15 years. The stories were extremely critical of the Army Corps, reporting that in a five-year period the Corps had approved 12,000 wetlands permits and denied one. The computer data was also backed up by extensive reporting, especially from disgruntled and former officials of the Corps. One was Vic Anderson, who said the Corps was "not protecting the environment. It's a make-believe program" (Dunne, 2005c, p. 1).

These journalistic tools can be powerful and the resulting stories can be dramatic. A word of warning. Finding documents and examining data are clearly important, but doing the reporting to obtain the human element is just as great a priority. Ron Nixon, a computer-assisted reporting expert, said too often reporters get carried away in thinking the story is only about the data. "You want to use this stuff for stories," he said. "Sometimes people get carried away with doing something for the sake of doing it" (O'Donnell, 2004, p. 21).

Study guide

1 Look up the laws on allowing access to records and meetings in your state, using the Freedom of Information Center website listed or another reference. What appear to be the strengths and weaknesses of the laws? Is there any effort underway to change the law? Write a news story about how the law has affected the environment or environmental policies.

2 Practice writing news leads based on the information on the *Philadelphia Inquirer*'s investigation of the toxic fire and its aftermath in Chester, PA.

3 Familiarize yourself with EPA's Envirofacts website that is located at www.epa.gov/enviro. Go to the area of the site called Quick Start. Insert your zip code and discover what the databases say about your neighborhood. Is there enough there to write a story? Are there any interesting leads that you can see?

4 Write several alternate leads based on the information at the end of the chapter about the *St. Petersburg Times'* "Vanishing Wetlands" series.

5 Look up the NICAR website which lists recent stories reporters have completed on several topics, including the environment. Click the environment button and review how environmental reporters most recently have taken advantage of computer-assisted reporting tools.

6 Write a story memo to your editor or instructor about how to report and write a story about EPA's Toxic Release Inventory and how it has affected your community.

7 For further reading, consider Eileen Welsome's *The Plutonium File* (1999), Javier Moro and Dominique Lapierre's *Five Minutes Past Midnight in Bhopal* (2002) and Brant Houston's *Computer Assisted Reporting, A Practical Guide* (2003).

Part III

Writing the beat

Chapter 9

Short news stories

The fire began on a warm, sultry afternoon inside Baltimore's Howard Street Tunnel. A 60-car freight train whose cargo included paper, wood pulp and a variety of chemicals was trapped in the 1.7-mile-long tunnel which ran beneath the heart of the city. Soon black acrid smoke poured from both tunnel entrances. Temperatures inside rose to 1,500-degrees Fahrenheit. Emergency personnel shut down key highways, causing rush hour gridlock, and ordered residents to stay in their houses with their windows closed and their air conditioning off (Ettlin & Wilber, 2001). Throughout the afternoon and evening a team of reporters from the *Baltimore Sun* covered the major story. Environmental reporter Heather Dewar and assistant state editor Tim Wheeler, a former environmental writer, knew they had to find out what chemicals were on the train. At first emergency officials were unable to provide the train manifest. Then names of chemicals came in either garbled or without confirmation. Finally, at a press conference shortly before deadline that night a *Sun* photographer took a picture of the manifest and editors back in the newsroom examined a blown-up print. The newspaper was able to report that nine of the freight cars carried chemicals including five that had acids (Wheeler, 2006).

The first and most important lesson in any news story, no matter what the time pressure or difficulty in obtaining the facts, is to get it right. Be accurate. Wheeler said that the newspaper had never encountered a story of this size and dimension. It produced four major stories that night, including one from its environmental reporter, Dewar, reporting that the city's emergency plan was hopelessly outdated and did not even address the issue of the train tunnel. The newspaper continued its reporting in the several days firefighters took to control the blaze. The environmental aspects also included a story about how the train was one of countless shipments of hazardous materials that went through the city by rail (Dunne, 2002d).

Story forms

The key to good writing is organization. To be clear in one's message one must have a plan before beginning to write. Journalistic writing, for better or worse, often falls into distinct organizational patterns or story forms. Some of the most common have been inverted pyramid, complex stories, hourglass, feature stories and explanation. There are numerous other names and formulas that journalists have devised over the years. Ultimately neither the names nor their rules will be as important as the plan the writer has devised for providing the information.

Inverted pyramid

This form is extremely common, especially in hard-news stories where the emphasis is on getting new and important information out as rapidly as possible. It is called inverted pyramid because the most important information is at the top and in the succeeding short paragraphs the remaining facts become increasingly less important. It allows the reader to stop reading before finishing the story, confident that the most important points have been conveyed. Its disciplined approach also helps the writer in constructing the story and laying out the facts. In addition, it assists editors in cutting the story, if necessary, knowing that the least important information should be at the bottom. In terms of criticism, inverted pyramid stories often repeat the most important facts three times, in the headline, the lead paragraph, and then by elaborating in the body of the story. Devised by newspapers in the nineteenth century, the story form can seem antiquated at a time when people often get their news from radio, television or the Internet. It also discourages people from reading the entire story, by placing the climax at the beginning. Many teachers and writing coaches dislike the form. They worry that writers put too much reliance on formula-writing, and results in a stale and uninteresting story. Despite the criticism, no one has been able to come up with a better form when it deals with breaking news (Itule & Anderson, 2007).

Complex news stories

This is a variation of the inverted pyramid, to be used when multiple facts threaten to overtax the writer, the editor and the reader. It may be especially helpful in writing about science or when there are several complex threads to the story. One of the dangers of the inverted pyramid is that the story might begin to jump from one point to another. For instance, the fire in the Baltimore tunnel had multiple elements including how many people were injured, the extent of the traffic gridlock and confusion in the city, the types of chemicals on the train and their dangers and when would the fire be extinguished (Ettlin & Wilber, 2001). Such a story could be organized around a lead and a secondary summary followed by a list of the main points. Subsequent sections of the story could then be organized around these main points, with background and minor issues buried deeper in the story. Transitions become clearly important in a story like this. Sometimes these lists are highlighted by bullets or by a one-word subject heading (Fedler *et al.*, 2005).

Hourglass

This form allows for a more natural story flow while also recognizing the reader's need to know the most important facts quickly. It is designed to bridge the difference between hard news and soft news where the time element and immediacy is not as critical, but the human interest element is important. The hourglass would show a small inverted pyramid on top followed by a much larger pyramid below. The story would begin with a summary at the top of the most important points and might even include a list of the main points. It would then convert into a more natural story, likely in narrative or chronological form, explaining how the situation developed. As it continued, it would build in interest, action, tension or all of these elements until it reached a climax. Some of the ending might have been disclosed at the top, but for the hourglass to succeed the reader needs a reason to continue until the end (Itule & Anderson, 2007).

Features

This story form deals with human interest. A feature story is soft news, but that does not make the subject matter less compelling or interesting to the reader. Unlike hard-news stories, the facts behind the story are not the selling points. The writing is less programmed. Either good descriptive writing, a tease, color or a good scene in the lead will get it started. After that the writing will have to pick up the pace. It can either be expository, moving from point to point, or narrative with a natural storyline leading to a conclusion. But it must move the reader forward and unlike the hard-news stories, it should have a strong ending. Some versions of these stories have what is called a nut graph, a device pioneered by the *Wall Street Journal* and sometimes called the Wall Street Journal approach. This formula began with a scene or anecdote which was followed by the nut, a succinct summary of what the story is all about. It is actually a delayed summary lead, similar to what one might find in the inverted pyramid, with perhaps a strong writing flair (Brooks *et al.*, 1996).

Explanation

Sometimes the best stories are the ones that simply put an issue in perspective. This story form is a variation of the feature and it may or may not have a time element tied to it. Sometimes it is related to a stronger summary story. In those situations it might be called a sidebar. It still begins with a strong lead but the story is organized around explaining or summarizing a main point (Fedler *et al.*, 2005). For instance, one of the stories in the Baltimore fire package was a profile of the Howard Street tunnel, describing it as an important conduit in shipping freight through the city even though unknown by local residents (Calvert, 2001).

Donald Murray, a veteran journalist and educator, once said that "writing is not a mystery. It is a process, a logical series of language acts that anyone who can write – and read what they have written – can perform" (Murray, 2000, p. 16). The first step is not to be intimidated. Journalists know that certain elements are needed in a story. Below are some of the most critical steps.

Leads

Ask any journalist, what is the most important paragraph in a news story? The answer will be the first one. Types of leads can vary significantly, especially in comparing hard-news approaches to soft-news leads. Still, all leads share some characteristics. They need strong verbs, details and color. Writers should strive for active, as opposed to passive, sentence construction. But no matter how hard one works on the writing, the reporting remains critically important.

Summary leads dominate most hard-news stories. At one time journalists were taught to identify the 5 Ws and the H and find the lead – the who, what, when, where, why and how. Some of those elements may make up the lead, but it is more important to find the most compelling, surprising, new or unusual fact. Consider this lead that ran the day after the Howard Street tunnel fire by the *Baltimore Sun*'s David Michael Ettlin and Del Quentin Wilbur:

> Civil defense sirens wailed and major highways into Baltimore were closed after a freight train hauling hazardous chemicals caught fire yesterday in a century-old railroad tunnel under Howard Street, shutting down much of the city's downtown.
>
> (Ettlin & Wilber, 2001)

Brevity is also important, especially in summaries. Many journalists prefer to keep leads to 30 or 35 words. Here is a lead from the *Grand*

Forks Herald in April, 1997 when flooding from several rivers deluged the downtown and threatened the city's supply of drinking water and hampered efforts to fight fires in the downtown area: "Water continued to drive residents of Grand Forks and East Grand Forks from their homes Saturday. Too much water, and too little" (Bradbury, 1997, p. 1).

Another way to write a summary is to step closer to an individual. In the aftermath of Hurricane Katrina in August, 2005, reporters from the *New Orleans Times-Picayune* found a victim who could poignantly demonstrate the plight of many in the ravaged city:

> Sitting on a black barrel amid the muck and stench near the St. Claude Avenue bridge, 52-year-old Daniel Weber broke into a sob, his voice crackling as he recounted how he had watched his wife drown and spent the next 14 hours floating in the polluted flood waters, his only life line a piece of driftwood.
>
> (Thevenot *et al.*, 2005, p. 1)

Sometimes feature and explanatory stories depend on summary leads. But they do not have to center on people. Seth Borenstein of Knight-Ridder News Service knew he had to work hard on this lead about clean coal technology.

> FORT LONESOME, Fla – Take dirty, old coal and smash it. Add water to make mud. Pour the mud into a 2,700-degree oven filled with pure oxygen. Voila, the coal mixture is transformed into a much cleaner-burning gas.
>
> (Borenstein, 2001, p. 1)

Borenstein said that he knew he would have some luck producing the lead when he found out that the dateline for the story was Fort Lonesome, a name seemingly perfect for a technology hardly anyone was embracing. This kind of story, based on a combination of science and engineering, is very common for environmental stories (Borenstein, 2006).

A range of lead options await the feature writer. Journalists and journalism educators have delighted in a series of names for these leads from description, anecdotal, narrative, contrast, mystery, teaser quotation, question, shockers, direct-address and the like. Most of these could also come under the term delayed lead. The purpose of the delayed lead is to begin with a powerful or interesting point that compels the reader into the story. Sometimes the drama in the story is still very evident, as in this story by Geoffrey Mohan of the *Los Angeles Times* about fires in 2003 in the nearby San Gabriel Mountains:

The fire broke over the mountain crest in sheets just before dawn Wednesday and whipped across the Rim of the World Highway like a cross-cut saw, foiling the plans of Fire Capt. David Shaw. He ordered his 20-man strike team into their trucks and told them to roll up the windows and wait.

(Mohan, 2003, p. 1)

Other times the writer uses a reader's curiosity to read further, such as Andrew Revkin did in this *New York Times* story about scientists working in Greenland.

SUMMIT CAMP, GREENLAND, May 18 – Two kinds of edgeless whiteness confront those who fly over the frozen, two-mile high, 1,200-mile long hump called Greenland: layers of low clouds and horizon-to-horizon sprawl of the ice cap itself. It is important to recognize the difference.

(Revkin, 2004b, p. 1)

Revkin in the next paragraph explained that some pilots "had flown into the ascending convexity of Greenland in years past, presuming it was another cloud bank" (Revkin, 2004b, p. 1). The writer's purpose is to arouse the reader's curiosity enough at this point to continue reading.

Attribution

It is critically important to the story to know who is providing the information. Attribution is not necessary if the writer observed what was taking place. But in other situations, knowing the information source helps the reader assess its accuracy. It lends credibility to the story. Attribution can be especially helpful in breaking news stories where the information is raw and not always confirmed. It also assists when controversies produce sides with distinctly different viewpoints. Attribution does not necessarily have to be in the lead, or otherwise prominently highlighted in the story.

The following section of the *Baltimore Sun*'s Howard Street tunnel story shows where the writers turned for guidance on both the hazard of the chemicals on the train and how the accident happened:

"Acids are very soluble in water, so when you breathe them in, it's as if you're pouring the acid right into your body," said Dr. Jeffrey Hasday, head of the pulmonary and critical care medicine division at the University of Maryland Medical Center.

The danger, said Bruce Anderson, director of the Maryland

Keys to writing a better news story

- short paragraphs.
- tight, concise, active sentences.
- a strong, compelling lead.
- vibrant verbs.
- powerful quotes.
- past tense (usually).
- clear attribution.
- fair and balanced reporting.
- consistent style.
- save something for the end.

Poison Center, depends on the extent of exposure to the chemicals. But there was no evidence last night any had leaked.

Hazardous materials experts from the Maryland Department of Environment tested the air repeatedly at both ends of the tunnel.

"There was no acid content in the smoke," agency spokesman John Verrico reported last night, adding that tests showed a significant wood-ash content.

"In the testing we've been doing, we have not found any compounds of concern," he said. "It's smoke from a fire which is going to be irritating, but we're not finding any acid compounds, which is kind of a sigh of relief."

Train conductor Edward Brown, 52, of West Baltimore, and engineer Chad Cadden, 27, of Stewartstown, Pa., said they did not know what caused the automatic brakes to activate.

"I don't really know what happened," Cadden said, recounting how the train stopped with the tandem locomotives three-quarters of the way through.

Robert Gould, a CSX spokesman said: "We do not know if it is a derailment or not; we just do not know."

The National Transportation Safety Board said it is sending investigators today.

(Ettlin & Wilber, 2001, p. 3)

In many of the latter paragraphs about the crash officials did not offer very much information about what had happened. Sometimes when the facts are not clear, it becomes even more important to add attribution. Likewise, in dealing with the potential hazards from the fire, the reporters clearly indicated where they were getting their information.

Quotes

Quotes are extremely important in a news story because they add flavor and color. Quotes go along with attribution in substantiating information. They allow the reader to hear various speakers. They can also break up a writer's narrative with a different viewpoint or outlook. Conversely, dull quotes can slow a story down. Capturing accurate comments by people is important. Using quotes selectively is also a priority. Quotes can be used to substantiate and highlight a lead. In Borenstein's lead about clean coal technology here is his next paragraph: " 'This is where the magic takes place,' said Tom Berry, the former chief engineer at the $650 million prototype electric power plant here" (Borenstein, 2001, p. 1).

Borenstein said he knew the moment Berry said the phrase that it was a very good quote and that he would use it high in the story (Borenstein, 2006). In the story by Mohan of the *Los Angeles Times* about the fire in the San Gabriel Mountains, he also used a quote directly after the lead: " 'A real honest-to-God firestorm,' Shaw said" (Mohan, 2003, p. 1).

Figure 9.1 A boat is left marooned atop a house and other devastation in Banda Aceh province in Northern Sumatra shortly after the December, 2004 earthquake and tsunami that devastated the area (source: courtesy National Science Foundation).

Quotes in these situations can serve as a transition between the lead and the next point. Quotes can also add a human interest element. Alan Sipress and Peter S. Goodman of the *Washington Post* were reporting on a massive earthquake and tsunami in December, 2004 when they wrote these passages:

> "People were coming up the roads, running and screaming that the beach was disappearing," said Borge Carlsson, a Swede who owns a guesthouse about 200 yards from the beach. "Cars were upside down, floating around. It's amazing to see anything like this."
>
> (Sipress & Goodman, 2004, p. 3)

Later there is this quote:

> "There were thousands of people on the beach then," said Richard Motein, a Canadian who runs a dive shop on Phuket. "I looked up and saw a wall of water coming at me full of lawn chairs, boats, umbrellas. It just totally wasted the beach."
>
> (Sipress & Goodman, 2004, p. 3)

Color

One journalism maxim is the concept of show, don't tell. As Mark Twain once said, "don't say the old lady screamed, bring her on and let her scream" (Murray, 2000, p. 167). Detail is critically important in all stories, but just like quotes, it needs to be selective. Bruce DeSilva, a writing coach for the Associated Press, said: "Description should never be there for decoration" (Rich, 2005, p. 214). In a story about research in the Arctic, Revkin of the *New York Times* arrived with scientists at a seasonal field camp in Greenland and described what they found:

> In some fields, science is not much more physically rigorous than doing a crossword puzzle. Arctic science is otherwise.
>
> They found the camp in tatters. Tarps over the three snowmobiles stored there all winter were shredded. Each machine's engine was packed with snow and ice, requiring gloves to be shed as the men opened air filters and carburetors in the bitter 25-knot wind.
>
> One of the three skylights brightening the plywood vestibule of the half-buried research bunker had been punctured. Snow had filtered everywhere. Icicles festooned the sandals hanging on pegs in the wall.
>
> (Revkin, 2004a, p. 1)

Normally color is captured by describing the visual. But a good reporter will fill a notebook with a plethora of observations, striving to use all of the senses. Consider these paragraphs from the fire story by Mohan of the *Los Angeles Times*:

> Around 9 a.m. Lucas sent a stream of foam onto the roof of the main house. Above it, the sky turned a muddy orange and smoke boiled across the horizon. About a quarter-mile upwind, two homes had erupted in flames, their timbers sighing and wheezing. Flames arced through the crowns of trees with a freight-train whoosh.
>
> (Mohan, 2003, p. 3)

This passage features both sight and sound and could easily have captured the smell of the fire. It helps place the reader at the scene.

Color and detail can include the whimsy. A few paragraphs later Mohan wrote: "A sign in front of one home that had so far been spared read: 'It's never too late to follow your dreams. Don't give up'" (Mohan, 2003, p. 4).

Background

One of the biggest challenges in writing environmental stories is how to convert complex, technical information into clearly understood writing. That does not mean writing down to the reader. It does require simplifying the language and sometimes the account. To accomplish this task the reporter needs to completely understand the concept that will be written about. It also requires the reporter to spend time with sources, to not make an error in the process of simplifying. Seth Borenstein had that challenge when he was trying to explain the concept of clean coal technology, one that was both complex and controversial. In the slightly condensed passage below he tried to discuss the technology in clearly understood terms.

> At heart, it's an effort to give an environmental makeover to cheap and abundant coal – which when burned normally spews pollution that causes smog, acid rain and global warming.
>
> As with any makeover, there's only so much you can do given what you have to work with. Clean coal is about 10 times cleaner than traditional coal. But it's also several times dirtier and far less energy-efficient than another abundant American fuel: natural gas.
>
> The latest hope is to turn coal into a gas and burn that. This process, called gasification, meets federal pollution standards, but there are only two such power plants in the nation: in Fort Lonesome and in West Terre Haute, Ind.
>
> Many attempts to build new plants that use other clean-coal processes have failed. Among the reasons: high design and con-

struction costs, technology problems, environmental misgivings, shaky investor confidence and risky business plans.

Washington's help, including support for retrofits to existing coal-fired plants to make them pollute less, has been generous.

Last year, investigators for the General Accounting Office, Congress' watchdog agency, found $588 million in unspent federal grants in a sample of 13 federally-aided clean coal projects. Some had failed before they spent the money; others were progressing too slow to use the money…

The real problem is simple, said Cena Swisher, the program director of Taxpayers for Common Sense, a Washington fiscal watchdog group that has targeted these projects: "There is no such thing as clean coal. Clean coal is an oxymoron," a phrase whose words contradict one another. "It's just not a good investment of taxpayers' dollars."

(Borenstein, 2001, p. 2)

Endings

For too long news stories ignored endings. Yet, there is no reason, even in an inverted pyramid story, not to attempt to wrap up the story. Many readers abandon hard-news stories before they reach the end because the writer encourages them to quit. A good, well-written story with concise and tightly constructed sentences should be able to compel a reader to go all the way to the end.

Endings are sometimes called kickers. There are nearly as many formulas for concluding a news story as there are for beginning a feature or soft-news lead. Some options include: using a strong quote; returning to the beginning of the story at the end; concluding with a surprise; telling an anecdote; looking to the future; or unfolding with a natural close or climax.

Quotes are a favorite way to end stories, although some writers complain that the device is overused and has become a cop-out. Still, there is a sense of satisfaction in hearing speakers observe or sum up the situation in their own words. The *Baltimore Sun* deadline story about the Howard Street tunnel ended by describing how the city's mayor had come to the scene of the fire from a political crab feast in a nearby community. He provided his assessment of the fire and the steps taken by the emergency personnel to keep everyone safe. The story ended:

The mayor praised fire personnel: "I thought about how lucky we are to have brave firefighters who grab a hose and walk into a tunnel with smoke billowing out of it, not knowing how far they'll get before there might be an explosion."

(Ettlin & Wilber, 2001, p. 4)

The *Washington Post* story about the earthquake and tsunami concluded with a powerful image.

> Severe flooding also struck the Seychelles, a string of islands off the east coast of Africa. A six-foot ocean surge disrupted power to hundreds of homes and abnormally high tides repeatedly littered the airport runway with fish, forcing firefighters to hose down the airfield between flights.
>
> (Sipress & Goodman, 2004, p. 4)

Craig Welch of the *Seattle Times*, in December, 2004, was reporting from Alaska where emergency workers were working to prevent an oil spill after a ship ran aground. His story quoted Dan Magone, who headed a ship salvage company, about how much progress Alaska had made in responding to such accidents. He chose an anecdotal ending that was mixed with a quote.

> For instance, he said, the 1986 wreck of the Chi Bo San, a small Korean freighter, sat so long on rocky shores less than three miles from the Selendang Ayu, with its contents streaming out, that rats multiplied until even the hardy salvage crews were afraid to board it.
>
> "It wasn't that long ago we were leaving wrecks on the beach," Magone said.
>
> (Welch, 2004, p. 3)

Revkin of the *New York Times* closed his story about the opening of the scientists' Greenland field camp at a natural end point, when the researchers completed their work to make the camp habitable for the next few weeks.

> The first sign of the finer side of Arctic science came as Nicolas Cullen, a team member also from Boulder, proclaimed it was time for tea.
>
> But nothing comes easy here.
>
> The prime ingredient, water, only exists in the frozen state.
>
> Mr. Cullen lit the stove, climbed out through the door in the ceiling, grabbed a shovel and blue barrel, and headed to the nearest drift.
>
> (Revkin, 2004a, p. 2)

One last word of warning when dealing with endings – writers should not try and sneak themselves or their opinions into the story at the end. Except for first-person stories, news stories work when the reporter stays out of the action. The same applies for endings. Any opinions should only be expressed by the news subjects.

Sequential deadline stories

In the summer of 1989 Bill Coughlin, the editor of the *Washington Daily News* in North Carolina, gave a copy of a statement that had been in his water bill to one of his four reporters at the afternoon daily. The town and the paper were small: the *Daily News* had a circulation of 10,500. The statement said that the town was testing for chemicals in its water system. When Coughlin gave the statement to reporter Betty Gray, she never anticipated she would receive such a quick environmental education. Working between other assignments, Gray learned that state environmental officials were testing for 42 chemicals in the water system, that at least one was carcinogenic, and that it had been found in the water supply in far greater quantities than what the EPA considered safe. However, since slightly less than 10,000 residents were hooked up to the city system, it was exempt from the requirements of the federal Safe Drinking Water Act. On Thursday, September 13, 1989 Gray scheduled an appointment with City Manager Bruce Radford. In the middle of the interview Radford broke off the talk, went to the newspaper, and tried unsuccessfully to place an advertisement. The ad admitted that the water supply contained "levels of certain chemicals which exceeded EPA requirements" (Wills, 1990. p. 4). Radford returned to his office, continued the interview, and Gray arrived back at the newspaper at noon. The front page was made over and the presses held for 30 minutes while Gray wrote her deadline story. It was the first of a series of breaking news stories Gray would write (Wills, 1990). Reviewing these stories demonstrates the power of short, sequential news stories. Journalists are often most proud of their lengthy, comprehensive investigative stories. But journalism's power is just as strong in gathering and dispensing the facts quickly. Each story helped produce new developments. Here is the top of Gray's first story on the city's water system

> Scientists with the state Division of Environmental Health are in Washington today investigating a cancer-causing chemical that has made its way into the city's drinking supply source, the *Daily News* has learned.
>
> But a spokesman for the N.C. Department of Environment, Health and Natural Resources said no one is in danger from the drinking water.
>
> "The consistency of the water is the same," City Manager Bruce Radford said in an interview today. "We have been drinking water

from the same source for 40 years and we don't have any cancer-related deaths so far."

(Gray, 1990a, p. 7)

The next day Radford sought to reassure local residents that the water was safe, appearing on television drinking a glass of water. The television news story said the reports of contamination were unconfirmed. Radford also told Gray that the city had known for a while of the chemicals in the water. But Gray kept digging for new information. Her story for Thursday began this way:

> While Washington officials were assuring residents city water was safe to drink, staff members of the state's Department of Environment, Health and Natural Resources were installing a bottled water dispenser in their Carolina Avenue office.
>
> Elevated amounts of trihalomethanes, a cancer-causing chemical, were known to be in the Washington water supply as long as three years ago, and the city was officially warned by test results in March.
>
> Nothing was said in public about that report until inquiries about the city water supply were made yesterday by the *Daily News*.

(Gray, 1990b, p. 9)

By the following Tuesday Gray had learned that a local Coca-Cola Bottling Company plant had discovered the water was contaminated three or four years earlier and warned the city. On Wednesday Gray obtained and published an exclusive report that a second carcinogenic chemical had been found in the water system. The story that day warned that a shutdown of the water system appeared imminent. As the coverage escalated, the state on Thursday afternoon summoned city officials to a meeting to warn of the drinking water's danger (Gray, 1990c). Here is the top of Gray's story on Friday, September 22:

> GREENVILLE – The cancer risk from the two toxic chemicals in Washington's contaminated water supply could be as high as one-in-250, not the much quoted one-in-10,000, the state informed city officials in a dramatic confrontation here yesterday.
>
> This means if 250 residents drank two litres of the water a day for 70 years one person from the group would contract cancer from drinking the water – or 40 cases of cancer over a 70-year period in a city the size of Washington. No city in the state has ever been told its water supply contained such deadly amounts, state scientists said.

"You have a cancer risk way above what we consider a safe level," Dr. Kenneth Rado, state toxicologist for the environmental epidemiology section of the N.C. Division of Health Services, said.

(Gray, 1990c, p. 18)

During the meeting city officials complained that state officials had disclosed too much information to the press. "Our citizens are ready to hang us," Washington Mayor J. Stancil Lilley complained (Gray, 1990c, p. 19). On Friday state officials told Washington residents not to drink the water, not to cook with it and not to take showers in it. On Saturday, September 23, only ten days after Gray's first story, a U.S. Marine convoy of water trucks arrived and began providing safe drinking water to the residents. In an election on October 10, the mayor and majority of the city council were voted out of office. By November 22 improvements had been made and the water system was declared safe. In the aftermath the EPA wrote new regulations so that smaller water systems were governed by the federal drinking water standards. In April, 1990 Gray and the *Washington Daily News* were awarded a Pulitzer Prize for their coverage of the water system (Wills, 1990).

Feature

Even when Candace Page of the *Burlington Free Press* was going to the press conference she knew she was going to have some fun with this story. She was having so few opportunities with environmental stories. "When you write about environmental policy, you just can't seem to have very many opportunities to poke fun," she said (Page, 2006). But Page liked to entertain as well as inform and the announcement that a rare Eastern racer snake was being released back into the wild seemed like an ideal opportunity. The racer was the rarest of snake species in Vermont; there were only eight that had been identified since the species was rediscovered in the state three years earlier. Fortunately, nearly everyone she needed to talk to was at the press conference, except for a veterinarian who had treated the snake after it had been injured. Page wanted readers to identify with the snake and she was hoping they had named it. She wanted to give the snake as much of a human personality, an identity, as possible. Unfortunately for her, they had not given the snake a name so eventually she had to stick to its official title, No. 039 (Page, 2006). Her story began:

HUNTINGTON – An injured black snake known as Eastern racer No. 039 went home Wednesday, after three months cosseting by a bevy of humans who saved him from certain death. It took X-rays, stitches, antibiotics, daily baths and frequent doses of cod liver oil.

If you think that makes No. 039 sound like royalty, or the last of his species, you're almost right.

(Page, 2005a, p. 1)

After explaining how rare the snake was and the extent of the injuries Page came back with a strong quote:

"Usually, this snake has a lot of attitude. It's a feisty, strong snake and it bites," said (herpetologist Erin) Talmage, who has cared for No. 039 for nearly two months. The injury sapped the snake's vigor, she said. "It hasn't had any attitude since I've had it. When I'd give it a bath, I had to hold its head up out of the water."

"We can't wait until it bites someone again," she joked.

(Page, 2005a, p. 1)

Page wrote more about how the snake was rescued and then added the following transitional phrase: "Dummerston veterinarian Dr. Ronald Svec took the case" (Page, 2005a, p. 1).

Page said she was trying to make people smile throughout the story. "There is nothing wrong with entertaining people, in letting them smile, even in a serious story," she said. While the story was light it was still extremely informative about wildlife and endangered species issues.

The ending was intended to give a sense of accomplishment while also talking about the snake's future:

Figure 9.2 Eastern Racer Snake No. 039 was the star at a press conference called by Vermont wildlife officials concerned about the survival of the rare snake species (source: courtesy *Burlington Free Press*).

After No. 039 posed for dozens of pictures Wednesday, the herpetologists headed for southwestern Vermont to take him home.

"I am really happy," Talmage said. "It is such a great feeling when you release an animal back out where it belongs."

(Page, 2005a, p. 1)

That would have been the end of the story, if No. 039 had not died a month later when it was run over by a truck. Instantly Page knew that she was going to write a tongue-in-cheek obituary, carrying the snake's human theme another notch. While the story mimicked an obituary one of the challenges was getting the snake's age, which usually goes high in such a story (Page, 2006). The lead: "Eastern racer snake No. 039, best known for a previous brush with mortality, died last week in Windham County of injuries suffered by being run over by truck. He was 15 or thereabouts" (Page, 2005b, p. 1).

That was immediately followed by a quote. "'It was very sad. We had hoped we could get that snake safely through the winter,' said Middlebury College researcher Jim Andrews, who first made No. 039's acquaintance last year" (Page, 2005b, p. 1).

The story recounted, as best as the author could, the snake's life and its short claim to fame. She wrote: "The snake lived most of its life in short grass, basking in the summer sun and denning up when the cold season came" (Page, 2005b, p. 1). Another line: "More docile than most of his nervous, quick-moving species, No. 039 is remembered with affection by the humans who cared for him this summer" (Page, 2005b, p. 1). Obituaries usually end with survivors, so the ending of this story was easy: "He is survived by a very small number of his species" (Page, 2005b, p. 1).

Explanatory

Seth Borenstein, of Knight-Ridder News Service, knew the story assignment would challenge the expertise he had developed covering science and environment from the Washington, DC bureau. Days after the powerful earthquake and tsunami struck the coasts of Asia and Africa in December, 2004 he was asked to place the event in perspective. It was hard to even contemplate the power of the natural disaster which had a death count approaching 150,000 at the time of the assignment. He had a day and a half to work on the story and he knew from his beat whom he wanted to talk to. He chose scientists who he knew could address the global and even spiritual aspects of this disaster (Borenstein, 2006). Among the scientists and comments were:

- Kathryn Sullivan, the first U.S. woman to walk in space and a former chief scientist for the National Oceanic and Atmospheric Administration, who said: "Mother nature will win when she wants to." When the forces of man and nature clash, she said, "you get reminded that the power of this planet is really there. We are, in our forces, implicitly nothing" (Borenstein, 2005, p. 2).
- Paul Richards, a professor of natural sciences at Columbia University: "It's what it means to be a member of planet Earth ... Does that inspire awe? Obviously it does" (Borenstein, 2005, p. 2).
- Rice University professor Neal Lane, who had been chief science advisor to former President Bill Clinton: "Nature is much more powerful, and we have precious little ability to influence what happens at that scale." Lane added that the majesty of nature inspired scientists. "I have always found it overwhelming," he said. "I think the mystery of nature is really what drives most scientists. That's why they don't sleep very well at night. Those mysteries are out there" (Borenstein, 2005, p. 2).

That mystical entry allowed Borenstein to consult the Bible's book of Job, and Job's questions of why he had suffered:

> Then the Lord answered Job out of the whirlwind: Who is this that darkens counsel by words without knowledge? Gird up your loins like a man, I will question you and you shall declare to me. Where were you when I laid the foundation of the Earth? Tell me, if you have understanding, Who determined its measurements – surely you know!
>
> (Borenstein, 2005, p. 3)

Borenstein was pleased to include a Bible passage in a story about tsunamis and science. "You usually have two ways to go with a story like this," he said. "You can either step closer and zero in on one aspect, or you can step back. This time I stepped way back." When he had completed his reporting, he sat and thought for about three hours on what he wanted to do. That's an unusual step, but he felt it was necessary in this story. He said he always struggled with his leads, and this time he played with the phrase of who was in charge, before finally settling for who was boss (Borenstein, 2006). The lead: "WASHINGTON – Man can dam rivers, build skyscrapers, even go to the moon, but sometimes mother nature needs only a split second to remind us of who's really boss" (Borenstein, 2005, p. 1).

Borenstein said his second paragraph was actually more important, and more difficult to write, because he wanted to place the natural disaster into context (Borenstein, 2006). The second paragraph: "Last

Sunday's tsunami offers yet another humbling lesson that the power of nature far exceeds the reach – indeed, even the imagination – of man" (Borenstein, 2005, p. 1).

Sometimes the simplicity of a sentence belies its complexity. The quotes and comments from the scientists make up the body of the story but before that Borenstein provided the facts to document those first two paragraphs. He next wrote:

> The earthquake and subsequent tsunami released as much energy as 1 million atomic bombs. It changed – slightly but perceptibly to modern science – the wobble and rotation of the Earth. It also redistributed Earth's mass, moving the North Pole 1 inch and causing the length of a day to shrink permanently by 3 millionths of a second, according to geophysicist Richard Gross of NASA's Jet Propulsion Laboratory. It also prompted prominent scientists to ponder the relationship between mankind, nature and God.
>
> (Borenstein, 2005, p. 1)

The story had so many powerful comments, he could have used several as his ending. He chose observations by Kathleen Tierney, a University of Colorado sociologist and the director of the Natural Hazards Research and Applications Information Center, about mankind's lack of respect for mother nature. She added a trace of hope. The ending:

> "Do we respect nature and do we live with nature? No, we want nature to do our bidding," said Tierney. "We live in a society that believes that technology can solve all our problems, that we can overcome our own human limitations through technology."
>
> When a tsunami comes, she said, it shows that Earth "doesn't care. It's nature."
>
> Disasters do, however, reveal another human power, one that can't be measured in energy released, physical destruction, or computer calculations of the Earth's spin.
>
> "What I see in disaster," Tierney said, "is the tremendous resilience of people."
>
> (Borenstein, 2005, p. 1)

Revision

When the writer reaches the ending the work is not finished. Begin by re-reading the story. If it was written on a computer, make a printout. Consider reading it out loud. Read it to someone else. Look for awkward phrases. Problems sometimes become more obvious when you read the story in a different form. Check the facts for accuracy. Look for omissions, or holes in the story, where more reporting is needed. Review organization, to make sure it is consistent and in focus. Spend more time on the lead. Good writers are not afraid to try five, ten, 15 or more leads before they are satisfied. Most importantly, writers have to give up ownership of their work, and to examine it skeptically and impassively. It is not easy. Donald Murray, the veteran journalist and educator, said "Effective writers turn traitor to their own copy, reading what they have written through the eyes of an enemy reader" (Murray, 2000, p. 163).

Study guide

1 Find an example of an inverted pyramid, complex story, hourglass, feature and explanatory news story. What did you like and dislike about each story? Should any of these have been written in a different story form?

2 Rewrite several of the leads in this chapter. Produce a minimum of five versions of each of them.

3 Find a news story with a good ending. Rewrite the ending, producing a minimum of five versions.

4 Betty Gray was successful at the *Washington Daily News* when she produced a series of stories on the town's water system. Compare the value of such sequential news stories to holding the facts and writing a longer, more comprehensive piece. Were there ethical issues which required Gray to write as soon as she had certain facts, or would she have been justified in holding them until she collected a complete story?

5 Compare a hard-news environmental story to a soft-news story. Convert a soft-news environmental story into a hard-news story.

6 Take a local environmental issue and do the reporting necessary to provide an explanatory story such as the tsunami story written by Seth Borenstein.

7 For further reading, consider Donald Murray's *Writing to Deadline, The Journalist at Work* (2000), William Zinsser's *Writing to Learn* (1988) and for fun, Carl Hiaasen's *Nature Girl* (2006) or *Stormy Weather* (1995).

Chapter 10

Longer news stories

Dina Cappiello of the *Houston Chronicle* kept getting the same skeptical response from some of her colleagues as she worked on her story about toxics in Houston's air. " 'You're going to tell us the air in Houston is polluted?' they asked. 'Yeah, right.' " Everyone knew that for years the EPA had rated Houston's air quality among the worst in the nation. Cappiello's reporting was finding that not only was the air foul but that the chemicals were endangering the health of people in many Houston neighborhoods. Despite this discovery, she feared that many readers would share that same cynical attitude as her colleagues. How was she going to overcome that reader skepticism? One day she sat with one of the newspaper's better writers to discuss the problem. At the end of the talk the writer wrote five words on a piece of paper – "It's worse than you thought." Cappiello wrote it on a card and stuck it at the top of her computer. She used that five-word message to mold her thinking about the six months of reporting and to guide what became a six-part series (Cappiello, 2006).

Longer news stories, usually called developed stories, can take anywhere from a few days to weeks, months or even years to produce. They can be produced either by an individual reporter or by the entire staff of a newspaper or news organization (one famous investigation of organized crime in Arizona was a joint project of reporters from around the country and the precursor to the Investigative Reporters and Editors organization (IRE, 2006)). Stories can be hard-hitting investigations based on an extensive search of documents or computer databases, written in an expository style designed to lay out the facts in a clear or comprehensive way. Or the story may rely on thorough reporting to tell a narrative, a natural story that the writer either observed or that had been reconstructed through interviews. In any of these approaches, the story can run in a single day or be part of a multiple series with numerous sidebars.

Planning what to write

Developed news stories are usually enterprise stories, which mean that they are proposed and initiated either by the writer or editor. The first step in launching a developed story is to do the homework. Reporters need to calculate the reporting requirements and to estimate when the writing can be completed. That may be accomplished by a one-sentence budget line. Or it could involve writing an extensive memo. Longer stories or projects require the writer to grasp both the story and the concept of why it should be told. The time constraints of other members of staff also need to be considered. Major developed stories may require multiple reporters, a story editor and copy editor, photographers, graphic artists and online technicians. Stories are usually driven by the writer, but not always. One series at the *Providence Journal* began after a photographer spent months taking pictures at a clinic that treated children suffering from lead poisoning. The photos were so compelling that the photographer convinced the editors that lead poisoning was a major environmental health issue in Providence (Power of Words, 2001).

Good stories require good reporting but it can be easy to lose sight of what the story is all about. Tom Meersman of the *Minneapolis Star Tribune* said that when he began reporting a major story he usually wrote a series of questions about what he hoped to learn. Once a journalist gets into the reporting he may lose that initial ignorance and no longer pursue the issues which interested him (Meersman, 2006).

Most journalists say organizing and keeping track of notes and documents are major undertakings. Filing is critically important. Reporters often write up their notes in memo or even story form immediately after interviews. Reporters sometimes get interrupted, and must put the reporting aside, when breaking news overtakes their beat. Some journalists like to write drafts of the story even as the writing continues. Each night when Heather Duncan of the *Macon Telegraph* was working on a series about the environment of Georgia's lowlands she would write some free-association notes of her observations from that day. She wrote about people's faces, voices and movements. "For me, it's very important to describe something while I'm looking at it, or as soon as possible afterwards," she said. "Trying to come up with a metaphor or simile from a remembered image just doesn't work" (Duncan, 2004, p. 21). Ged Carbone of the *Providence Journal* sometimes wrote those metaphors or similes while he was taking notes out in the field (Carbone, 1994). Knowing when the reporting should end may be difficult to determine. Covering a big story is like exploring and illuminating a dark cave with many chambers. It seems like there is always another path to explore, another cavern to brighten. John McPhee, a longtime writer for the *New Yorker* who has often written about the environment, said he knew it was time to wrap up the research when he heard the same stories and comments from sources for the third time (Howarth, 1976).

Organization

Probably no task can be more formidable in the writing process than focusing on what the reporting has produced and finding a way to organize it. "The most important thing in the story," said Thomas Boswell of the *Washington Post*, "is finding the central idea ... Once you find that idea or thread, all the other anecdotes, illustrations, and quotes are pearls that hang on this thread" (Scanlan, 1995, p. 2).

Reporters have many techniques. Many journalists start by finding a short, simple phrase that frames the story. It need not be more than a few words and it can be done early, sometimes even during the reporting. However, framing the issue too soon may prove faulty if the reporting does not develop as planned. Roy Peter Clark, a writing instructor with the Poynter Institute, said that when he began a series of stories about a woman whose husband died of AIDS, he wrote a mission statement. He scribbled it on two pieces of legal paper, describing what he was writing about and how he wanted to write it. He said it began: "I want to tell a human story, not just about AIDS, but of deeply human themes of life, love, death, sorrow, hope, compassion, family and community" (Clark, 2004, p. 1). He also described how he wanted to frame the story and the shape of the story form. "I cannot overstate the value of this exercise, which took only 10 minutes," he said afterwards. "It gave me a view over the horizon before I began drafting the story" (Clark, 2004, p. 2).

Compressing the story into a few short words or phrases is the first step towards creating an outline. When thinking of structure, consider the concept of the plumb line. A plumb line is used by carpenters, painters and wallpaper hangers to create a straight line by holding a string at the top of a wall. The string has a weight at the bottom and gravity makes a straight line. That's what the aim of writing is, to follow that straight line. When the writing veers off to the right or left, even if the material is good, if it does not follow that plumb line it is creating a disservice to the reader. It needs to be edited out so that the story can get back on track. Writers have various terms for this, but the most popular are "killing your babies" or "killing your darlings." The phrase pretty much sums up the dilemma. The great sports writer Red Smith once had this to say about the task: "There is nothing to writing. All you do is sit down at a typewriter and open a vein" (Murray, 2000, p. 85).

Story outlines will vary. They can be formal, with Roman numerals and capital letters heading main points, or they can be informal, with just the most salient details jotted down. Christopher Scanlan of the Poynter Institute suggested writers should "make a list of the elements you want to include in your story. Number them in order of importance. Structure your story accordingly. They can be extremely elaborate" (Scanlan, 1995, p. 2). McPhee, the *New Yorker* writer, said that when he returned from months of research out in the field he would type up his notes, producing a huge mound of paper. He would consider the topics that his reporting had discovered and write those on small index cards, until he had a pile of them. Then, he would carefully go through the cards, ordering them and posting them near where he was working. Finally, he would attack the pile of typewritten notes with scissors. He would cut them up, dividing them into sections that corresponded with the index cards, eventually placing them in folders. When he was finished he would have a file of folders. Each would be consulted when he reached that point in the story (Howarth, 1976).

Writing beginnings and endings sometimes can help writers organize. McPhee said the other tool he used to organize was to write the beginning of the article early. Leads "shine a flashlight into the story," said McPhee (Scanlan, 1995, p. 2). When Doug Fischer of the *Oakland Tribune* in 2004 was writing a series about the chemicals found in the bodies of a typical California family that had agreed to testing, he found himself in an unusual writing situation. "Deadlines and delays in getting the family's results meant I had to write part three first," he said. "By the time I got to part one, knowing exactly where this series was going proved immensely helpful. Unorthodox? Yes. But it worked here" (Dunne, 2005b, p. 22). Fischer still wrote an outline; he just did it backwards.

Sometimes novice writers think their literary talents will be more liberated, if they write without an outline. Jon Franklin is a leading practitioner of narrative writing. He aims to return the art of storytelling to journalism. Yet Franklin believes in the value of planning. "For beginners, it's total nonsense not to outline," he said. "It's like flying an airplane without a flight plan" (Soennichsen, 2004, p. 6).

Leads

Writers have more options in starting longer stories than they usually have in shorter, deadline stories. In a developed story, some writers set the strongest facts out immediately, in short declaratory sentences. The focus is on what the writer found and the lead avoids attribution or the opinions of others. Consider the lead that David Ottaway and Joe Stephens of the *Washington Post* wrote in 2003 about the Nature Conservancy. The top began this way:

The Arlington-based Nature Conservancy has blossomed into the world's richest environmental group, amassing $3 billion in assets by pledging to save precious places. Known for its advertisements decorated with forests, streams and the soothing voice of actor Paul Newman, the 52-year-old charity preserves millions of acres across the nation.

Yet the Conservancy has logged forests, engineered a $64 million deal paving the way for opulent houses on fragile grasslands and drilled for natural gas under the last breeding ground of an endangered species.

The nonprofit Conservancy has traveled far beyond its humble beginnings, when it relied on small donors and acquired a few small plots at a time. Its governing board and advisory council now include executives and directors from one or more oil companies, chemical producers, auto manufacturers, mining concerns, logging operations and coal-burning electric utilities.

Some of these corporations have paid millions in environmental fines. Last year, they and other corporations donated $225 million to the Conservancy – an amount approaching that given by individuals.

Today, the million-member Conservancy itself is something of a corporate juggernaut, Big Green. It is also the leading proponent of a brand of environmentalism that promotes compromise between conservation and corporate America.

(Ottaway & Stephens, 2003a, p. 1)

The writers used the Conservancy's philosophy in soliciting corporate assistance to protect the environment as a contrast to what the newspaper found about the organization's record. The lead continued with one-paragraph summaries of some of the Conservancy's more controversial moves followed by a defense of the organization by its president and other officials. Hard-hitting investigative pieces often begin with this approach.

Dina Cappiello said it was how she drafted her first lead about Houston's air pollution. "My tendency as a writer is, if I have something important, is to say it right out," she said. "Don't back into it" (Cappiello, 2006). But her chief editor did not think that the lead was working. He wanted a softer approach, not quite a delayed lead, but one that raised other issues. "He told me to imagine as if I were a director working on the movie. What would be my first shot? Putting it in that visual frame helped" (Cappiello, 2006). She thought of one particular neighborhood and the fences that she had noticed that had dominated the scene. She wrote:

Mary Guerra lives in a community of fences. Chain-link, picket or wrought-iron varieties surround nearly every house, as well as the nearby refinery and chemical plant. Some have vines growing on them, others are topped with barbed wire. Many have signs – "No trespassing," "Beware of dog," – in English or Spanish.

The fences are meant to keep out the strays that wander the streets of Houston's Manchester neighborhood, the prostitutes who sometimes strut down its block and the drug dealers who residents say have settled into some of its run-down trailers.

What the fences don't stop are the sharp, sometimes sweet odors that waft from the chemical plants and refineries on the nearby Ship Channel, or the black dust occasionally released by the stacks that ring this working-class community just outside the East Loop.

(Cappiello, 2005a, p. 1)

She had often been struck by the fences when she was in the neighborhood reporting the story. "I just thought it was a great metaphor for this entire subject," she said (Cappiello, 2006).

John McQuaid and Mark Schleifstein of the New Orleans Times-Picayune studied, in 1995 and 1996, how the world's fisheries were increasingly endangered. They could have begun their eight-part series with a lead just as forthright as the Post's story about Big Green. But they wanted their readers to read their series for eight days. That story, written by McQuaid, began with an anecdote that delayed the lead:

Tom Shelley piloted his flat-bottomed boat through the sunlight one recent morning on his way to the oyster beds he depends on for a living. The marsh air was warming but the wind had a sting to it and the water had taken on a wintry blue cast.

After beaching the boat, Shelley and his mate, Timmy Kirk, paused to orient themselves by the tidal eddies and southwest wind. Then they lumbered through the water, backs bent, their eyes scanning the marsh floor. Reaching down with gloved hands, they picked up oysters and tossed them into the rowboat they pulled behind them.

The going was easy that morning. But it isn't always. Sometimes a fast-moving tide brings the water up to their necks. Sometimes the water recedes and they must drag the boats across desolate, wind-whipped mud flats.

Shelley can adapt to the changing mood of the marshes. It comes with the job. But he and thousands of other fishers are helpless before the man-made changes tearing across the Gulf of Mexico, leaving a swath of wrecked lives and ecological havoc in their wake.

(McQuaid, 1996, p. 2)

What is remarkable about this lead is that it does far more than transport the reader out to the oyster flats. McQuaid provided significant foreshadowing that began with the "sting of the wind" and the "wintry blue cast." The foreshadowing became more direct in the third paragraph when McQuaid warned that the work was not easy, although the metaphor was not clearly explained until the fourth paragraph. By then the lead was moving into the nut graph, the summary of what the story was all about.

Sometimes a delayed lead can be a misnomer. Consider this lead written by Jon Franklin when he was working for the *Raleigh News & Observer*:

> DURHAM – It was dawn when David Brewer arrived at the Duke Primate Center to find two cars parked outside the loading doors. One belonged to Cathy Williams, the primate center veterinarian, and the other to her assistant. David knew instantly that something was wrong.
>
> (Franklin, 1998, p. 1)

The story waited another 400 words to provide an answer to what was wrong. It involved one of the primate center's most valuable and endangered animals, a golden-crowned sifaka or lemur. The revelation arrived with a quote: " 'Oh, no,' David said. 'Oh shit. She died' " (Franklin, 1998, p. 1).

By then the reader already had guessed what had happened. Franklin's strong hint in the lead had been layered with more suggestions in those next 400 words. A good delayed lead is more than a tease, more than an exercise to display a writer's talents for description or narrative. It needs to connect the reader to the story.

Nut graphs

Invented by the *Wall Street Journal*, nut graphs are especially critical for many types of delayed leads in developed stories. Readers quickly grow impatient when the story's direction begins to waver or if the narrative becomes confusing. Newspaper writers worry whether the reader will continue with the story if it jumps onto another page and the reader sees how much more he has to read. The nut graph needs to be as tight and succinct as possible. Journalists disagree about how far into the story it should go. Some like to see it by no later than the third or fourth paragraph, fearing that if the lead stretches out too long, the writer will lose the reader. Others argue that is too formulaic. Rick Jaroslovsky, a reporter and editor at the *Wall Street Journal*, recalled a colleague who was an excellent writer but who resisted writing nut graphs. He argued that putting the nut graph in "will only slow down the story, and if you have done your job well, the reader will know why the story is important ... without your having to hit him over the head with it" (Clark, 2002, p. 1).

The lead on the *Times-Picayune* fishing story earlier in the chapter moved flawlessly into the nut graph. It continued:

> Part of a global sea change in fishing, the forces include disappearing fish and marshlands, a flood of cheap seafood imports and gill net bans. They threaten millions of livelihoods and the Gulf's unique fishing culture.
>
> (McQuaid, 1996, p. 2)

The nut graph for the Houston air pollution story was:

> The *Houston Chronicle* tested the air in public parks, playgrounds and neighborhoods bordering some of the state's largest industrial plants and found the air in Manchester area so laden with toxic chemicals that it was dangerous to breathe.
>
> (Cappiello, 2005a, p. 1)

Writing with authority

In March, 2001 Julie Hauserman of the *St. Petersburg Times* wrote a story about the dangers of pressure-treated lumber. An excerpt:

> All over the state, pressure-treated boards and posts are leaking arsenic into the soil. The arsenic comes from chromated copper arsenate, or CCA, a powerful pesticide brew that is injected into the boards to give them long life against the elements.
>
> Arsenic is leaking out of huge wooden playgrounds that volunteers built all over Tampa Bay. It's leaking beneath decks and state park boardwalks, at levels that are dozens of times – even hundreds of times – higher than the state considers safe. And discarded pressure-treated lumber is leaking arsenic out of unlined landfills, state experts say, posing a threat to drinking water.
>
> If you've never heard of this before, you're not alone.
>
> Most people who buy the popular wood don't have a clue that it contains toxic pesticides.
>
> They don't know the wood has been banned in several countries. They don't know that some companies that sell arsenic-filled wood in the United States make another kind of pressure-treated wood, one that doesn't have arsenic in it, and sell it overseas.
>
> Americans haven't demanded a more environmentally friendly

product because the bad news about pressure-treated wood isn't widely known here.

Most Americans don't know that they are supposed to wear gloves and a dust mask when working with the wood. They don't know they are supposed to clean up the arsenic-laced sawdust and wash their clothes and hands after building with it. They don't know that a burning pile of pressure-treated lumber gives off toxic smoke.

(Hauserman, 2001, p. 1)

It was powerful writing, similar in approach to the top of the *Washington Post* story about the Nature Conservancy. What gives writers the license to write stories that so unceasingly condemn problems and point fingers? Writers need to be fair and write balanced stories. But if the reporting has been thorough, a developed story should allow them to write with authority. While an explanation from the aggrieved parties needs to be included, it does not have to be as early in the story or as prominent as the details about the problem. Hauserman said she was trying to make a strong point in this section. "It did hammer you," she said. "Oh my God, Oh my God, Oh my God. By the time you get to the part where the people were constructing them, the case was made" (Dunne, 2001, p. 23). While the story clearly had a point-of-view, it was justified by overwhelming evidence. The story included arguments by industry officials who contended that the wood was safe. They were also provided an opportunity to produce information backing that contention. However, the story also mentioned numerous studies, including testing conducted by the newspaper, which indicated that the wood was dangerous.

"Writing with authority comes from talking to so many people and finding so much common ground that you do not have to attribute that kind of information to particular people," said Meersman of the *Minneapolis Star Tribune*. "You don't say it as an opinion, but as a fact that is later backed up by the facts all the way through" (Meersman, 2006).

This type of writing should not be confused with advocacy journalism which will be addressed in Chapter 15. This is forceful prose backed up by strong reporting and an abundance of facts.

Endings

Some writers like to work backwards. They construct the ending first, and then write to that conclusion. If nothing else, the practice illustrates just how important some writers value endings in developed stories. The strongest endings are essential for each part in a series. Writers know that a strong ending, especially a cliffhanger, will be the best way to convince the reader to return for the next installment. In 1996 when Clark of the Poynter Institute wrote his series called "Three Little Words" about a woman who was married to a man who died of AIDS, he broke the story into 29 parts. Each part was no more than 850 words and could be read in five minutes when published in the *St. Petersburg Times* (Clark, 2004). Clark was trying to revive the serial, a literary form with long history that included writers like Charles Dickens and characters such as Flash Gordon. A major reason serials were so successful was because they closed with a cliffhanger, with the main subject virtually about to plunge off a cliff. Early in the series written by Clark the husband told his wife that he had AIDS. After the realization sunk in, the story ended with the woman wondering if she too had the disease. The next part ended as the doctor was about to tell her the test results (Clark, 1996).

Clark needed cliffhangers for 28 of the 29 days. While they are effective, there are many other ways to end a story. Cappiello of the *Houston Chronicle* said she knew she had a strong ending for the first day of her series. She had been asking public officials if they would be willing to live where many poor people resided and the toxic fumes were especially bad. Virtually everyone said no (Cappiello, 2006). One official with the Texas Commission on Environmental Quality was especially articulate on the point and she used it like this:

> "Are you kidding?" asked Chris Jones, a chemist with the TCEQ.
>
> Posed with the question one night while he was monitoring toxic emissions along a dark road lined with industry, Jones said it wouldn't be worth the risk.
>
> "I have a family," he said.
>
> "There are no regulations to speak of," he added and without a clear definition of what's good or bad "over time, its cancer, man."
>
> (Cappiello, 2005a, p. 10)

Working with an editor

Working on a developed story, investigation or series over weeks or months can be a lonely experience, even if a team of reporters is assigned to the task. It can be difficult to recognize where to go next and when to stop, both with the reporting and with the writing. At times like this a story or project editor is especially valued. Writing coach Donald Murray said there are at least four different types of editing:

- Idea editing, when the editor works with the writer to hone and shape the direction of the story or stories.

- Reporting editing, where the writer stays in touch with the editor on a regular basis, consulting and getting help so that the reporting does not go off on tangents.
- Structural editing, when the editor helps guide the way the material stays organized.
- Language editing, where the story editor and the copy editor carefully review and improve all aspects of the writing, from spelling, grammar, style and especially accuracy. Often one editor will fill some or even all of these roles (Murray, 2000).

Developed projects involve others besides just the writer. The project editor heads the team of writers, editors, photographers and graphic artists. The editor calls regular meetings of the team to keep everyone informed on the project's progress. Jean Plunkett of the *Providence Journal* was project editor for the series on lead-poisoned children. In a discussion with the lead writer, Peter Lord, it was obvious that the two approached the production of the series in a collaborative process. Besides meeting regularly with Lord, editors, and those working on the visuals and online version, Plunkett kept track of every draft as it progressed (Power of Words, 2001).

"This project really had drafts for every story," recalled Plunkett. "I would write little notes to Pete, like: "This ending is really weak.""

"If I'm getting dense or losing her, Jean didn't mind saying so," said Lord.

"I tend to use notes and talk to the reporters," added Plunkett. "It might be: It needs a really good ending. He would take them and think about them" (Power of Words, 2001, p. 4).

Such collaborations do not end when the story is completed to both the editor's and writer's satisfaction. Other tasks are mandatory, such as fact-checking. Writers should always do their own fact-checking, but it is often required in consultation with an editor on major stories. Reporters should also monitor and have a role in the pictures, graphics, headlines and captions, the design and display of the pages and even the promotion of the story.

Expository writing

Besides terms such as hard news and soft news, deadline and developed, there is another classification for stories – exposition and narrative. Expository writing is non-fiction prose that sets forth facts, ideas and arguments (Grow, 1999). Much of journalism is exposition and a good example is the inverted pyramid for shorter news stories. While the inverted pyramid does not apply for longer developed stories, the style is similar. A more common approach is to begin with a summary lead, although a delayed lead can also be used in exposition. The main distinction with exposition is to convey facts in an order that the writer believed would be both compelling and important. In contrast narrative is usually chronological, told in the order of how events occurred. The information in an exposition story is often written in sections, but they are not necessarily linear or chronological. Instead, their primary purpose is to supplement and substantiate the lead or premise. The form is especially common in investigative stories. Whole sections can be devoted to sub-points of the main thesis. Characters and subjects can be introduced, described and their findings or actions explored before the writer moves on to another sub-point. Examples of exposition writing would include Cappielli's Houston air pollution story, the *Washington Post*'s investigation of the Nature Conservancy and the *New Orleans Times-Picayune* series about over fishing.

Exposition – a case study

In June, 2004 when Meersman of the *Minneapolis Star Tribune* completed a series called "Invaded Waters" his intent was to warn readers that the environment of the Great Lakes was being permanently altered because of public and government inaction (Meersman, 2004). While he knew it would be a hard-hitting wake-up call for his readers, he was not sure until fairly late in the process how the stories would be organized. While management discussed options, Meersman began writing pieces of the series. The possibilities ranged from a five- or six-day series to a package of stories that would all run on the same day in a special section. Finally his editors decided on a three-day series (Meersman, 2006). Meersman and his editors planned for the first day to be a strong overview of how vast populations of fish and other sealife – so many no one knew the number – had invaded the Great Lakes. The second day explained how invasive species were arriving in the ballast water of ships. Officials were required to inspect the ballast water, but the inspections program was severely flawed. The third day described how biologists had been warning about the problem for years but government had failed to respond. The series also had nine sidebars, numerous photos, and a large graphic detailing some of the problems in the Great Lakes.

The first day began with a strong, direct summary:

> The Great Lakes have become a giant outdoor biology experiment – with no one in charge.
>
> In the space of a few decades, an evolutionary snap of the fingers, vast populations of foreign fish, mussels and other creatures have invaded and damaged irreversibly an ecological design that took thousands of years to evolve.

Figure 10.1 A loon lies dead along Lake Erie near Dunkirk, NY. The loon is a victim of invasive species that increasingly have become an environmental problem on the Great Lakes (source: courtesy *Minneapolis Star Tribune*).

These unwanted guests in the largest freshwater system on the face of Earth have muscled out native species, killed thousands of loons and other migrating birds, devoured food resources, clogged water-intake pipes and begun to spill into many of North America's premier lakes and rivers.

Many scientists say the invaders are a worse problem than the industrial contamination that fouled the Great Lakes in the 1960s.

(Meersman, 2004, p. 1)

Meersman said that the intent of this opening was to incorporate all of the important threads that the series would examine. His editor used the rather inelegant term of "top cramming" to describe it. "What I was doing was not just a nut graph or a traditional news lead as much as it was a sweeping nut graph," he said. "The top was like a giant nut graph" (Meersman, 2006).

What followed were individual sections, some of which had been written weeks before. Some had been longer and were trimmed, while others were expanded. The order and topic of each section was:

- The invaders killed many native species.
- New species have grown rapidly.
- How the new species arrived in ships.
- The costs to society.
- How the arrivals have spread beyond the Great Lakes.
- Government's failure to stop the problem (Meersman, 2004).

As the writing and editing of the first story continued some of the sections changed in their order of priority. For instance, the section high up in the story about the death of native species described how countless loons had died on the shores of Lake Erie. During the loons' migratory flights each spring and fall many had stopped at Erie and consumed a fish called the goby. It was a European species that was new to the lake and toxic to the loons. In five years 50,000 loons had died. Meersman said that this section had been deeper in the story, but his editors urged him to write about the loons earlier because it told the threat to wildlife so convincingly. A picture of a dead loon became a signature photo for the series. Sections like this allow flexibility in tinkering and altering the organization of the story (Meersman, 2004).

Writing a series may also permit a reporter to find a use for those non-essential elements, the "babies" or "darlings" killed in the main draft. Sometimes they make good sidebars. In Meersman's series the most powerful sidebar described how a U.S. Fish and Wildlife manager, Jerry Rasmussen, was reassigned because he was attempting to place restrictions on the invasive Asian black carp as it migrated north. Two Arkansas aquaculture farmers who raised black carp pressured the agency, although federal officials said Rasmussen was reassigned because of budget concerns. Meersman said he originally planned to make the story of Rasmussen a longer story and a key part of the series. It had been designed to show how agencies such as Fish and Wildlife could have separate and at times conflicting orders. In the Rasmussen case the clash was between the need to stop invasive species against efforts to encourage aquaculture and the cultivation of new species (Meersman, 2004). One drawback of sidebars can be their short length. In this case, Meersman said he may have cut too much out of the final version of the sidebar (Meersman, 2006).

The main stories in the other two days centered on more specific issues. Meersman said his favorite was the third day. It described how scientists proposed building an electric fence to prevent the goby from leaving the Great Lakes and migrating through the shipping canal southwest of Chicago that eventually connected with the Mississippi River. Government officials delayed so long that the fish had already passed the gate by the time it was completed in 2002 at a cost of $1.2 million. But Meersman did not end the story there. The second half told of the Asian black carp's migration north up the Mississippi towards the Great Lakes and the effort to build a second fence to stop it (Meersman, 2004). Not surprisingly, officials were not optimistic the fence would be completed in time. Meersman said the story went so much further than others had in describing the problem. "Our story took it further in offering an explanation of why this is happening and why we as a society are not grappling with it in a timely manner," he said (Meersman, 2006). It ended on a strong note:

> The efforts to block the carp and gobies are small skirmishes in what scientists see as a larger war.
>
> Phyllis Windle, senior staff scientist for the Union of Concerned Scientists, said that battle strategies need to change.
>
> "It's hard for me to see that this continuing, piecemeal, one-species-by-one-species approach is going to get us where we need to go," she said. "There's been no real fundamental change in the last 30 years in the way the U.S. thinks about the damages of these species and how important it is to prevent them."
>
> (Meersman, 2004, p. 12)

Meersman said he was trying in this close to emphasize a major point raised in the series. "You need to underscore the fact that this is not a high priority issue," he said. "People were talking about the need for new laws, but what I found is that many of the existing laws are not even being enforced" (Meersman, 2006).

Narrative

Narrative writing is both celebrated and scorned by journalists. It is pursued by some writers and misunderstood by others. Yet it can produce compelling journalism that is embraced by readers, even if they may not know it by name. Narrative means storytelling. Bryan Gruley of the *Wall Street Journal* said:

> It's what I do when my wife asks me how golf went and I describe how it was that I nearly birdied but eventually bogeyed the last hole of the day, shot by shot, with insertions about the weather, the conditions, my state of mind, the unfairness of life, how I set out to reduce my stress and wound up creating it.
>
> (Scanlan, 2003, p. 3)

Obviously Gruley could have just reported on his golf score but his narrative was far more entertaining – at least that was his hope. Mark Kramer, writer in residence at Harvard University, runs a program on narrative writing and has listed the elements of the form. Kramer said that at a minimum a narrative must have set scenes, characters, action that unfolds over time, the interpretative voice of a narrator, a sense of relationship to the reader and finally a tale that leads the reader to a point, realization, or destination. Janet Rae Brooks of the *Salt Lake Tribune* said "narrative is what I come up with when I put my niece to bed and she says 'Tell me a story.' I tell her a story, I don't tell her an article" (Scanlan, 2003, p. 14).

One of the foremost apostles of narrative is Jon Franklin, who won two Pulitzer Prizes as a science writer and who now teaches journalism at the University of Maryland. Franklin said that even the reporting for a narrative is different than other types of stories, because the writer must focus more on characters and the actions they take. "The character confronts something, struggles with it, usually realizes something and then brings it to a conclusion," he said (Soennichsen, 2004, p. 5). Tom French, of the *St. Petersburg Times*, said narrative stories must have an engine, a writing device that pushes the tension towards a climax (Clark, 2005).

Not all journalists embrace the narrative story. Many are uncomfortable because some of its characteristics are similar to those used by the creative or fiction writer. Telling stories through scenes is important in narrative. Some writers witness and report on what they observe. Another common tactic is to reconstruct scenes where the writer has not been present. Reconstructions rely on the memory of those who were there. But memories can be faulty, especially from days or weeks afterwards. Narratives also take more time in the reporting and writing than many editors are willing to grant.

Narratives can be written about environmental subjects just as easily as any other subject. No issue is too technical or complicated, if it has the correct vehicle. A celebrated narrative has been Franklin's "Mrs. Kelly's Monster," a story that was awarded one of his two Pulitzer Prizes. It was a story about a woman's brain surgery. Franklin said that nothing can be certain when beginning a narrative. While the writer may produce a hypothesis, often he cannot be certain of the story until he completes the reporting. In this case, he assumed Mrs Kelly would be the protagonist, and the surgery that he observed was only going to be preliminary to a larger operation, where she would finally overcome a brain aneurysm and relieve her pain. But Mrs. Kelly died following the operation. Franklin said "the story ended up being about what it is like to be a surgeon who just killed somebody" (Soennichsen, 2004, p. 3).

Getting on and off the narrative train

Some reporters deal with the challenges of narrative by combining it with elements of exposition. Mark Kramer has likened the story process to a train which begins its journey as a narrative. At the journey's first stop the writer and reader get off the narrative so that the writer can provide important background details. Then, both get back on the narrative train and continue their journey. The technique should be used sparingly. Too many delays could send the narrative train off on a side track that could end in a derailment.

The challenge of moving on and off the train confronted Lord of the *Providence Journal* in 2001 when he wrote his series about lead-poisoned children. The project had begun after photographer John Freidah had spent months shooting pictures of children and their families. The pictures clearly told the human story, one that Lord and his editor Plunkett wanted to capture. Plunkett said: "No one can turn away from a wonderful image of a child. We moved to have one child each day whose story would illustrate an aspect of lead poisoning" (Power of words, 2001, p. 1). It was that image that helped form the lead to the first day of the story, which began:

> PROVIDENCE – Shonnell Jordan bursts into the examination room, rushes by the doctor and grabs at toys, stethoscopes, tongue depressors – anything he can get his hands on. He's small for a 3-year-old, but he's like a miniature storm.
>
> A nurse hands him raisins and they spill to the floor. He dives after them and pops each one into his mouth. When she won't give him any more, he tries to bite her.
>
> Dr. James "Jeff" Brown, who has headed this clinic in Providence for 30 years, struggles to hold Shonnell with one hand, but he wriggles away. Finally Dr. Brown sits down, pins Shonnell between his knees, quickly puts the stethoscope to Shonnell's back and chest and peers into his ears and mouth.
>
> Shonnell seems healthy, but he won't stop moving. It is late July, a time when many Rhode Island families are at the beach. But Shonnell visits doctors. He was even hospitalized for three days, along with his sister.
>
> He is lead poisoned.
>
> (Lord, 2001a, p. 1)

The nut graph for the lead poisoning story came one paragraph later after the writer mentions Shonnell's two siblings, Maurianna and Mark:

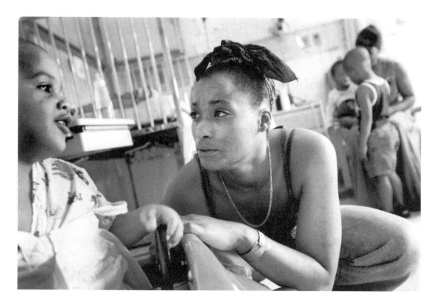

Figure 10.2 Shonnell Jordan is one of the main characters in the series written by Peter Lord of the *Providence Journal* about how lead poisoning was sickening children in Rhode Island (source: courtesy *Providence Journal*).

> Shonnell, who is now 4, Maurianna and Mark, are among nearly 3,000 Rhode Island children under the age of 6 who were diagnosed with lead poisoning last year. They are among the hundreds who were considered significantly lead poisoned – triggering mandatory state inspection of their homes in a search for the cause.
>
> (Lord, 2001a, pp. 1–2)

At this point Lord got off of the narrative train, providing about 500 words of background. He said that while he wanted to tell the human side of the tragedy, he was also compelled to report why this could continue to happen. Year after year another 3,000 poor children were being poisoned. Among the points he produced in this block of copy was:

- The rate that children in Providence were lead-poisoned was four times higher than the national rate.
- Poisoning could significantly affect intelligence and struck hardest at children under six.
- Government officials had failed to respond to what had become the greatest environmental health threat in Rhode Island (Lord, 2001a).

Then Lord returned to the narrative, telling how the misfortunes had first began for Burnadette Jordan, the young mother of Shonnell and his siblings, when she had moved into her own apartment. The gas stove immediately broke, the bathroom pipes had burst and the paint cracked when the heat came on. But those problems were nothing in comparison to what happened when she took her two young children in for a routine health checkup. Their lead levels were so high that the children had to be hospitalized. After they were released, Jordan searched frantically and unsuccessfully for a new place to live. By the end of the story her son, Shonnell, was still struggling. She took him to a Little League tryout but he was not allowed on the team after league officials saw him try to bite his mother. Burnadette landed back at her mother's apartment, hoping to find a new home and health and educational help for her children (Lord, 2001a).

Both reporter and editor said their intent was to focus the story as much as possible on the family. Plunkett, the editor, said: "I urged Pete to resist the urge to start off with an anecdote and abandon it and go to the facts and figures, but to keep it on Shonnell and do it that way" (Power of words, 2001, p. 1). Lord said he wanted to work with the families, but first he spent weeks understanding lead poisoning. He was pleased with the help he got from the families (Power of words, 2001). The first story was an overview; subsequent stories described how the dilapidated housing stock contributed to the problem, the burden lead poisoning placed on the educational system, how the health system struggled with lead-poisoned children and how government and courts failed to find solutions. Each issue was framed around one particular lead-poisoned child (Lord, 2001a–f).

Lord believes the format chosen, and the very human stories they told, were what made the difference the following year when the state legislature adopted a bill requiring landlords to clean up apartments containing lead paint and requiring the state to focus additional resources on the children being poisoned. He said: "It wouldn't have worked without them opening up their lives, and they became characters. People got choked up about individual characters" (Power of words, 2001, p. 4).

Study guide

1 Discuss how Tom Meersman could have converted his story about invasive species in the Great Lakes into a narrative story. Discuss what steps Peter Lord would have had to take to write an expository developed story about lead poisoning.

2 Take the Meersman or Lord story and write a one-sentence guiding summary of what you think the story should be about. Write a mission statement about each story.

3 Good resources for developed stories can be found at www.pulitzer.org which lists every Pulitzer Prize-winning story with links to the more recent ones and at www.nieman.harvard. edu/narrative, which is the Nieman Narrative Digest with a listing and links to recently published narrative stories.

4 Find a story you particularly admire at the Pulitzer or Nieman online site, or elsewhere, and write an outline of that story. Take that story and write a 500-word story. What does the reader lose and gain from this shorter story?

5 Consider contacting the writer of that article or series that you admired. What questions would you ask the writer?

6 Watch a film. Stop the tape often and notice how and when the director lines up scenes and moves the action forward. Outline the film. Write a lead for it.

7 For further reading, consider Jon Franklin's *Writing for Story* (1994), William Howarth's *John McPhee Reader* (1976) and *Literary Journalism* by Norman Sims and Mark Kramer (1995).

Chapter 11

Side beats

Steve Grant noticed that his canoe was gliding faster than normal. It took him a few minutes to realize that he was paddling with more force than normal because he was so caught by his emotion. On the shore people waved and clapped, boat horns sounded, and people snapped pictures. A mile before Saybrook Point other canoes came abreast. The paddlers included his wife and two children. Finally, on shore, his editor handed him a cup of champagne and poured the rest of the bottle over Grant's head. Speakers at the podium praised Grant and his canoe (Grant, 1991).

Figure 11.1 Steve Grant of the *Hartford Courant* portages his canoe and equipment around a dam on his trek down the Connecticut River. Grant wrote a series about his trip down the river (source: courtesy *Hartford Courant*).

It was June, 1991, and Grant, a reporter for the *Hartford Courant*, had just completed a 410-mile canoe trek of the Connecticut River from its source on the Canadian border to where it emptied into Long Island Sound. He had written stories about the journey three times a week for each of the last five weeks. The first-person reports had seized Connecticut readers' attention. The newspaper was already getting hundreds of telephone calls and letters. "It was the most popular story I have written in my career," Grant said. "It will be in my obit" (Grant, 2006).

First-person stories have that ability to connect with readers. So do many of Grant's other stories which feature nature and the outdoors. Environmental journalism is not confined to the traditional beats of newspapers and television stations. It can be found in a range of journalistic beats, from nature writing to travel to agriculture and even food.

Nature writing

From John Muir to Annie Dillard to Bill McKibben, readers have always identified with nature and those who write about it. McKay Jenkins, a nature writer and teacher, said that nature writing "is one of a nonfiction writer's best chances to explore the ephemeral, the unseen, the mysterious" (Jenkins, 2006, p. 234). He added that writing about nature allows a writer to discuss such fundamental issues as life and death and also to explore mankind's position in the world. Nature can be a metaphor, a window towards the exploration of universal themes. Noted nature writer David Quammen wrote: "A trout is both a fish and an idea, a representation of something larger, in this case an entire ecosystem. The trick for the nature writer is to remember both the trout and the watershed" (Jenkins, 2006, p. 231).

The spectrum of nature writing is broad. The largest group of practitioners may be the outdoor writers whose beats center on fishing and hunting in their community. Many write for local newspapers and belong to the Outdoor Writers Association of America. Many magazines have also specialized in coverage of nature, from slick monthlies like *National Geographic* to small niche quarterly publications such as *American Forest*, owned by the conservation group American Forests. Publishers have always found a market for books centering on nature, even though rumor has it that Norman MacLean's *A River Runs Through It* was rejected by one New York publishing house because the book "had too many trees in it" (Jenkins, 2006, p. 231).

Steve Grant carved out a slightly different type of nature beat at the *Hartford Courant* and found it wildly popular. The former environmental and political bureau chief proposed the nature beat after he discovered he could not abide editing or being stuck in the office all day.

Grant said that when he first proposed a beat that centered on nature, editors were not convinced that readers would be interested in stories about plants and animals. But they gave him a chance. He wrote about how thousands of crows congregated each winter in a few old gnarled trees in a Hartford neighborhood. He described how after a century of growth the forests of Connecticut were aging and in decline. Soon his executive editor at the time, Mike Waller, was moving the stories budgeted for inside to page one. Grant's proposal to canoe the Connecticut River had been kicking around for years. One day a deputy editor jokingly raised the issue as part of a casual conversation with Waller and Grant. Intrigued, Waller ordered Grant to write a detailed memo and a day later he approved it. His only orders were "do it and take as long as it takes to do it right" (Grant, 2006). Since then Grant has done similar series hiking the entire Appalachian Trail, traversing the New England coast, and circumnavigating Long Island Sound. He believes his smaller, more manageable stories are just as effective in helping readers connect with the environment. "We're never going to save the environment unless people get engaged," he said. "If we can make it accessible in stories such as these, then maybe we have a chance" (Grant, 2006).

While Grant's Connecticut River series was written in the first person, nature stories can be written in either first person or third person. A writer should have a good reason for including himself in the story. The writer's presence should not be gratuitous. Writing in the first person allows the reporter to more easily make observations and judgments. For instance, in the story where Grant had canoed the Connecticut River he was standing at the crowded podium when struck by a thought. He wrote: "I thought how different the first week of the trip had been from the last. The first week had been so quiet, the last week so celebratory" (Grant, 1991, p. 16).

Sometimes the writer's experience is so unique that third person would not be appropriate. Burkhard Bilger was researching a story about unusual wildlife dishes in the south. In a story called "Braised Shank of Free-Range Possum?" he shared a meal with Jeff Jackson, a professor of wildlife management at the University of Georgia:

> Now chewing on another rich yet fibrous flab of mystery muscle, I wonder what it is, exactly, that makes something inedible. Is it just a matter of physiology, of nutrient deficiencies and taste-bud densities, or is it more psychological – a habit of mind changed by culture, temperament, and parents telling us to eat our vegetables? Taste is a mind–body problem of the most intractable kind, and nothing brings it into focus as vividly as eating something unknown and potentially disgusting. Jeff, smiling faintly, informs me that this particular mouthful is armadillo meat. Why should that make my

throat constrict and my stomach leap into my diaphragm? Does the fact that some southerners call this "possum on the half shell" make it less palatable?

(Bilger, 2002, pp. 11–12)

Edward O. Wilson said that nature writing has evolved into its own distinct art form (Wilson, 2001). Writers like Annie Dillard, who won the 1974 Pulitzer Prize for *Pilgrim at Tinker Creek*, have added immeasurably to the form. First-person writing about nature adds perspective beyond what many conventional stories can achieve by adding value judgments. Consider this excerpt from Dillard's book:

I live by a creek, Tinker Creek, in a valley in Virginia's Blue Ridge. An anchorite's hermitage is called an anchor-hold; some anchor-holds were simple sheds clamped to the side of a church like a barnacle to a rock. I think of this house clamped to the side of Tinker Creek as an anchor-hold. It holds me at anchor to the rock bottom of the creek itself and it keeps me steadied in the current, as a sea anchor does, facing the stream of light pouring down. It's a good place to live; there's a lot to think about. The creeks – Tinker and Carvin's – are an active mystery, fresh every minute. Theirs is the mystery of the continuous creation and all that providence implies; the uncertainty of vision, the horror of the fixed, the dissolution of the present, the intricacy of beauty, the pressure of fecundity, the elusiveness of the free, and the flawed nature of perfection.

(Dillard, 1974, pp. 2–3)

Nature writing must also be factual. The beauty and poetry should be offset by the stark reality of what is happening to the environment. Mark Cherrington traveled to Israel to write "To Save a Watering Hole." The story was about Dalit Yosef's efforts to save a wildlife refuge from development in an area that had become a major resort. It detailed Yosef's fight to defend the refuge against those who made death threats and burned down his research station. One day he discovered the family dog hanging from a chain, dead, with a paper attached that said "Get Out." The refuge had become an important resting place for migratory birds traveling from Europe, Asia and Africa. Those traveling through Israel each spring included: three million raptors, 800,000 honey buzzards, 460,000 steppe buzzards, 142,000 lesser spotted eagles and 1.2 billion songbirds and waders. Cherrington then wrote:

They come here from the Sahel, the Sahara, and the Sinai where the desert is so dry people have died of dehydration in eight hours. The birds come by the tens of thousands, great swirling clouds of them, sunbaked and exhausted, desperate to reach this piece of land. Even under the best of circumstances, 60 percent of some migratory species may die en route, and some survivors arrive with all their fat and most of their muscle metabolized. For birds flying south, the sanctuary is a last, crucial pit stop. For birds flying north, it's a life-saving oasis.

(Cherrington, 2001 p. 11)

Sometimes writers are intimidated by nature. McKay Jenkins taught a college class in Delaware called "The Literature of the Land" and found that his journalism students were having difficulty producing nature stories. One explained that the problem was that there was "no nature in Delaware." Americans' increasing distance from the natural world may be a challenge, but it offers numerous opportunities. James Eli Shiffer of the *Raleigh News & Observer* had covered the cop beat in the past, but his decision to write about canoeing 235 miles down North Carolina's Neuse River provoked far more concern for his safety from friends and relatives. Shiffer said the unpredictability of the river, its wildlife, and the characters who lived on it were a tremendous asset. "Covering an environmental story in such an intense and personal way reminded me that rivers are complex creatures, more than the sum of their fish, dissolved oxygen levels, and flood stages," wrote Shiffer (1998, p. 14).

Environmental travel writing

Some of the best travel writing of the nineteenth century was written by Thoreau, Walt Whitman, Herman Melville and Mark Twain. More recent writers include Jack Kerouac, Dillard, Jon Krakauer, Paul Theroux, and Bill Bryson, to name just a few. Travel writing can be split into two divides: basic guides and armchair travel. The former provides valuable practical information including lists of hotels, restaurants and places to see. This section will deal only with armchair travel, a genre that is less focused on whether the reader will journey to the destination and that is far more intent on trans-porting the reader to the place through words. While environmental travel has become popular, armchair travel tells a story. The Internet has been significantly changing the travel industry including opportunities for travel writing. Newspapers and periodicals have been losing advertising to online travel sites. That switch has been reducing the demand for armchair travel, even though the form remains popular with readers. Anyone seriously interested in pursu-ing travel writing should know that many resorts, travel bureaus and destinations arrange for tours by accredited travel writers and pay for all of their expenses. Some publications accept stories that are a result of such expense-paid tours, while others have strong prohibitions against them. To avoid such potential conflicts of interest, major publications are usually willing to pay the expenses of established travel writers.

Good travel writing depends on anecdotes, vivid descriptions of places and people and a mechanism to place those observations in perspective. Pico Iyer, author of several travel books, said that "travel writing anywhere involves an extension of the passing into something more durable, and the elaboration of an incident that would be humdrum at home into something that is revealing both of setting and of self" (Iyer, 2004, p. xviii). For some, self-discovery works best in exotic settings. Mark Jenkins, writing for *Outside* magazine, was traveling illegally in northeast India. Jenkins was trying to get across Burma and into China on the Stilwell Road, if it still existed. Built during World War II, it had vanished into the jungle. In "The Ghost Road" Jenkins had just evaded the border police by jumping into a vintage white Ambassador automobile. He wrote:

> I find myself sitting beside a large Buddhist llama in maroon robes. I adjust my disguise and scan the crowd outside.
> "You are being chased," said the llama.
> "I am."
> The llama speaks to the chauffeur. The chauffeur taps his horn and maneuvers around a brahma bull seated in the road, speeds up. In the outskirts of Ledo, we roll onto a long green grassy driverway, pass a freshly guilded stupa, and stop in front of a group of wooden buildings. The llama lifts his frock above polished black shoes and steps out.
> "My name is Aggadhamma," he says in a British-accented English. "This is the Namsai Buddhist Vihara, a monastery for boys. You are safe here."
>
> (Jenkins, 2004, pp. 129–130)

This passage demonstrates how much good dialogue can help a story. While exotic locales are nice, they are not essential. Just like there truly is nature in Delaware, there are also opportunities to write about travel at home. Increasingly Steve Grant of the *Hartford Courant* has been asked to do travel stories about local natural and cultural resources. One day he drove north of Hartford to Bartholomew's Cobble, a 329-acre outcropping of rock that featured 800 plant species and 240 bird species. Located near untended hay fields, Grant wrote:

Check for bobolinks. They are not hard to identify, even if you haven't the foggiest what a bobolink is. They are a curiosity in the bird world; the males have black bellies and a back that appears mostly white, with a dull yellow nape. In the bird world the opposite – a pale belly and a dark back – is the norm.

Bobolinks are noted for their song, often described as cheerful and bubbly, and their commute. They are among the truly long-distance migrants, wintering 5,000 or more miles away in Bolivia, Paraguay and Argentina. While not rare, they're not a bird you're likely to encounter unless you have a field of hay nearby that remains unmown into summer.

(Grant, 2004, p. 2)

Agriculture journalism

In the early 1970s more than nine million people in Michigan were found to have "measurable levels" of a dangerous chemical, poly-brominated biphenyl or PBBs, in the tissues of their bodies. PBBs are not meant to be ingested, they are a highly toxic fire retardant. The sequence of events that led to these people being exposed to the chemical began early in 1973. A truck driver known as Shorty was supposed to deliver 50-pound sacks of a food additive to Farm Bureau Services, which operated the biggest feed plant in Michigan. Instead he delivered sacks of the crystallized PBBs and it was not until months later that the error was discovered. By then countless cows had ingested the chemical. Tens of thousands of the cows were slaughtered and buried in pits and hundreds of farms were found to contain remnants of the PBBs. Humans had consumed the PBBs either from milk or other products produced by the cows. Hundreds of people reported symptoms of severe toxicity while the rest of the population was told they were at risk in the future to a series of long-term diseases (Eggington, 1980).

While the extent of the pollution and the health threat was comparable to Love Canal or Chernobyl, the PBB crisis in Michigan never received the same attention. Even in Michigan the local press was slow to catch on to the story, not reporting it in any detail until months after the problem was discovered. Ultimately the *Detroit Free Press* published three detailed stories about the PBB accident, but not until 1977 (Eggington, 1980).

America is increasingly an urban society that does not understand rural or agriculture issues, even when it comes to such basic subjects as where people obtain their food. In 1850 agriculture employed 65 percent of all Americans. By 1990 the number was 2.7 percent with expectations that it could fall below 2 percent by 2005 (Pawlick, 2001).

News organizations have cut the number of reporters covering agriculture and one survey found only 16 agriculture journalism academic programs in the U.S. and Canada (Pawlick, 2001). Coverage of food production has been left to such beats as business and the food page. Still, it is foolish for environmental reporters, even large-city or suburban reporters in the northeast or the west coast, to ignore what is taking place on the nation's farms.

William Allen, a journalism professor at the University of Missouri's agriculture journalism program, said he and others often struggle even defining the term ag journalism. A better term might be the ag beat, he said, and it is important to recognize that it covers a range of disciplines including science, economics, the environment and politics (Allen, 2007). Stories on the ag beat extend far beyond the farm.

Hot topics

Two of the biggest issues in the beat for environmental reporters in the first decade of the twenty-first century have been biotechnology and ethanol.

Biotechnology is defined by U.S. Department of Agriculture as "a range of tools, including traditional breeding techniques, that alter living organisms...; improve plants and animals; or develop microorganisms for specific agriculture uses" (USDA, 2005, p. 1). Most of the developments in this area have centered on genetically engineered crops. The first commercial crops of genetically engineered products occurred in the mid-1990s and they have become increasingly common since then. In 2004 they accounted for 46 percent of all corn plantings in the U.S., 76 percent for cotton and 85 percent for soybeans (USDA, 2005). Yet a poll taken by the Pew Initiative on Food and Biotechnology in 2006 indicated that Americans were "still generally uncertain" about genetically modified and cloned food. Virtually everyone in the U.S. by then had been exposed to some processed foods containing gene-altered foods, yet only one-quarter of those polled thought they fit into that category. The poll found that 34 percent of the 1,000 people polled thought the crops were safe while 29 percent labeled them unsafe (Weiss, 2006).

One reason for the concern is that it is difficult to segregate genetically altered crops. In 2000 researchers discovered that StarLink corn, which was unapproved for human use, had made its way into many food products. In addition, U.S. long-grain rice has been contaminated by other experimental varieties (Weiss, 2006). The Agriculture Department also concedes that there are "potential risks" from genetically altered crops that must be monitored closely, including unanticipated environmental impacts to other species (USDA, 2005).

Ethanol is another technological development in agriculture, although its origins are far older. Ethanol was first used as a lighting fuel in the 1850s and its fortunes have risen and fallen several times. Revived interest in ethanol as a transportation fuel began in the 1970s after the international oil embargos of 1973 and 1979. Its prime benefits are that it comes from a renewable resource – usually corn – and it can be domestically produced. Its handicaps are that it can be expensive to produce in comparison to some fossil fuels and vehicles have to be modified to use it (EIA, n.d.).

In 2005 and 2006 energy prices rose dramatically and ethanol's fortunes rose again. Investors began spending billions of dollars on new ethanol refinery plants, with the number estimated under construction in 2007 ranging from 65 to 79. That caused concerns about whether enough corn would be left for uses beyond ethanol. "We're worried that there will be less to feed the world if we're using too much corn to make fuel," said Lester Brown, president of the Environmental Policy Institute. "The U.S. ... supplies 70 percent of the world's corn exports" (Clayton, 2007, p. 1). The demand was also driving up the price of corn to record levels. In November, 2006 a bushel of corn hit $3.70, a ten-year high and 77 percent increase from the year before (Rutledge, 2006). That was affecting a range of foods that use corn as a feedstock, especially beef and pork. Experts warned that if the price of corn remained that high it would make ethanol production unprofitable.

Both of these examples demonstrate not only the complexity of the issues in the agricultural and food fields but their breadth. Ag journalism stories are often staring reporters in the face. They just need to recognize them. For instance, the decline of the small farm has been told many times, but how many writers have examined the land-use issues raised as a result of these economical and social changes. Food pages and restaurant reviewers have described the increased interest among consumers to buy more locally grown items. Such stories have obvious energy and environmental angles. Rachel Carson's *Silent Spring* was an ag journalism story and so was the Alar story about pesticides on apples (see Chapter 7). Pat Stith of the *News & Observer* in Raleigh, NC, also had no idea he would be writing an ag journalism story in 1994 when he got a tip about a state veterinarian.

Boss Hog

Pat Stith's tip was that a state veterinarian was taking junkets from large pork producers in the state (Sill, 2005). Stith and reporter Joby Warrick soon learned that the pork producers were becoming increasingly powerful in North Carolina. Family farms were going out of business and the land was being sold to large corporations. Those companies were winning exemptions from regulations and taxes. As the firms grew so did the millions of pigs they were breeding as well as the waste coming from the animals. The reporters found that the state did not have the ability to regulate the pigs or the resulting waste problem.

The lead for their first story began:

> Imagine a city as big as New York suddenly grafted onto North Carolina's Coastal Plain. Double it.
>
> Now imagine that city has no sewage treatment plants. All the wastes from 15 million inhabitants are simply flushed into open pits and sprayed onto the fields.
>
> (Warrick & Stith, 1995, p. 1)

The story reported that this "vast city of swine" produced 9.5 million tons of manure each year that was stored in thousands of lagoons. Wendell H. Murphy, a former state senator who had become the nation's largest hog producer, maintained that the lagoons safely contained the waste. But the reporters found studies indicating that contaminants from the lagoons were getting into the groundwater (Warrick & Stith, 1995).

Reporters in the past had produced stories about the odor complaints. But no one had looked into it in the depth of the *News & Observer* reporters. They told how the residents of Browntown, NC, suffered through church services while smelling the acrid odor of the hogs (Sill, 2005). They also described how studies showed that large amounts of ammonia gas from the hog farms returned to earth in rain. The ammonia was linked to algae growth explosions in local rivers and estuaries (Warrick & Stith, 1995).

The five-part series, called "Boss Hog," prompted state officials to create a special commission. At one point the commission appeared to be stalled until a huge lagoon collapsed, causing a large fish kill. The state imposed a moratorium on new farms, implemented a series of regulatory reforms as well as providing research to find alternate uses for the waste (Sill, 2005). The series won the Pulitzer Prize in 1996.

Study guide

1 Write a story about yourself in first person. Then rewrite it in third person. Compare the two stories. What are the advantages and disadvantages of each?

2 Nature can be found in Delaware or anywhere. Compile a list of at least five nature stories that you could write based in your local area.

3 Write an armchair travel story. It can be based on a trip you have taken or on a local site.

4 Many college students have insisted that dining facilities offer organic food options and buy more locally produced food. What is happening at the local college or university on that issue? Is there a story?

5 Read the "Boss Hog" series that can be found in its entirety at www.pulitzer.org. What reporting and writing elements worked for the reporters?

6 For further reading, consider Annie Dillard's *Pilgrim at Tinker Creek* (1974), Paul Theroux's *The Great Railway Bazaar* (1995), Michael Pollan's *Botany of Desire* (2002) and *The Best American Science and Nature Writing* and *The Best American Travel Writing* that have each been published annually since 2000.

Chapter 12

Opinion

John Oakes became an editorial writer at the *New York Times* in 1949. From 1961 to 1976 he was editor of the editorial page. Besides developing the concept of the op-ed page, now a common feature in newspapers around the country, Oakes changed the editorial page voice of the *Times*. For years editorials had sounded like "the voice of a family doctor" (Columbia University, 2006, p. 1), according to Robert McFadden, another longtime *New York Times* writer. Oakes urged writers to take firm stands based on strong reasoning and language. Oakes also developed an environmental column, which he proposed after stepping down from running the editorial page. Editors at first wondered if readers would have enough interest in the environment. This prompted Oakes to offer to write it for free. It quickly became one of the most popular columns in the *Times*. Oakes wrote in a voice similar to his editorial writers. He complained that the policies of James Watt, then Interior Secretary, were "radical, inflationary, economically unsound and environmentally degrading." He also lamented the government's failure to respond to the threat of acid rain, which he called "aerial sewage." He was not always critical: he praised efforts to develop more public lands and parks (Columbia University, 2006).

In columns and editorials opinion is expected. Writers take varying approaches but the idea is to make the writing lively and the subject interesting. John McCormick, deputy editorial page editor of the *Chicago Tribune*, said that there was nothing worse in an editorial than a writing voice that was "stuffy, omnipotent, often pompous" (Woods, 2003, p. 1). He said the key was to write essays, not editorials. "Never let your editorial page become the dull place some readers, and some journalists, feel that it is," he said (Woods, 2003, p. 2).

For years Edward Flattau and Paul H. MacClennan wrote columns in favor of the environment, often pushing both government and business to do more. Flattau became a nationally syndicated environmental columnist in the early 1960s and his column has been carried over the years by various news services. Former *Los Angeles Times* Washington

Bureau Chief Jack Nelson said that Flattau's writing carried "the passion of an environmentalist, but with a journalist's reverence for the facts" ("Syndicated Columnist," 2004, p. 1) In a column in 2000 Flattau ridiculed "think tanks of right wing and libertarian persuasion" for their opposition to government regulation. He wrote: "They preach that trees are worse polluters than factories and that swamps are cesspools of pestilence we would do well to replace with shopping malls" (Flattau, 2000, p. 1). MacClennan's writing voice was similar in tone and political leaning. A longtime writer for the *Buffalo News*, MacClennan wrote a weekly column until he retired in 1997 ("Buffalo News," 1998). Since then he continued to produce occasional columns. In 2004 he was so upset about the state of the environment that he wrote "we appear to be entering the Decade of Environmental Shame." He described greater Buffalo:

> The area has a rotting, toxin-infested Buffalo River and while a group is focused on this, the entire environmental community should be raising hell about it. Same for the lingering nuclear waste at West Valley or the fact that the Buffalo waterfront remains a public wasteland.
> And Niagara Falls – it's a scenic disgrace given over to billboards, towers and other eyesores.
>
> (MacClennan, 2004, p. 2)

A strong writing voice is essential, no matter how portions of the column are drafted. Betsy Marston wrote a column for *High Country News* in Paonia, CO, called "Heard around the West." It is composed of news briefs and reports of environmental and other issues from states around the Rocky Mountain region, with Marston's editorial zip added. Writing about a Colorado land developer, Marston began: "Real estate developer Tom Chapman must relish his work, which can be summed up as pulling the Forest Service's chain with one hand while using the other to extract large amounts of money from the wallets of taxpayers" (Marston, 2005, p. 1).

Conservative columnists write about the environment in voices just as authoritative as their colleagues on the left. One of the most forthright was the late Warren Brooks, a longtime syndicated columnist with the *Detroit News* and a free market advocate. Another is Michael Fumento, a nationally syndicated columnist, who sometimes has used a sense of humor to skewer what he saw as a hapless or biased press and an environmental community that was overly alarmist. In one column he recalled how the press had termed 2001 the "Summer of the Shark" because so many news stories reported that swimmers were being shredded. Actually, he said, there were 11 fewer attacks than the year before.

In the same column, he discussed a dead zone that developed each year in the Gulf of Mexico and killed fish. Some scientists believed it was from fertilizer run-off from farms on the Mississippi River. Fumento maintained that theory was unproven and overly simplistic and touted by headline-seeking scientists. Here is how he described the quest of one scientist: "The dead zone is to Louisiana marine biologist Nancy Rabalais what the Redcoats were to Paul Revere. But for the one, nobody would have heard of the other" (Fumento, 2004, p. 1).

Sometimes it pays to not get too serious in writing opinions about the environment. Dave Barry, a nationally-syndicated columnist begin-

---

Be clear

John McCormick of the *Chicago Tribune* said that while it is good to express opinions in columns, selling those ideas is not easy. He said writers need to carefully organize the debate and to provide enough background for the reader to understand the context. He said writers of editorials and opinion articles should ask themselves seven questions as they develop the article. They are:

- Who is the target of this article? Is it being written for opinion leaders, the average reader, or just for the writer?
- What is the correct tone or attitude? Should the writer be angry, perplexed or befuddled?
- What is the article trying to accomplish? Does it seek a response from an official, a public change in attitude or is it just for entertainment?
- What will this article contribute to the debate? Will the article offer new facts, new arguments or new dimensions? McCormick said that the power of voice comes from the strength of the facts and the reasoning that drives the arguments.
- How new are the issues being raised in the article? Is it more than warmed over wisdom, does it offer a solution?
- Attack your own premise. Make sure your position withstands critical comments. What would be an opponent's most compelling argument?
- Are we creating a three-bowler? McCormick uses this phrase to make sure the article is not boring. The phrase means that the reader will be so bored by an article as he sits eating his cereal that his face flops into the bowl not once, not twice, but three times in his sheer boredom (McCormick, 2003).

ning in 1983 at the *Miami Herald*, learned early how easy it was to poke fun at the environment. One favorite issue he repeatedly turned to was animal flatulence. In a 2002 column Barry wrote:

> As you know if you have ever stood outdoors in the Midwest, cows give off methane gas. We don't know why. Maybe they're bored. Maybe they're trying to spoil humanity's appetite for hamburgers. All we know is, scientists believe that methane gas is a major factor in global warming.
>
> (Barry, 2002, p. 1)

Opinion – a case study

Tom Philp of the *Sacramento Bee* sometimes has written about water issues. His discoveries of questionable spending by several water agencies were detailed in Chapter 6. For years Philp had accepted the fact that Yosemite had a second valley nearly as grand as the centerpiece of the national park and that the valley had been lost forever. The valley's name was Hetch Hetchy. In 1913 Congress had agreed to allow San Francisco to build a dam and flood the Hetch Hetchy valley so that the city would have a source of drinking water.

In 2002 Philp began to hear that the Environmental Defense group had run a computer study showing the dam at Hetch Hetchy was no longer necessary. The study indicated that there were enough other water resources available without the Hetch Hetchy reservoir. He wrote a column about the environmentalist responsible for the study. The following year he heard that a second study had been undertaken by researchers from the University of California at Davis. This computer analysis also showed that dams downstream of Hetch Hetchy could contain more than enough water for San Francisco. In early 2004 Philp wrote a memo to his editors proposing an editorial series about the issue. He tried to break down the number of editorials that would be needed to spell out all of the technical issues. "This is like a case of mental chess," he said. "You have to know your idea enough to produce a game plan" (Philp, 2006). Shortly afterwards, editors approved the plan.

Philp spent weeks researching water issues, engineering reports, and water law and politics. "I forced myself to understand all of the technical issues," he said. "My early drafts were excessive in making a technical case." He was slightly overwhelmed by the challenge. "I was making a case for something that was way out of the box," he explained. "None of our readers even began to understand how you could restore Hetch Hetchy and how it would affect water quality and supply" (Philp, 2006).

Figure 12.1 The O'Shaughnessy Dam today contains the reservoir that has flooded the Hetch Hetchy reservoir. Editorials by Tom Philp of the *Sacramento Bee* prompted new discussions on whether the reservoir should be drained (source: courtesy Ron Good, Restore Hetch Hetchy).

He wrote drafts of most of the planned editorials and went on vacation. When he returned, his editor warned him that he still had work ahead of him. His editorial voice was too technical. She suggested he write more like John Muir, the naturalist who had explored Yosemite and who had bitterly campaigned against the Hetch Hetchy dam. "It was brilliant advice," said Philp. "It really helped in the persuasion of each article. It also helped because by the end, all of the articles read the same. They read with the same voice" (Philp, 2006).

Philp had hoped that in one editorial he would be able to interview someone who had seen Hetch Hetchy before it was inundated. It would have had to be someone who worked or visited up there, who was a teenager at the time, and who was now close to 100 years old. Over time he realized he was not going to find that person and that Muir's voice was especially powerful. "I knew I could not out-Muir John Muir," he said. So he decided to interview the naturalist who had died in 1914. He went to the University of Pacific library in nearby Stockton, where Muir's papers were stored and found remarks that would answer Philp's questions.

The first editorial was designed as an introduction. It began:

> Here is the best kept secret of Yosemite Valley: It has a twin.
>
> This little brother, as the late naturalist John Muir called it, has a thundering waterfall named Wapama, a feathery cascade named Tueeulala and a towering peak called Kolana. Below Kolana, a valley snakes between granite walls for eight miles to reach a staircase of rock known as the Grand Canyon of the Tuolumme.
>
> Yosemite's little brother has a name. It is called Hetch Hetchy, derived from the Indian name for its native grasses. But despite its grandeur and its presence in a park that is a national treasure, few people know Hetch Hetchy exists and few visit it.
>
> There is a reason for this remarkable obscurity. Hetch Hetchy is underwater.
>
> (Philp, 2004a, p. 1)

Philp believes that editorials have to bridge two distinct audience groups, the opinion leaders and the average reader. "A great editorial has to be bifocal," he said. "You can't just write editorials for the inside crowd because you will quickly lose all of your 300,000 readers" (Philp, 2006). Still, it is a challenge to create that bridge. Philp said he liked to talk to people about the project, especially to his father-in-law, to learn how to communicate with the average reader.

McCormick (2003) also pointed out that the writer needed to know who would be in opposition and what they would be asked. In his first editorial Philp explained the history of the dam and the fact that Yosemite was becoming increasingly popular with four million visitors a year. Then he introduced the opposition:

> San Francisco first set sights on this river for water in 1901. The city's leaders and residents would understandably be nervous and resistant to change today. Water and electricity are still precious commodities. Hetch Hetchy provides nearly 85 percent of the city's water and about a sixth of its electricity. It also supplies a large portion of the water for Alameda, Santa Clara and San Mateo counties.
>
> (Philp, 2004a, p. 3)

Philp followed this quickly with the arguments in favor of removing the dam. He wrote:

> Ninety years ago, the senators' collective clairvoyance was spotty. They had no way to anticipate that in 1971 the new Don Pedro

Dam, creating a reservoir more than five times the size of Hetch Hetchy's, would be built downstream. They had no way of knowing that an invention called the computer would reveal to UC Davis researchers that the big downstream dam could do the work that Hetch Hetchy does now. They had no way to know, in other words, that they were making a decision that might someday be undone.

(Philp, 2004a, p. 3)

Notice the language repeated in that paragraph. Philp was attempting to mimic Muir's voice. It was effective writing. Good opinion articles need to be tight and concise. Each of Philp's editorials on Hetch Hetchy averaged about 750 words. In the series introduction he was telling readers about issues he would explore in further articles. Writers need to end pointedly but gracefully. The reader needs to know the writer's opinion, but the writer need not be intrusive. Philp's first editorial ended:

In short, Californians don't have to be prisoners of a 90-year-old debate. Change is coming to the river. As part of that evolution, it is no longer unthinkable to imagine reuniting Yosemite's twin valleys. Something magnificent and unexpected could actually happen. A river could be allowed to run free through a glacial valley, just as it did before Congress locked it away nine decades ago.

(Philp, 2004a, p. 4)

Philp wrote 11 editorials about the removal of the Hetch Hetchy dam between August and November of 2004. Some of the subsequent editorials explained the specifics of the computer modeling showing how downriver dams could replace Hetch Hetchy (Philp, 2004b); how San Francisco considered itself so liberal and "green" and yet how it opposed unblocking the Hetch Hetchy reservoir (Philp, 2004c); how San Francisco only paid the federal government $82.19 a day for the rights to Hetch Hetchy (Philp, 2004d); how the valley contained very little silt and how vegetation would quickly be restored if the water was drained (Philp, 2004e); and the complexity of water rights in California (Philp, 2004f).

In the midst of the editorial series, political leaders responded. Two key state assembly leaders announced support for a study to reopen Hetch Hetchy. By the final editorial on November 14, California Governor Arnold Schwarzenegger agreed to that review (Philp, 2004g). The decision was gratifying to Philp. "I told my editors, 'I have no idea how this is going to be received.' I was nervous about it," he said. "It was really not on the radar except for a couple of blips on the screen. That's one reason we decided to move forward on it" (Philp, 2006).

Philp's Hetch Hetchy series was awarded the Pulitzer Prize for editorial writing in 2005 (Pulitzer.org, 2006). But prospects for the dam remained unclear. Philp had prepared readers in his last editorial that any decision would take time. The key, he said, was that the dialog had at least begun. He wrote "gone is the ability to dismiss the idea of restoring Hetch Hetchy as a far-fetched fantasy" (Philp, 2004g, p. 3).

Study guide

1 Write a news story. Then rewrite it into an opinion column or editorial. Compare these two versions.

2 Research the status of the efforts to drain the Hetch Hetchy reservoir and open up the valley.

3 Dave Barry has long been one of the nation's best humorists. Humor and the environment do not often coexist. Brainstorm and produce ideas on how you could write about the environment using humor, either in news stories or opinion articles.

4 For further reading, consider John Muir's *My First Summer in the Sierras* (1911/1998) and Dave Barry's *Boogers Are My Beat* (2003).

Chapter 13

Broadcast journalism

A buffalo scampered out of a hot spring as steam rose in the cold winter air. The camera panned to snow-covered hills, with tufts of white powder coating the branches of conifers.

"Yellowstone National Park in winter," declared reporter Natalie Pawelski of CNN from off-camera. "Hot springs, wildlife in the snow, the hills alive with the sound of snowmobile" (RTNDA, 2003).

Pawelski said her story about the battle over whether snowmobiles should be allowed in Yellowstone Park was a natural for television. "You've got stunning visuals – geysers and bison steaming in the snow," she said. "You've got great sound – the silence of a winter post-card, cut by the whine of snowmobiles and the throaty growl of a tailpipe as blue smoke spits into the air" (RTNDA, 2003). Plus the main characters were passionate. The snowmobile riders were excited about being able to traverse great distances in the vast park. Environ-mentalists were upset that Yellowstone's air quality was worse than Los Angeles'. The residents of nearby West Yellowstone worried that their economy would sink if the park banned snowmobiles (RTNDA, 2003).

All television news stories about the environment should be so visual and so compelling. Unfortunately, some have not been. Television is highly dependent on what the camera can see. Radio succeeds with what the microphone records. All environmental stories cannot offer the visual feast depicted in the Yellowstone story. Instead, many are technical and complex. Broadcast observers believe that environmental coverage, especially for television, peaked around 1990 in the aftermath of a series of environmental calamities including the Chernobyl nuclear accident and the *Exxon Valdez* oil spill. Environmental reporting appeared to be making a comeback until the September 11, 2001 terrorist attack refocused the attention of many news organizations. Then major hurricanes struck the east coast in 2004 and 2005. The visual evidence mounted that the environment was warming up. "We are seeing visible pictures on television of arctic ice melting and glaciers retreating," said Christy George, a producer for Oregon Public Radio.

"Global warming in the past was a story without pictures. It was a slow motion disaster, which was very difficult to cover." That has changed and George and others believed that television was poised to deliver the big environmental stories of the twenty-first century (George, 2006).

Broadcasting's limitations

Scott Miller, a former environmental reporter for KING-TV in Seattle, remembered proposing a story one day about a court ruling that would force improvements in the salmon runs on the Columbia River. "Does this mean the salmon are saved?" a producer asked. "If not, it sounds like a process story" (Miller, 2003, p. 16). A process story plays out over a long time, typical of most environment stories. Miller said environmental stories offer complexity – no clear storylines or obvious winners or losers. He remembered a television consultant who came to his station one day and declared "Every TV story needs a good guy and a bad guy" (Miller, 2003, p. 16). For years consultants drove television coverage with plans that emphasized personalities and studio sets. When consultants addressed content in a news program, environment was often significantly down the list of priorities (Willman, 2005).

As environmental issues fell in popularity, the number of reporters assigned to the environmental beat, both at the networks and at local stations, declined during the 1990s. CNN at one point had 15 staffers assigned to environmental coverage. Besides covering breaking stories the reporters produced stories for two regular broadcasts, *Earth Matters* on CNN and *Network Earth*, which aired on the affiliated channel, TBS. Both channels were owned by Ted Turner's Turner Broadcasting. The 30-minute *Earth Matters* program, which ran on Sundays, ended in 2001 after AOL purchased Turner. Camille Feanny, CNN's last surviving environmental journalist left in 2005. She said that she appeared to be the last remaining reporter at any network assigned to the environment (Dawson, 2005).

The few environment reporters at local stations found themselves increasingly doing more general assignment work. Matt Hammill at WQAD-TV in Moline, IL in the mid-1990s was doing a major environmental story every week but over the next ten years he said that interest in such stories dwindled both at the station and from the audience. By 2006 he found himself producing more general interest stories that were mixed with environmental themes (Hammill, 2006). Vince Patton, who covered the environment at KGW-TV in Portland, OR, said that at best he only spent about 50 percent of his time on beat stories. Shortly after the 2001 terrorist attacks, that work fell to 20 percent (Patton, 2006b). Alice Jacobs, vice president of news at WSVN-TV in Miami, seemed to sum up the views of many news managers in a 2004 interview. "Should there be a story we need to cover such as (an event in) the Everglades or an oil spill, we assign a general assignment reporter," she said (Whitney, 2004a, p. 9).

General assignment reporters have excelled at times in producing environmental stories. But some science background and understanding helps, especially in interviewing scientists. Television stories rarely run more than two or three minutes, making it difficult to explore issues in as much depth as in print stories. That has bothered many scientists, who worried that their comments would be taken out of context. Television also needs clear and concise speakers. "You must not only get the information, but you need it to be spoken in plain English," said Patton. "Lots of scientists have problems with that. They are absolutely brilliant, except when it comes to talking to the public" (Patton, 2006b).

When broadcast works

Broadcast journalists who described problems in the field could also tout just as many successes. Pawelski said that CNN's *Earth Matters* worked because the program stayed away from preaching about the benefits of recycling and the complaints of environmental activists and instead it stuck to storytelling narratives. "We mixed solid reporting with techniques of fiction – character, setting, plot and theme," she said. "The stories concentrated on people, not policy" (Pawelski, 2004, p. 87). Hammill said that wildlife stories can be extremely popular. He produced a news story about a peregrine falcon nesting downtown. Afterwards the station set up a live camera that broadcast continuously over the station's website. "It brought great interest from parents and kids and school groups as they watched the chicks hatch out, lose their fuzz-ball look and eventually gain enough feathers and confidence to take that first step from 15 stories up" (Hammill, 2006). Patton said what has helped maintain the beat in Portland was the area's strong interest in the environment. "I think people in the northwest have always had an enormously special relationship with the environment and it cuts across political boundaries ... A lot of people live here because of the environment" (Whitney, 2004a, p. 10).

Miller said it is important for television environmental reporters to work hard to maintain the beat. He said he would keep a list of 150 to 200 stories and never get discouraged, even though 70 percent were rejected by editors. One key was to use big breaking news as a way to write about the environment. One year forest officials were expecting a big fire season and he convinced his editors to produce a three-part series. He went to Idaho to report about prescribed burns, to Oregon to describe efforts to thin overgrown forests and to Montana to show how

Broadcast writing guidelines

Print and online journalism share many of the same qualities as broadcast journalism. Accuracy remains the primary requirement of all media and reporting. On environmental stories reporters still need to understand the basics of science, government regulation, and advocacy positions. Also, all three fields demand good writing. The fundamental difference between print and broadcast is that writing for the latter needs to be more conversational. Broadcast writing is aimed for the ear, not for the eye. Another fundamental difference is that the material gathered by the camera or the microphone is the primary content to shape the story (Stovall, 2004).

Other ways to help in writing for television or radio include:

- Use simple sentences and familiar words.
- Keep the subject close to the verb.
- Avoid pronouns.
- Eliminate unnecessary words or phrases.
- Write primarily in the present tense.
- Avoid including time elements if possible.
- Place attribution before quotes.
- List titles before names.
- Avoid direct quotes if possible.
- Round out numbers and statistics.
- Avoid symbols such as $ and %. Write them out.
- Avoid the passive voice.
- Use as little punctuation as necessary.
- Avoid abbreviations.
- Spell difficult words phonetically, placing the pronunciation in parentheses.

(Redmond *et al.*, 2005)

Yellowstone had responded after a disastrous fire season. By the time he returned, fires were beginning in Washington. He said: "If I tried to pitch that in a vacuum, they would say 'What are you talking about?'" (Whitney, 2003c, p. 38).

Broadcast reporters said they spent a great deal of time pitching stories. "It sounds crass, but you may need to think more like a promotions writer than a journalist," said Patton (2006a, p. 1). Pitching stories during the sweeps period when TV-ratings services evaluate viewership levels has been one of the most important times to find responsive news managers. Reporters also need to get creative at times.

Jeff Burnside, a television news reporter in Miami, FL, said he was unable to convince his producers to let him do a story about how seagrass beds were being restored. But a few months later he was able to sell them on doing a story about how boaters were paying big fines when they ran aground. What he did not tell them was that the fines those boaters were paying financed the restoration of the seagrass beds. "In TV news, the art of story telling begins with the story selling to your managers," said Patton (2006a, p. 1).

SEJ each year runs an environmental journalism awards contest and receives many entries from television and radio stations. Among just a few winners were:

- NBC's Stone Phillips found an interesting way to report on the federal government's decision to no longer require electric utilities to upgrade aging power plants. He interviewed Bruce Buckheit, who was so outraged by the decision that he resigned from his position in charge of EPA's Air Enforcement Division. Phillips also talked to John Ramil, chief operating officer of a Tampa utility. Buckheit had pressured Ramil's company until it agreed to spend $1 billion to upgrade its old coal-fired plants. Ramil praised Buckheit, saying he had done the right thing and the air would be cleaner in Florida as a result. Buckheit had wanted to clean the air elsewhere, but the Bush Administration's decision ended that and so he quit (Cooperman, 2004).

- A tanker truck leaked 2,500 gallons of liquid asphalt on Thanksgiving Day 2003 onto a city street and into a storm drain. When Paul Adrian of KDFW-TV learned of it, he knew he had more than a minor breaking news story. The tanker was owned by the City of Dallas and for the last month Adrian had been working on a story about how the city's environmental inspectors had two standards. They fined private companies up to $240,000 for such environmental infractions. But when the city was involved, they waived any enforcement or penalties. Shots by the station's helicopter crew showed how the Thanksgiving Day leak ran not just into the storm drain, but from there into the nearby Trinity River. The comprehensive deadline story forced changes by city and state environmental regulators (Whitney, 2004b).

- Craig Cheatham of KMOV-TV in St. Louis took a story about a lead smelter in Herculaneum, MO, that was causing sickness amongst local residents into a story with international ramifications. Local newspapers and television stations were already covering the pollution record of the facility owned by the Doe Run Company and a proposal to buy up local homes because of the pollution. In March 2002 Cheatham reported that the company knew when air monitors would test the plant's emission, raising the possibility the firm could increase toxic releases at other dates. He then showed that the company had a pattern of environmental problems. He traveled to LaOroya, Peru, and he described the pollution from the Doe Run smelter there, especially how its fumes had poisoned children under six (Whitney, 2003a).

• Sarah Bennett was a student at Missouri State University when she produced a seven-minute television documentary that won a first place award from SEJ. The story was about a community park in Springfield, MO, that had been built over a zinc and lead mine turned illegal dioxin landfill. The state had dumped 18 inches of sand and dirt over the dump and turned it into a park. Since then, records showed it had rarely been inspected to see if that "cap" was still in place. SEJ judges said they were impressed with Bennett's work, which included all of the research, reporting, photography and production. They said: "Despite these constraints she produced a seven-minute documentary that is rock solid journalism" (SEJ, 2003).

• A two-part story for public radio's Living on Earth program about the struggles over Alaska's Tongass National Forest began with the sound of water. The trickle of water grew into a steady flow as Richard Nelson, an Alaskan writer, talked about the rainforest: "Rain is the god here. Rain is what makes this forest. Rain is to southeast Alaska as sun is to the desert" (Hand & Ballman, 2001a, p. 1). Producers Guy Hand and Chris Ballman talked to loggers, wildlife biologists and others who described the conflicts over the biological wealth of the forest (Hand & Ballman, 2001b).

Public radio and television meteorologists

Steve Curwood, a Boston journalist, in 1990 produced the first pilot for a PBS show called *Living on Earth*. The show began airing weekly a year later and by 2006 it was broadcast on up to 300 affiliates. In the broadcast field, it set the standard for continuing coverage of the environment. A typical 30-minute broadcast offered a variety of stories, including at least one long piece and several shorter stories. One week the lead story was about whether the country was going to be building a new generation of nuclear power plants. There were shorter stories on whether to build a road in a wilderness area, the threats to Florida's Lake Okeechobee and the remaking of the Los Angeles River (*Living on Earth*, 1991–2006).

National Public Radio also often highlighted environmental stories on its news programs such as *All Things Considered*, *Morning Edition*, and *Marketplace*. Local public radio stations have had fewer resources. One exception has been the Great Lakes Radio Consortium, which produced daily radio offerings about the environment for listeners in the upper midwest. Great Lakes described its mission as working to reveal "the relationship between the natural world and the everyday lives of people in the Great Lakes region" (GLRC, 2006, p. 1). A typical week included stories about feasting on backyard weeds, hybrid-car owners, how EPA was tightening air emission rules for dry cleaners, an examination of what a USDA organic label meant and what was the relationship between race and the location of waste facility sites. The consortium was carried by 140 stations with 40 million listeners (GLRC, 2006).

Local television stations, while preferring to use general assignment reporters, have always had specialists for sports and the weather. Increasingly some local news directors have called on their weather staff to do more environmental news coverage. The decision was not surprising, considering that broadcasters who forecast the weather were already familiar with at least one branch of science. Plus, atmospheric science was at the lexis of the biggest environmental story – climate change. If climate change caused storms to become more severe, this trend may intensify. Staff at the Weather Channel, following Hurricane Katrina in 2005, began reporting about how environmental issues contributed to the storm. Most of the coverage was about the loss of wetlands on the Gulf Coast and whether their presence might have slowed down the storm (Whitney, 2005).

Elsewhere a number of television stations assigned their meteorological staff to work at least part-time on environmental stories. J.C. Monahan at WCVB-TV was the weekend meteorologist and covered environmental issues on weekdays. She reported on such issues as cleaning up pollution on the Charles River, street trees affected by road salt and a community program encouraging residents to use rain barrels to water garden plants. WCMH-TV Columbus, OH, had a similar arrangement with its weekend meteorologist, Marshall McPeek, who did weather-related environmental stories on weekdays. WGN-TV in Chicago already had its chief weather expert, Tom Skilling, discussing science issues in a special report called "Ask Tom Why," when it decided to expand into environmental issues. "Going into environmental areas has kept the segments fresh," explained Pam Grimes, the producer. "We're lucky because we have an hour of news, so we have the time to go into some of these things" (Whitney, 2003b, p. 39).

Public radio environmental programs and the advent of television meteorologists as environmental specialists were two of the most promising areas of broadcast journalism. Good reporting was produced in many ways. The following pages highlight the techniques reporters have used to produce a variety of broadcast stories. They include a radio story, a live broadcast, a short daily story, a longer reporting project that resulted in a two-part series by a local television station, and a documentary.

Carbon black

Vicki Monks, a freelance reporter in Oklahoma City, began her story on public radio's *Living on Earth* with the sound of a gate clanking, a bucket scraping and sheep bleating. "Natural sound is critically important in engaging the listener and making the listener feel that they are there with you," she said. "It puts the story into context" (Monks, 2006). Monks had been reporting this story for months when she sat down to write the script and edit the tape. One of her first tasks was to compile a list of all of the natural sounds she had taped. She knew she would use these sounds as breaks or transitions in the story. She chose the one with the sheep because it was so important. It led in to the farmer, John Hough, whose strong Oklahoma accent described how he felt about his sheep. The script began:

MONKS: On a small acreage just south of Ponca City, Oklahoma, John Hough runs a herd of white-faced sheep, a breed prized for pure white wool. Problem is, these sheep appear closer to black – an oily, sooty black.

HOUGH: That one right there in the middle, look at her nose, around her nose nostrils, look how black it is. And up past her eyes, see them streaks up past her eyes? That all should be white. It's a pathetic thing to see some kind of an animal like that.

(Monks, 2005, pp. 1–2)

The animals and everything else on the Hough property were coated with a black film suspected of coming from a nearby plant that produced carbon black, a fine particle used to strengthen the rubber in tires. Monks' story reported that California had listed carbon black as a suspected carcinogen. A UCLA toxicology professor described the potential threat. Monks produced that interview after numerous phone calls to other scientists less willing to go on the air. But she found even stronger statements when she talked to Thurman and Thelma Buffalohead. The couple, both members of the Ponca Indian tribe, had lived on the Ponca reservation next to the plant since it opened in 1953. A company official had assured them it would never pollute. The script continued:

THELMA: I said, "Will it get everything black?" "No, no, no, it'll be all right," he said.

THURMAN: I hate to say it, but that's a lie, telling people that and then it's dirty. I tell you it's dirty, still that way.

MONKS: Thurman Buffalohead has a Ponca word for that.

THURMAN: Eeooshista – that's what liar means, lying means. Eeooshista and eegah moneeteday.

(Monks, 2005, p. 3)

(a)

(b)

Figure 13.1 Oklahoma farmer John Hough with several of the sheep whose coats have taken on a black tint (a). Hough and others blame the black particles on a nearby plant south of Ponca City (b) that creates a product called carbon black, which is used to strengthen the rubber in tires (source: courtesy Vicki Monks).

Monks had struggled to pare her script down to 16 minutes, which for radio is a long broadcast. She had had to cut key interviews, including one with Karen Howe, whose daughter had severe respiratory problems and had not been allowed to play outside in the five years they had lived in the Ponca housing project near the carbon black plant. Monks said that keeping the Buffaloheads' talk in the Ponca language was important. "The sound of the Ponca words expressed the essence of this elderly couple better than anything I possibly could write," she said (Dunne, 2005d, p. 24).

Monks had been working on a story outline that was primarily based on the interviews. Radio stories are built around these interviews and she had to include several viewpoints. A company official denied that the plant was responsible for the pollution. Also, a spokeswoman for the Oklahoma Department of Environmental Quality surprised Monks when she admitted that the agency's testing for carbon black was inadequate. The department had received complaints for years, sometimes as many as 100 a month, but it had never been able to confirm in lab tests that the black particles were carbon black. Those lab tests, the spokeswoman said, were useless. Monks said she brought a stack of documents with her to the interview. She wondered if those files influenced the spokeswoman. "It was important for the spokeswoman of DEQ to understand that glib answers were not going to work," said Monks (Monks, 2006). The story ended with Carter Camp and other Ponca tribal leaders talking about the tribe taking over environmental regulations of the carbon black plant, which was on the reservation. The script:

CAMP: "We're still here and we're going to be here in the future and we're going to clean up our land and we're going to ask the American people to ally themselves with us and help us to clean up this land then finally maybe we'll clean up America. Ya-ooh!"
MONKS: In January, Continental Carbon paid a $5,000 fine, the first in its 50-year history.
(*Ponca war dance music*)
MONKS: For *Living on Earth*, I'm Vicki Monks.
(*Ponca drums*).

(Monks, 2005, p. 7)

Monks said she purposely did not comment on the fine, which she felt was paltry, because she was certain most listeners would agree and be upset.

In the story I painted a picture of a company engaged in egregious pollution with lax oversight by regulators. The amount of the fine says a lot, without me having to say anything. You always walk a line in this business between being clear and hitting people over the head. I prefer putting the facts out that are in context and letting the listeners come to their own conclusion.

(Monks, 2006)

Live above Mount St. Helens

Around nine in the morning on October 5, 2004, Mount St. Helens, which had been rumbling for days, awoke with a huge cloud of steam and ash. Within minutes Vince Patton of KGW-TV in Portland and the station's Chief Cameraman Karl Petersen were in the station's news helicopter. As they approached the mountain from the south, they went live showing ash and steam billowing away from the mountain. The volcano vented for an hour. Regular programming was suspended while the station broadcast the live shots. Patton explained what they were viewing. Then it took another two hours for the clouds to clear before they could see the crater floor (Patton, 2004).

As the station's environmental reporter Patton had become an expert on volcanoes and Mount St. Helens. Two years earlier he had received special permission to fly into the crater and land. He had produced a report for the evening news about a growing glacier and ice caves inside the crater. Mount St. Helen's was already America's most famous volcano after its eruption on May 18, 1980. Now scientists said that the mountain was due for a much greater explosion.

Patton said he tried not to think of that as he broadcast live pictures from the new eruption. The camera peered into the crater and viewers could see a blast hole vent had developed and that it was covered with glacial ice water. Also, a large dome was thrusting up. Patton realized it was where he had walked through ice caves two years earlier. Smaller vents spewed steam. Viewers were aided by the helicopter's two gyro-stabilized broadcast-quality cameras. One was a FLIR Ultramedia II that zoomed in on the trail of ash and into the crater. The other was a FLIR Safire I which provided live infrared thermal images in black and white which showed the hot spots in the crater.

Patton, Petersen and Pilot Brian Sonnier were alone in the helicopter, but as the station broadcast the images it called on experts to comment at the station in Portland and elsewhere. Carl Thornber of the U.S. Geological Survey stopped at one of the station's satellite trucks near the mountain. He became excited, watching the live images from the helicopter.

KGW aired the live broadcasts throughout the morning, during the noon news and again for the 5 p.m. and 6 p.m. news broadcasts. With nightfall coming the helicopter returned. In the following two years

Patton would go up another dozen times whenever the mountain stirred. All three men knew the rides above the mountain carried a degree of risk. The 1980 blast erupted suddenly, flattening 230 square miles of forest in three minutes and killing 57 people (U.S. Forest Service, 2003). A helicopter in the air could not survive such a force. Yet Petersen said the risks were worth it. "This is breathtaking, always spectacular," he said. "I'd rather do this than be on the ground miles away" (Patton, 2004, p. 12).

Knotweed invasion

Scene: Sound of water splashing. Workers in boots and rain gear walked down the shallow Sandy River on a gray, overcast day.
PATTON: The Nature Conservancy weed team knows exactly where to find its prey.

(RTNDA, 2003)

The camera panned to a clump of green plants with large leaves that rose up to 15 feet above the river. They were Japanese knotweeds, not very well known, but extremely invasive. The camera showed Patton standing on the river bank as he explained that the plant's size gave "it such a huge advantage over other plants" (RTNDA, 2003). The camera panned down to the flowing river and then underwater showing a startled fish and a rock-covered bottom.

The camera shot was eye-catching, a trick in which a camera was placed inside an empty glass aquarium tank and then partially submerged into the river. It was an old camera trick and the last by KGW, because Patton later that day accidentally cracked the tank's glass. The station subsequently bought an underwater camera. Patton said the one minute, 45-second broadcast was typical of what he did most days. He and a cameraman spent about two hours on the Sandy River with the Nature Conservancy crew. He wrote the script and helped edit the film and it aired that evening.

The story focused on the crew and its efforts to control the knotweed. Cutting it down the year before had encouraged more growth. The camera showed the weed crew cutting each trunk and then carefully dabbing a herbicide on it. It was painstaking work, and Patton said that was why the story had attracted him and allowed him to sell it to his station manager.

It ended with Jonathan Knoll, the manager of the weed team, who said: "I'm comfortable that we found that balance. We are using the appropriate method for each spot that we find on the landscape" (RTNDA, 2003).

Sprawl

Mark Hammill of WQAD-TV began his story by interviewing Bill Christman, whose job was to remove unwanted wildlife from a home-owner's residence. It began:

Scene: Christman climbing the ladder at a house.
CHRISTMAN: She's going to come flying out of there.
HAMMILL: He's been attacked by snarling raccoons...
Scene: Christman uses metal tool to capture a raccoon that scrambles on the roof of the house.
HAMMILL: Blindsided by owls...
Scene: Close-up of the face of an owl.
CHRISTMAN: He swooped down and attacked me.
HAMMILL: He really did?
Scene: Christman raises arm.
CHRISTMAN: Yeah, he got the back of my arm.
HAMMILL: And he has faced the worst of all occupational hazards.
Scene: Close-up of Christman.
CHRISTMAN: I got sprayed by a skunk yesterday.

(RTNDA, 2003)

If ever a story seemed ill-suited for television, it would be the two-part series that Hammill produced about urban growth and sprawl. Yet the story won several television awards. It worked, primarily because of the pictures of wildlife and the surprising story about how they were invading people's homes. Or, as Hammill said in the story, it was about how people were invading the animal's habitat. Cute pictures of a fawn and baby possums competed with a snarling trapped raccoon and a large deer seen during the night. A graphic popped up showing that 25,000 vehicles in Iowa and Illinois had hit deer the year before and five people in the two states had died from such accidents (RTNDA, 2003).

Towards the end of the wildlife segment, Hammill took a canoe ride into a swamp with wildlife biologist John Stravers. Stravers climbed a tree and found four rare and healthy red shoulder hawk chicks. The hawks looked startled, but did not budge from their nesting place high in the tree. Hammill said it demonstrated that there was no such thing as a worthless acre. The story continued:

Scene: Stravers sitting in canoe.
STRAVERS: That's exactly what a red shoulder has to have is a mosquito-infested, nettle-growth, poison-ivy, old-growth floodplain forest and if they do not have a big enough one they aren't here.

Scene: Four hawk chicks sit in perch and begin squawking.
STRAVERS: All right, here we've got four red shoulder hawks, buteo lineatus. That, my fellow Quad Citians, is the sound of wildness here in the willy bottom.
HAWK: Squawk, squawk, squawk.
Scene: Stravers on a rope swings away from the tree and rappelling down.
Scene: Distant camera shot of hawk chicks high up in their tree perch.
HAMMILL: The sound of wildness that John Stravers hopes will never disappear under concrete.

(RTNDA, 2003)

As powerful as the camera scenes were, Hammill's writing was also strong. Sometimes the simplicity of a sentence or paragraph can make a larger impact than prose that is more elaborate. Hammill began his second segment about urban growth, called "Corn or Concrete" with sparse words and familiar images. The script:

HAMMILL: It is called the price of progress when this turns…
Scene: Green corn waving in the wind in a field.
HAMMILL: Into this.
Scene: Men in suits shoveling dirt at a ground breaking.
Scene: A wetland.
HAMMILL: Or this…
Scene: A wetland.
HAMMILL: Makes way for this.
Scene: Tractor scoops up raw earth in a field.
HAMMILL: But as our Quad City environment changes and our commutes get longer, some are questioning our quality of life. And they argue that the price has gotten too high.

(RTNDA, 2003)

The story featured two mayors. One argued development was necessary to build the local economy. The other worried that it was costing the community more in new services than the development was producing in taxes. The story also presented a farmer whose rich agricultural land was about to be purchased and converted into an industrial park by a local community. Visual images were important for the story. The television station hired a helicopter for the day to show new homes standing next to farm fields. Another strong scene closed the second portion:

Scene: Hammill walks past large road grader.
HAMMILL: While debate continues, so does the development. Farmers out in this area have always had an old saying but they say it has

never rung so true. They say that if you live so close enough to town that you see the city lights, you probably live too close.
Scene: Camera pans past Hammill and the road grader to a field of raw dirt.

(RTNDA, 2003)

Documentary stories

Longer documentaries have been a stable of the networks since the dawn of television, and lengths and formats have varied. The most popular were shorter pieces, such as those on such programs as *60 Minutes*. But the networks have also aired news specials of one hour or more. Public television over the years has been a leader in environmental documentaries. Wildlife stories have been popular on such programs as *Nature* and science-related pieces have aired on *Nova*. Cable television stations have done their share of environmental stories, from CNN to the Discovery Channel. The weekend following Hurricane Katrina, Discovery devoted three hours to a series of stories about whether hurricanes were getting stronger, how hurricanes developed, and the early hurricane warning system on the Gulf Coast (Whitney, 2005). In July, 2006 it broadcast a two-hour story narrated by former *NBC News* anchor Tom Brokaw about climate change (Abbott & Bristow, 2006). The format of documentaries often broke down into the same choice that print reporters faced with longer, developed stories, discussed in Chapter 10. It was between expository and narrative stories. Expository was explanatory nonfiction prose that set forth facts, ideas and arguments. Narrative was storytelling.

Natalie Pawelski, who preferred narrative in her stories for CNN's *Earth Matters*, described a story she did about mountaintop removal mining in West Virginia. "The mountain state is losing its mountains" (Pawelski, 2004, p. 87) the script began, as aerial shots showed a colorful West Virginia landscape in early fall. Then chunks of mountain were blasted away and the camera moved from the scenic foliage to raw earthen plateaus. Coal companies were blasting 400 to 600 feet off the top of the mountains to harvest the coal. It was economical because companies needed fewer workers, but it also dumped rocky residue into hundreds of miles of streams.

The story did not center on the competing views of residents, coal mining officials and government officials. Instead, it concentrated on stories from several characters. One was a man who stood in a mountaintop cemetery and looked down at the debris below which had been the next mountain over. In another scene a former miner cried, remembering a once pristine and now damaged stream where he had swam and fished when he was a boy. A mountaintop-removal miner told about how he had a better paying job to support his family of three children, and a safer job than if he was underground. Finally, there was the story of a mined-out mountain that a coal company said had been restored. It was still flat, but it was covered with grass and supported some trees. To build a connection with the audience, the script reminded viewers that most Americans got their electricity from coal.

Pawelski, in remembering that story, said such pieces built a strong case for television coverage of the environment. "Even oozing stories have their dramatic moments and good environmental reporting is beautifully suited to television," she said. "The visuals are often stunning, the characters are usually compelling, and the questions raised strike at the way all of us live our lives each day" (Pawelski, 2004, p. 88).

Study guide

1 Read a news story out loud. Then, using the guidelines provided in this chapter, convert the story into a script for a television news story. What interviews or visual scenes would the story need?

2 For that same news story consider what sounds could be recorded to enhance it for a radio story?

3 Knowing that visual scenes are important, produce a list of possible television stories about the environment. What kinds of stories are most common on your list? What subject areas, if any, appear to be missing?

4 Examine a week of local television news or a network news program. Often the stories are listed on a news organization's website. How many environmental stories is the television station or network missing? Were there any environmental stories that same week produced by the local or national newspapers?

5 The archives for Living on Earth are located at http:loe.org. Listen to a broadcast. What works on the program? What does not work?

6 Climate change has been difficult for television stations to cover, especially at local news stations. Brainstorm and produce ten broadcast stories, with either strong visual or audio elements, that would work for a local television or radio news program.

7 For further reading, consider Roone Arledge's Roone (2003), Fred Friendly's Due to Circumstances Beyond Our Control (1967) and an audio tape produced by National Public Radio, The Best of NPR, Writers on Writing (1999).

Chapter 14

Online journalism

Amanda Griscom Little admitted she was "a tad creeped out" when the audience of more than 800 erupted and gave, with much shouting and hand signals, a Wal-Mart chant. (Give me a W … A … L … M … A … R … T … What does that spell?… Who do we love?) She was in Bentonsville, AR in 2006 at the corporate headquarters of the world's most successful retailer. Wal-Mart fascinated her, but not for its financial success (Little, 2006f). What intrigued her was Lee Scott, Wal-Mart chief executive officer, who had announced that the company wanted to run on 100 percent renewable energy and produce zero waste. Since then, the company had proposed mandatory caps on greenhouse-gas emissions. Little had interviewed Scott in a story titled "Don't Discount Him" (Little, 2006b). His comments were at odds with a company often accused of creating suburban sprawl, producing mountains of waste and promoting gratuitous consumption. On the day Little was in Arkansas, the Wal-Mart executives were all watching *An Inconvenient Truth*, a documentary on the threat of climate change. They were about to hear from the man behind the film, former Vice President Al Gore (Little, 2006f).

What makes this tale of Little and her adventures at Wal-Mart distinctive is where the story ran – *Grist*. The online publication was founded by Chip Giller who had previously helped start *Greenwire*, an environmental news daily. Giller's work with the Earth Day Network led him to begin *Grist*, which has specialized in reporting about the environment with a touch of attitude and humor (Brodeur, 2006). As the publication pointed out, reading environmental journalism "too often feels like eating your vegetables. Boiled. With no butter" ("About Grist," 2006, p. 1). *Grist* said it not only buttered the vegetables it added salt and strained the metaphors.

In 2003 Little began writing a column for *Grist* called "Muckraker." It started as three small news briefs each week and then it evolved into longer weekly pieces that tried to explore environmental issues that others were ignoring. One week she would write about the decision by

Massachusetts Governor Mitt Romney to oppose efforts by his and other northeastern states to reduce greenhouse gases. Pundits believed Romney feared supporting a greenhouse emissions standard because it would not play well if he ran for President (Little, 2006a). Another week she wrote about the unusual but growing alliance between the Sierra Club and the steelworkers union (Little, 2006d). A third examined whether the feds should regulate and reduce farm pollution (Little, 2006e). The pieces often had a political angle, but Little said she tried to avoid the type of insider language that she too often saw in political or environmental stories. While the column was popular, by far the most sought-after feature in the online publication was Ask Umbra. The column was a Dear Abby-type feature where readers pose such questions as whether it was all right to use pesticides on their lawn. Umbra's sometimes reasoned, sometimes snarky response would provoke comments on the accompanying weblog Grist Mill which generated even more debate (Little, 2006c).

Figure 14.1 *Grist* likes to promote its light-hearted approach towards coverage of the environment (source: courtesy *Grist*: www.grist.org).

Grist is one of several environmental news periodicals publishing on the Web. Others have included *TreeHugger.com*, an online magazine founded by Graham Hill (*TreeHugger.com*, 2007), and *IdealBite.com*, which is designed to offer tips on how to live a more environmentally friendly lifestyle (*IdealBite.com*, 2007). One of the positive features of the Web is that sites can easily be designed for specialized audiences. Online journalism is still in an early evolutionary stage, but it does promise to bring changes in how news is generated, compiled and disseminated. As old media have lost readers and viewers to this new media, a range of opportunities have been opening up for journalists willing to take risks. The prospects range from working for a website run by mainstream news organizations to building one's own website or weblog into a new business. Even more profound is the possibility that the Web would dramatically change journalism from a one-way system where reporters and editors talked to readers. News organizations and websites have been experimenting with a range of options where the communication is two-way, and where readers not only respond to the news but in some cases helped report and disseminate it.

News goes online

The Defense Department first began developing what is now called the Internet in 1969 as a way to communicate if a nuclear attack wiped out the conventional phone system. The Advanced Research Project Agency (ARPA) connected computers and computer networks, although the system developed slowly. A hypertext system that allowed people to share on the Internet through hypertext markup language, or HTML, in 1991 further hastened the development. This led to the creation of the World Wide Web. By the mid-1990s commercial and public use began to increase significantly (Stovall, 2004).

From its beginnings, the Internet was an obvious medium for conveying news. However, mainstream news organizations and many Internet companies hesitated to develop Internet news sites, especially those that produced news reporting or content. The websites that newspapers, television and radio stations built in the mid to late 1990s usually were simply digests of what had already appeared in print or on the air. Such formats were quickly called "shovelware." While the content on these sites was quick and easy to produce, it ignored the ability of the Web to combine written information with sound, still photographs, video and to link to other sites. News organizations resisted spending money because advertising Web sales were disappointing. Newspapers were also reluctant because news that had been sold at newsstands and through home delivery was now being given away free on the Web. Internet companies were more interested in developing market areas they believed would be more financially lucrative than news (Stovall, 2004).

The realization of the Internet's potential as a news source occurred when the terrorist attacks struck New York and Washington on September 11, 2001. While television was the most widely watched medium, reliance on websites increased dramatically. The CNN website that had been getting 14 million hits a day, was getting 19 million hits an hour the day after the attack. MSNBC reported that 12.5 million people logged onto its site that day, three times the highest number of any day before. Yahoo reported its traffic increased by 40 times on that day (Stovall, 2004). Other major events, such as the 2004 East Asia earthquake and tsunami, and Hurricane Katrina in 2005 further bore out that lesson.

Major news organizations got the message. A study in 2005 that examined news content on websites for one day found that major news organizations and Internet sites such as *NYTimes.com*, Google and CNN.com were repeatedly updating their stories as the day progressed. Between 9 a.m. and 9 p.m. the *Times* site had updated or replaced the six top stories and 31 of the 67 stories posted. The study said that the *Times* site was like watching a virtual newsroom throughout the day as reporting came in and news evolved. It suggested the website's motto should be "all the news that's fit to post" (Project for Excellence in Journalism, 2006, p. 1). Google had the greatest resources, able to tap 4,500 different news sources in a process called news aggregation. Yahoo was also an aggregator, and it competed with Google by allowing users to designate what types of news they wanted to receive (Project for Excellence in Journalism, 2006).

Other media companies, such as the Tribune Company and Newhouse Newspapers, were experimenting with innovative sites. The Tribune embraced the concept of convergence, of combining the best of what was being offered in a community such as Tampa from the newspaper and a local radio station and offering them in print, on the air and online (Gordon, 2003). Newhouse separated its online news organizations from its local newspapers, producing sites such as *Cleveland Live* (clevelandlive.com) and *NOLA.com* in New Orleans (Stovall, 2004).

News organizations increasingly found that online sites complimented what they produced in type or on the air. Internet sites were capable of housing thousands of images, stories or documents, allowing news consumers to obtain far more information than could be offered on the printed page or the air waves. Plus articles or video could be archived so that consumers could refer to them long after they were no longer considered news. The full capabilities of convergence, of combing the best of print and broadcast online, were still being explored.

The other great strength of the Internet was to open journalism to more players through weblogs and wikis. There were signs that this might happen. For instance, freelance writer Christopher Albritton was able to raise enough money from his blog in 2003 to finance a trip and cover the war in Iraq (Gahran, 2005a). In addition, existing organizations could now find a voice online. The Center for Public Integrity, a Washington, DC-based non-profit research and journalism organization founded in 1989 by a former television reporter, used to produce news stories, reports and books that it sent to various news organizations. Since the arrival of the Internet it now posts those articles online. For instance, in 2004 it produced a fairly typical report about how U.S. oil and gas companies had at least 882 subsidiaries located in tax havens such as the Cayman Islands, Bermuda and Liechtenstein. The story posted on its website featured an interactive map showing the tax havens and naming the companies that had been using it. Company names were in hypertext so that readers could click the type and find even more information about the firm (Williams & Werve, 2004). Contest judges at SEJ were impressed enough that the story took first place in the organization's Internet story category (SEJ, 2005).

Displaying the environment online

One early discovery of the strength of the Internet has been how websites could become community resources. Stephen Farnsworth, a political scientist from Georgetown University, studied one such development in Albany, NY. Residents who lived along the Hudson River were getting tired and confused by the unending chorus of charges and counter-charges about a plan to clean toxic waste from the river bottom. For years the EPA and environmental activists had been fighting to get General Electric to dredge and clean up the waste in the Hudson. Views had polarized. Advocates for both sides had posted websites with contradictory data and positions. The GE website, called Hudson Voice, did not make it clear that this was the company's forum. Newspapers, television and radio all served as neutral guides in such disputes. The problem was that newspapers, and especially broadcast news organizations, are perishable. The content they provide rarely is retained in an easy way to reference. But a website run by a respected news organization, the *Albany Times-Union*, showed that it could be a reliable guide in such controversies. The dispute had been continuing for several years when Farnsworth discussed it in 2001 and he said the website was making a profound difference. The newspaper had produced a collection of answers to frequently asked questions that it posted on its website. Also, it ran a fully indexed archive of previous stories about the dredging issue. Farnsworth said readers were able to see how the story had evolved and how positions had changed over time. He said it was an important reality check, and he believed it would also discourage future disinformation from either side. "This approach can also help build the newspaper's most important asset: its credibility," he said. "The newspaper Web page can be, and should be, the best place to go for the most comprehensive and most objective information on controversial topics like the Hudson River dredging" (Schwartz, 2001, p. 11).

Besides news stories, many news organizations also have posted other materials including extra pictures, audio, video, documents and entire databases on their websites. Sometimes the amount of material posted dwarfed the original story. A website can also serve as a reference point for subsequent stories on the issue. Hypertext can provide links and even more details about specific facts. Here are some examples of several stories already discussed in the text, and how their message was enhanced on the Web:

- James Bruggers worried that he might have overstated his conclusion in his *Louisville Courier-Journal* story about air pollution. He wrote that the risks from some air toxics in the city were dangerously high. Two subsequent risk assessments were even starker about the risks than Bruggers' story. Both were appended to the website with Bruggers' story, along with a form that readers could click if they wanted to ask a question (Bruggers, 2003).
- Julie Hauserman of the *St. Petersburg Times* surprised readers when she wrote about the dangers of pressure-treated wood that contained arsenic. It also drew strong reactions from residents, the lumber industry and eventually federal regulators. About 50 stories about the issue followed over the next two years and each was added to the website in a list along with the initial story. The links to those stories created a far deeper, more complete report on the issue (*Sptimes.com*, 2001).
- The *Seattle Post Intelligencer* relied on numerous databases when it investigated how successful government officials had been in cleaning up Puget Sound. When the story ran on the website, it included a database maintained by the state about water quality. Readers could enter a location to find details about who in their area had the most environmental infractions (Seattlepi.nwsource.com, 2002).
- When the *St. Petersburg Times* wrote about vanishing wetlands in Florida it had planned to include an interactive map so readers could see satellite imagery of their area and how it had changed. That proved to be too ambitious, but the staff was able to show satellite images of particular areas, such as the resulting disappearance of a wetland where a Wal-Mart had been allowed to build.

That site also featured audio of an official from the Army Corps of Engineers defending wetlands decisions and video of once pristine areas that had been developed (Dunne, 2005c).

Most of these online presentations were done at the end of the reporting project with reporters playing a peripheral role. It is not yet clear whether reporters, who in the past carried a pencil and notepad, will soon also be asked to tote digital tape recorders and cameras. Or whether television reporters, who edit tape, will have to learn languages such as html and/or special Web-oriented software programs. Some reporters have, but roles are still evolving. The future may depend on technological changes as high-speed access to the Internet increases, computers get faster, and software becomes even smarter.

Peter Lord of the *Providence Journal* in 2005 was working on a traditional newspaper series when he met with the newspaper's online staff. He found a group of talented professionals eager to convert the news series into a dramatic online presentation. The story was about Capt. John R. "Rob" Lewis and his 20-year effort to protect open space on his native Block Island (Lord, 2005a–f). Going into the project,

Figure 14.2 Capt. John R. "Rob" Lewis and his wife pose in Block Island, RI. Peter Lord of the *Providence Journal* used old tape recordings of Lewis to enhance the online presentation of his newspaper series about the island (source: courtesy Tobee S. McMellon).

newspaper editors knew they wanted to display far more pictures online than they had room for in the paper. Photographer John Freidah, who had worked with Lord on the lead poisoning series detailed in Chapter 10, had taken pictures over the course of a year on the island. Besides running the newspaper stories, the online site presented the pictures, with music from a local folk group, and narration from Lord. Each section was two to three minutes long. Lord was asked not to write a script. Instead, he studied his stories and then told the story spontaneously on tape in two to three minute increments. "It was an interesting and very different way of doing story-telling," said Lord. "I found that as I told the story my voice and the way I spoke corresponded to what was happening. When Rob left one day in the story, my voice hesitated. When I got to an exciting event, my voice did get excited" (Lord, 2006).

Lewis had died several years earlier but Lord found a tape recording he had made years before when he spent a day on Block Island with the former merchant marine captain. It had defects, he could hear Lewis' wife in the background making lunch and not everything Lewis said was useful. But the staff was able to run excerpts with a montage of family pictures of Lewis. "People really like it," said Lord (2006).

Reader participation

The boldest experiments center on websites that invited readers to participate. They ranged from community bulletin boards, to news aggregators who allowed the audience to vote on what was most important, to experiments in what has been called crowdsourcing. Consider these examples:

- *iBrattleboro.com* was set up in Brattleboro, VT, as an "original, locally-owned citizen journalism site" where the audience was invited to write their own stories, interviews and announcements (*iBrattleboro.com*, 2007, p. 1). A typical day on the site displayed the weather, local news about U.S. Senator Bernie Sanders and a global warming forum, comments such as the value of paved versus dirt roads, a weekly poll, and a list of upcoming events.
- Online sites such as *Digg*, *Reddit* and *Newsvine* where stories or links of stories are posted and then evaluated by each respective site's viewers. For instance, on Digg participants selected online articles, videos or podcasts, wrote a short summary of the item, and posted it on a range of categories from technology, science (including an environmental sub-list), business, sports, entertainment and gaming. Other viewers would check out these stories and designate which ones they especially liked. The most popular stories would move to the homepage (*Digg.com*, 2007).

Whether these sites succeed, some say they represent a significant change in how news is gathered. "The kind of news audience that mostly prefers to absorb news is rapidly aging and shrinking," said Amy Gahran, an online journalism consultant.

> They're being replaced by what Jay Rosen (a press critic and journalism professor at New York University) calls "the people formerly known as the audience." This is an engaged mosaic of communities who prefer to actively seek out news and information from many sources, directly verify at least some of that information, converse with other people publicly, and share their own news or perspective.
>
> (Gahran, 2007)

Gahran said traditional news organizations have been having difficulty understanding this concept, and of breaking from the mindset of publisher to one of serving as a community leader. "News organizations that do embrace this evolution will survive and even thrive," she said. "Those that don't will shrink or disappear" (Gahran, 2007).

In the fall of 2006 one of the more conservative, traditional newspaper chains dramatically embraced this new direction. Gannett, which published *USAToday* and 90 other dailies, announced it was converting its newsrooms into "information centers." Editors said that instead of being organized into separate metro, state, or sports departments, staff would be assigned to one of seven departments that would carry names such as data, digital and community conversations. These new departments would carry out four goals: emphasize local news over national; disseminate more audience-generated content; place more resources on the websites and less on the daily newspaper; and use crowdsourcing techniques to gather more news (Howe, 2006).

Crowdsourcing is designed to use readers as reporters in a range of stories and Gannett's best example of how it could work had occurred earlier that year at *The News-Press* in Fort Myers, FL. In May readers had complained to the paper that they were being asked to pay up to $28,000 to connect newly constructed homes to water and sewer lines. Rather than assign a reporter to this issue, editors asked readers to find out why the costs were at that level. The response was overwhelming. Accountants voluntarily examined balance sheets, retired engineers reviewed blueprints and a whistle-blower leaked documents suggesting bid-rigging. "We had people from all over the world helping us," said Kate Marymont, editor-in-chief at the *News-Press* (Howe, 2006, p. 4). Website traffic was unprecedented and it continued for six weeks until the city agreed to cut the fees by 30 percent and one official resigned.

Despite that success, veteran journalists have many reservations about turning over news stories or investigations to readers. An example of what can go wrong occurred when the *Cincinnati Enquirer*, another Gannett newspaper, asked online readers to work on the murder of a three-year-old foster child. Readers quickly condemned the foster parents, even though no charges had been filed, and the message board had to be closed until charges were filed. Gregory Korte, an investigative journalist for the *Enquirer*, said "It's very hard to separate fact from fiction online, and some people expect that whatever's on our site undergoes the same degree of scrutiny as what appears in the paper" (Howe, 2006, p. 5).

Non-traditional news organizations are also experimenting with crowdsourcing, such as the Los Angeles-based *BrooWaha*. Ariel Vardi founded the site while still attending graduate school at Georgia Institute of Technology and he hoped to establish similar *BrooWaha*'s in San Francisco, Atlanta and New York. "In newspapers there aren't enough journalists to cover everything," he explained. "On campus, there were so many students; they see everything that happens. I thought giving them the tool to share everything they see would be really helpful" (Saar, 2006, p. 2).

Blogs

Blogs are another way that the Web is changing journalism. Rohit Gupta and two colleagues made a blog and got it online in December, 2004 hours after the earthquake and tsunami struck South Asia. "We realized that people were looking for information and there was not much out there," Gupta said. "Our idea was to set up a clearing house for all the information that we were collecting" (Srinivas, 2005, p. 1). Gupta, working with Peter Griffin and Dina Mehta, all of Mumbai, India (formerly Bombay) began with text messages they were receiving from a television producer in Sri Lanka who had survived the tsunami. Google established a link and soon people were finding the site. Other survivor accounts arrived, posted by email and text message. Many of these stories were more emotional than professional, but the writers were clearly and quickly conveying what was happening, often better than more established news sources. Within days the South-east Asia Earthquake and Tsunami Blog (SEA-EAT) had over 200 volunteer bloggers posting entries with translations available in Chinese, French, German, Italian, Japanese, Korean, Portuguese and Spanish. The *Online Journalism Review* said it was "the first time hundreds of ordinary people produced powerful coverage of a huge news event along with traditional media" (Srinivas, 2005, p. 1).

Blogs have become a powerful force on the Internet. Even as they have become more popular and well-used they have often been misun-

Figure 14.3 Devastation is strewn everywhere near the coastline of Banda Aceh province in Northern Sumatra after the earthquake and tsunami struck in December, 2004 (source: courtesy National Science Foundation).

derstood and dismissed as nothing more than personal online diaries. They are far more. Blogs have been described as a type of website, featuring material produced by a group, organization or individual. The information can range from facts to rumors. They may be well-edited or simply sloppy prose. The usual format has been for them to run in reverse chronological order with the most recent items at the top. Each blog item was assigned a unique, persistent Web address or URL which allowed people to link easily to the site. They usually provided for a comment section and they sometimes included feeds. Many websites look like blogs and many blogs look like websites. Gahran, in her blog discussing blogs, wrote: "There is no clear line where blogging ends and other forms of publishing begins. There's a lot of overlap" (Gahran, 2005a, p. 2). She said the best way to determine was to ask the creator of the site if it was a blog.

Blogs have changed significantly since the 1990s, when they were only Internet diaries. They have played a strong role in politics. Bloggers publicized Senate Majority Leader Trent Lott's praise in 2002 of Sen. Strom Thurmond, with some commentators saying that Lott's comments amounted to sanctioning racism (McClure, 2006). Bloggers and journalists have had their scandals too. Ben Domenech left his blog at the *washingtonpost.com* in 2006 when outside bloggers discovered examples of past plagiarism. Michael Hiltzik of the *Los Angeles Times* lost his blog after critics discovered that Hiltzik was posting comments under false identities (Niles, 2006). Many journalists have produced blogs. The *Greeley Tribune* in Colorado produced an editor's blog, which allowed readers to get an inside look at how the paper was produced. NBC News anchor Brian Williams wrote a similar type of blog about the network (Gahran, 2005a). A search engine, Icerocket, has been designed specifically to search out various types of blogs (Icerocket.com, 2007).

Environmental writers have used blogs in a variety of ways:

- Wendee Holtcamp, a Texas-based freelancer who has written about the environment for such news outlets as *Audubon*, *Sierra* and the Discovery Channel, wrote a blog called Bohemian Adventures. It was a personal narrative with subjects ranging from her colonoscopy to kayak fly-fishing on the San Saba River (Holtcamp, 2006). She said it was set up more for personal reasons and to communicate with friends. But it was also a public site and she knew both her editors and readers sometimes read it because she would get comments either on the blog or privately. "I'm kind of a prolific writer," she explained. "It's a way to express myself and be creative" (Holtcamp, 2006).
- Contentious, produced by Gahran, was more of a professional sounding-board. Gahran, based in Colorado, consulted for online clients and also pursued environmental journalism. The blog was an advertisement demonstrating Gahran's knowledge in the field while also serving as a communication tool. For instance, the information about both blogs and podcasting mentioned later in this chapter was taken partly from Gahran's blog (Gahran, 2005a).
- Dateline Earth, a blog produced by Robert McClure and Lisa Stiffler of the *Seattle Post-Intelligencer*, featured environmental news. They tried to post daily. The news ranged from national or international stories to quirky local items. Begun in November, 2005, within months the writing style had already grown looser. McClure compared the blog to his earlier career at United Press International wire service when news had to be compiled and sent out quickly. He said the amount of reporting on the blog varied. "What we offer is perspective and analysis to inform readers quickly about developments that are intriguing or important or yes, it's a big part of the blogsphere – at least a little bit funny," he said (McClure, 2006, p. 23).

Wikis

Wikis, taken from the Hawaiian term *wiki wiki* which means quick, are online sites where one or more individuals can make contributions to a posted entry. In some situations the wiki has been open to anyone to make additions or modifications while in other situations a gatekeeper has controlled access and the editing. Online wikis have featured cookbooks and collections of quotations. Probably the best-known wiki is Wikipedia, an online encyclopedia that was loosely controlled by its founder, Jimmy Wales, and a consortium of about 200 volunteers (Hafner, 2006). Wikipedia rapidly expanded into other cooperatively-supported ventures including: Wiktionary which offered an online dictionary; Wikiquote which provided quotations; Wikisource billed as a free library; Wikiversity offering free learning tools; and Wikinews. Unlike some other sites that purposely stray into opinion, the group of volunteers working on Wikinews said that their stories were designed to be written from "a neutral point of view to ensure fair and unbiased reporting" (Wikinews, 2007, p. 5).

News organizations and online sites have experimented with wikis with varying degrees of success. The most famous failure was in 2005 when the *Los Angeles Times* began a wikitorial option for online readers. It posted an editorial urging a better defined plan for withdrawing troops to Iraq and urged readers to add their thoughts. Many did but others added foul language and sexually explicit photos which finally forced the editors to suspend the service (MSNBC, 2005). The *Online Journalism Review* has used wikis, including one that allowed a series of invited guests to weigh in on the future of broadcast television. Access was limited to the invited guests, but readers could watch as the debate developed over several days (Glaser, 2005a). The publication *Wired News* assigned a story about wikis and when reporter Ryan Singer finished the editors did something unusual. They took the unedited story and posted it as a wiki, inviting readers to "whip it into shape" (Gahran, 2006, p. 1). Quotes could not be changed, but readers were allowed to reorganize the story, make cuts and tinker. Gahran concluded that "wikis are great for projects where the goal is comprehensiveness, inclusiveness, or consensus" (Gahran, 2006, p. 1).

Podcasts

Podcasts are audio files that can be received online and played on computers or portable MP3 players. Many of the best environmental podcasting sites are the same as those broadcast on the air, such as *Living on Earth* and Great Lakes Radio Consortium (Gahran, 2005b). Others, including environmental groups, have audio podcasts. For instance, the

Nature Conservancy produced what it called Nature Stories Podcasts. One posted on their website was called "The Secret Life of New York's Bees" and it described how beekeepers illegally maintained hives in New York City. Another, "Private Lives of Wolves," was the story of an Idaho couple who spent six years living near a captive wolf pack (Nature Conservancy, 2006).

An ambitious onetime podcast was produced by the *Atlanta Journal-Constitution* in 2006 in conjunction with its narrative journalism series about two New Orleans hospitals during and after Hurricane Katrina. The series was called "Through Hell and High Water." The podcast featured 22 episodes each running up to 20 minutes and it was released on the newspaper's website as well as being sold as a four-hour CD. The newspaper hired a radio announcer, Tom Opdyke, to narrate the scripts, which featured plot twists and climaxes at the end of each chapter (Scanlan, 2006). Chapter 19 of the series began this way:

> By Friday morning, September 2, Dr. Ben deBoisblanc was nearly a one man physician on auto pilot. As long as helicopters continued to land on the roof of the Tulane hospital's parking lot across the street, the impassioned physician was going to get his patients over there. Wednesday he had managed to get four patients from Charity Hospital evacuated by choppers. Thursday about 30 more. All were critical and three had died, two while waiting in the garage. But Friday more than 200 patients remained entrapped in Charity as well as about 800 employees and their families. Four days after Hurricane Katrina, they were nearly out of food, water and medicine.
>
> (Hansen, 2006)

After completing the series, Opdyke reported he received many favorable comments from people who said they preferred to hear the audio as opposed to read the series. Opdyke said that he hoped to do more podcasts. "My initial response is to put up anything you think is interesting, produce it the most attractive and friendly way you can and learn from each venture" (Scanlan, 2006, p. 6).

That is the adventure of the online world. Something new seems to be happening every day.

Study guide

1 Review the *Grist* magazine site at www.grist.org. What do you like and dislike about the content? Are there ways the site can be improved?

2 Compare the approach traditional news organizations take on their websites. Review such sites as www.nytimes.com, www.washingtonpost.com, www.wsj.com, www.NOLA.com and www.clevelandlive. com.

3 SEJ has an extensive listing of weblogs at www.sej.org. Read a range of environmental blogs. How can they be effective in producing news stories?

4 Find information in an environmental weblog to produce a story. Do not rely on the facts in the blog. Verify them from other sources. Do original reporting and attempt to localize the issue.

5 Consider setting up your own blog. Instructions can be found at several sites on the Internet including Google's blogger.com, LiveJournal at livejournal.com and Gather at www.gather.com. Another option is offered by Typepad.

6 For further reading, consider James Glen Stoval's *Web Journalism* (2004), James Wallace's *Overdrive: Bill Gates and the Race to Control Cyperspace* (1997), *Where Wizards Stay Up Late: The Origins of the Internet* by Katie Hafner and Matthew Lyon, (1996) and *The Internet Handbook for Writers, Researchers and Journalists* by Mary McGuire, Linda Stilborne, Melinda McAdams and Laurel Hyatt (2002).

Part IV

Understanding the beat

Chapter 15

Fairness and advocacy

In 1990 journalists, environmentalists and newsmakers converged at a conference sponsored by the magazine *Utne Reader* to debate their respective roles. Much of the dialog centered on how far journalists should go in expressing their opinion in stories about improving the environment. Should journalists present both sides of an issue, or should they tell readers which was right? Author and futurist Hazel Henderson complained that the press already did the latter. She said mainstream news organizations were too dependent on advertising to be fair and balanced. "Never have we needed to look further ahead than now, yet journalism schools still teach bean-counting, tedious overload of details, and warn about leaving interpretation to others," she said. "The mass media put up their guard against advocacy" (Meersman, 1990–1991, p. 6). Journalists had varying viewpoints on the issue. Barbara Pyle, an environmental editor for the Turner Broadcasting System, said that she had abandoned any pretense of being an "objective journalist" years earlier. She said that the world's environmental problems were simply too urgent and enormous to do otherwise (Meersman, 1990–1991). Amal Kumar Naj of the *Wall Street Journal* questioned how journalists could engage in advocacy when the scientific evidence on so many environmental issues was so uncertain. "The scientists themselves don't know," he said. Teya Ryan with Turner Broadcasting contended that "advocacy journalism is a misnomer" because "who is opposed to a better environment?" ("Contributors," 1990–1991, p. 7). Since no one is, she said "you can't take an advocacy position on the environment" ("Contributors," 1990–1991, p. 8).

A dozen years later the debate erupted again on the pages of the *SEJournal*. Brian Hodel, editor of *TheNaturalResouces.org*, questioned whether environmental writers were only "producing a white-coat journalism that interests only the cognoscenti, eliciting yawns from everyone else" ("Are we," 2003, p. 19). He said that H.L. Mencken, the longtime writer for the *Baltimore Evening Sun*, was never afraid to express his opinion and it was time for environmental journalists to do the same. Paul Rogers, of the *San Jose Mercury News*, responded that Mencken had been an opinion columnist, not a reporter. He said reporters should trust no one, including environmentalists, because "nobody has a monopoly on knowing the best way to solve environmental problems" ("Are we," 2003, p. 19). Others joined the debate in a story that ran for pages ("Are we," 2003).

The discussion was not new. Journalists and others have been deliberating the merits of objectivity and advocacy since the days of Benjamin Franklin and the flat-bed press. The issue was severely tested in the 1950s when Sen. Joseph McCarthy successfully manipulated the press and its extremely rigid definition of fairness and objectivity. Journalism reported on McCarthy's charges of Communist conspiracies, but reporters failed to add context and perspective that would have demonstrated that McCarthy's crusade was not substantiated by facts (Friendly, 1967). Journalists learned that they must go beyond the role of he-said-they-said reporting to add background, interpretation and analysis. Most of the mainstream journalism profession has settled on this role, although some in the alternate press, cable television and the Internet seem more willing to take stronger advocacy positions.

Journalism organizations, including the American Society of Newspaper Editors, the Society of Professional Journalists and the Radio-Television News Directors Association, have all established codes of ethics (Bowles & Borden, 2004). ASNE's standards stressed that journalists needed to be independent, impartial and be able to report truthfully and accurately. Some highlights included:

• Journalists must avoid impropriety and the appearance of impropriety as well as any conflict of interest.
• Every effort must be made to assure that the news content is accurate, free from bias and in context, and that all sides are presented fairly.
• Sound practice demands a clear distinction between news reports and opinion (Bowles & Borden, 2004).

Environmental journalists also believe that they need to be as fair and objective as other journalists. Surveys of 364 newspaper and television journalists in four regions of the nation found that all but two felt that they needed to be objective. Those surveys also found that only two journalists felt that there was no need to be fair to corporations or environmental activist groups (Sachsman *et al.*, 2006).

Yet the public believes that the press does distort messages. An ASNE survey in 1998 found that 80 percent of those polled believed that the news media was biased. A comparable number thought that powerful individuals or organizations could either stop a story or have it spun to their advantage (Bowles & Borden, 2004).

There are several reasons for the distrust. Too often journalists get the facts wrong and the errors have made readers and viewers distrustful (Meyer, 2005). Also, a number of reporters have plagiarized or made up facts. Jayson Blair, a reporter at the *New York Times*, in 2003 was caught lifting facts from other publications and fabricating entire scenes before his misdeeds were discovered and he was fired (Rieder, 2003).

Environmental reporters have another problem. The issue, as it was mentioned in Chapter 1, is whether environmental journalists, because they write about the environment, are pro-environment. The discussions that broke out both at the *Utne* conference and in the *SEJournal* demonstrate that it is not just the public that is struggling to find the answer. The environmental beat is both complex and challenging. It is a combination of science and politics. Public policy issues produce rabid advocates on each side. Environmental journalists are called upon more often to provide needed interpretation. The demands are so great that some either rebel from the profession's ethical standards or have found it convenient at times to ignore them.

Promoting advocacy

Michael Frome, a longtime journalist and professor, for years urged journalists to be environmental advocates. Beginning in the 1940s Frome carved out a freelance writing career producing stories about the environment for such publications as *American Forests*, *Field & Stream*, the *Los Angeles Times* and *Defenders of Wildlife*. He also wrote about a dozen books. Much of his writing centered on preserving America's natural wonders and historic and cultural treasures. Later he became an environmental journalism professor for Western Washington University. Now retired, he was an unabashed proponent of environmental advocacy journalism. Frome said that when he was a writer he worked tirelessly with others to save and protect scenic and wild areas. In 1956, when he won a $5,000 award for his work, he gave it to grassroots organizations. "What the heck, they deserve it more than I do," he said later (Frome, 1992, p. 13). He encouraged students to learn the basics of journalism while also adopting the emotion and power of environmental activists. He said:

> I do teach a different kind of journalism, advocacy journalism in behalf of the environment, yet hewing to basic principles of literacy, accuracy, fairness and meeting a deadline ... Advocacy is a word that we have been taught to avoid. It marks a bias, something most

journalists are convinced should not be acknowledged, despite the fact that it is inescapable. But my point is that we ought to be advocates for the health and safety of the planet.

(Frome, 1998, p. ix)

In 1998, Frome wrote *Green Ink: An Introduction to Environmental Journalism*, which espoused his theory of combining advocacy and journalism. He urged students or aspiring writers to volunteer at the local Audubon or Sierra Club as a way to build contacts and learn of the most pressing environmental issues. Frome acknowledged that most mainstream journalism organizations and publications did not embrace his views, but he argued that they should in the face of the world's increasing environmental problems (Frome, 1998).

Suggestions of bias

Frome also said mainstream journalists should embrace advocacy because many were already being accused of writing biased, one-sided accounts in favor of environmentalists and their movement (Frome, 1998). One reporter who was accused was Philip Shabecoff, who for 14 years covered the environment for the *New York Times*. Towards the end of his tenure on the beat Shabecoff said he began to hear complaints that he was too tight with his environmental sources and that his reporting focused too much on environmental threats. He was told, "I was writing too much about how economic activity was harming the environment and not enough about how the cost of environmental regulation was harming the economy" (Shabecoff, 2004, p. 54). In 1990 he was reassigned to cover the Internal Revenue Service. Shortly afterwards he quit. Shabecoff said he thought his experience had been unique. Then he began to hear from reporters at other newspapers who had similar experiences. Bill Kovach, a *New York Times* Washington bureau chief, told Shabecoff his problem had been that he had been "ahead of the curve" (Shabecoff, 2004, p. 54).

These clashes between environmental reporters were especially prominent in the 1990s and at smaller, mostly western newspapers. Some attributed this trend to a conflict between the older, more conservative managers of newspapers and broadcast outlets and younger, more liberal reporting staffs (Loftis, 1992). Stephen Stuebner said he was surprised when his editors at the *Idaho Statesman* in Boise complained in August, 1991 that he was too pro-environment. He said the complaints came unexpectedly after five years of coverage. He said he pressed but received few specific examples. Two months later he was pulled off the beat. He resigned instead (Stuebner, 1992). The then executive editor of the *Idaho Statesman* responded that Stuebner had been repeatedly warned about bias in his writing. "His response to this constructive criticism may have been laughter," said Bill Steinauer, the editor. "We were not laughing" (Cox & Carmody, 1992, p. 7).

Some news organizations have allowed reporters to cross the line between straight reporting and offering opinions. That decision can confuse readers, who have to wonder whether the journalist's reporting has been as biased as his writing. Paul H. MacClennan covered the environment for years for the *Buffalo News* both as a reporter on weekdays and a columnist on Sundays. MacClennan, who retired in 1998, said he never heard any complaints from editors or sources about blending the reporting and column roles in his beat. "I thought writing a column helped me to enlarge and broaden readers' understanding," he said. In his news stories he said he separated fact from fiction. "But in the column I could go beyond the scope of the straight news story" ("Buffalo news," 1998, p. 2). Such allowances are increasingly rare.

Trade secrets

To preempt accusations of bias, journalists covering environmental issues need to be as thorough as possible. In March, 2001 the Public Broadcasting System broadcast a two-hour documentary about the chemical industry. Produced by Sherry Jones and narrated by Bill Moyers, "Trade Secrets" described how the chemical industry from the 1950s to the 1970s produced vinyl chloride and other chemicals even though it knew the substances could harm human health and the environment. The story also detailed how the industry had engaged in a systematic campaign to deceive the public of those hazards. The story was based on documents assembled by a lawyer representing several families who had sued the chemical industry (Jones, 2001). The broadcast drew a counterattack from the chemical industry, which charged that Jones and Moyers had produced an unbalanced and unfair story. Industry officials complained that the authors of the company documents were not interviewed and that industry defenses were limited during the first 90 minutes of the broadcast. Instead, industry officials along with environmentalists and others were invited to the last 30 minutes, a panel discussion of the issues raised in the story. Industry officials complained they were not given adequate time to prepare. In several news stories about the furor over the broadcast, Moyers reported that he tried but failed to track down the authors of the documents. He said that the panel discussion seemed the best way to represent industry's views (Davis, 2001). He also feared that the chemical industry's public relations specialists would obscure the point of the story. "Ida Tarbell didn't go to the public relations person at the oil

Figure 15.1 *Columbia Journalism Review* felt that the issue of objectivity in news was so important that it made the issue its cover story in its July/August 2003 issue (source: courtesy Michael Mabry, *Columbia Journalism Review*).

company … You just get propaganda and information," Moyers said (Dunne, 2002b, p. 16).

By failing to interview industry officials and include their viewpoints in the main story, much of the focus of what was reported was diverted to Moyer's ethics. Timothy Wheeler, an environmental reporter and editor at the *Baltimore Sun*, watched the controversy with great interest. The name of Wheeler's father, a longtime chemical company executive, was attached to some of the documents cited by Moyers. At the time, Wheeler's father could have been reached. Wheeler said he did not want to sound like an industry apologist, but he questioned how the story could be complete when no one tried to contact his father. "You don't know how important fairness is until you or someone close to you is the subject of an investigation," said Wheeler (2001, p. 17).

Anti-environment

Reporters have also been accused of being anti-environment, although fewer have been removed from their beats or dismissed because they were too friendly to business and industry groups. John Stossel of ABC News is one whose work invited such criticism. Once a respected consumer and environmental reporter, Stossel said he had an awakening and realized that some of those stories had been overly alarmist. He then began producing stories that he said compensated for his earlier leanings by openly accusing environmental activists as fringe radicals and environmental regulations as needlessly costly to society. Stossel went on the lecture circuit, accepting fees of $20,000 or more from industry groups, as he described the dangers of such regulatory agencies as the FDA and the EPA ("From Jekyll," 1995). Stossel's work for ABC's 20/20 and other television news specials was repeatedly criticized for its biases and journalism tactics. For instance, he was criticized harshly for his questionable tactics in interviewing elementary school students for a program called "What's Wrong With Tampering With Nature?" The special ridiculed environmentalists as "preachers of doom and gloom" who had helped brainwash U.S. schools into becoming "environmental boot camps." Parents of several children at a California school complained that Stossel's questions to students were misleading, repeating questions until he got the answers he wanted. Because of the criticism, the network pulled the interview of the California children, but it backed Stossel's reporting. Network defenders contend that Stossel is more entertainer than journalist and that his performance fits a tabloid style designed to boost his ratings (Coen, 2003).

Even the network could not defend another controversial story Stossel produced in 2000 called "The Food You Eat," which warned that organic produce might be more dangerous than conventional produce. The story maintained that increased levels of E. coli bacteria were found in organic produce in tests commissioned by ABC. The news story also reported that there were no pesticide residue on either organic or regular produce, eliminating a prime reason some consumers prefer organic. But the Organic Trade Association contended that the tests on E. coli did not distinguish between dangerous and benign strains of the bacteria, which was a crucial difference. Plus, the scientists commissioned by ABC said they never tested the produce for pesticides, only for bacteria. ABC reprimanded Stossel and the show's producer, suspended Stossel for a month, and forced Stossel to make a lengthy on-air apology (Coen, 2003).

Getting the science wrong

Similar concerns arose in the early 1990s about the environmental reporting of Keith Schneider, who followed Shabecoff in the environmental beat at the *New York Times*. Schneider was not an advocate journalist. He was a prize-winning journalist who at the time was writing for one of the nation's best newspapers. But he was accused of making controversial conclusions in some of his news stories, conclusions that many reporters and scientists said were inaccurate. Most of the criticism centered on Schneider's reporting on dioxin. The chemical, a chlorine-based substance that forced the 1982 evacuation of Times Beach, MO, had often been called one of the most dangerous manmade chemicals. But Schneider's stories in 1991 said that research was showing that the chemical was not as hazardous as originally suspected. In 1993 he advanced that thesis in a five-part series called "What Price Cleanup?" that explored whether the government's efforts to protect health from dioxin and other threats were working properly. Schneider wrote that exposure to dioxin "is now considered by some experts to be no more risky than spending a week sunbathing" (Monks, 1993, p. 1). That statement, along with Schneider's reporting on dioxin, was harshly criticized by some scientists who said the comparison was inaccurate (Monks, 1993). Scientists were also upset because the analogy was used repeatedly in the *Times*, one of the nation's most influential newspapers, but also was picked up by other publications (Carmody, 1995).

At the time Schneider defended his work, arguing that for too long journalists had always sided with environmentalists. "Environmental journalists have to regard environmental groups with as much skepticism as we have traditionally regarded polluters," he said. The controversy over Schneider's reporting ended in 1995 when he resigned and moved back to his home state of Michigan to work on land use issues. He created the Michigan Land Use Institute which was both an environmental and journalism organization championing "smart growth" over "suburban sprawl." The Institute produced a news service and its stories advocated environmental positions with a point of view. Weekly newspapers and radio and television stations sometimes used the stories ("Keith Schneider's," 2004).

Alternative media

So far this discussion has centered on mainstream journalists who have either stepped beyond the established ethical norm or been accused of bias. The standard is not the same for journalists who report for a variety of alternative news organizations. These can include alternate newspapers, magazines and newsletters aligned with environmental or industry groups carrying points of views, columnists, talk show hosts, cable television commentators, and Internet correspondents. Many of these journalists and news organizations clearly state their political biases and readers know they are getting a point-of-view, whether it is *Sierra* magazine or FOX television news commentator Bill O'Reilly. "Opinion journalism can be more honest than objective-style journalism because it does not have to hide its point of view," Michael Kinsley, the founding editor of *Slate*, wrote in the online publication. "It doesn't have to follow a trail of evidence or line of reasoning until one step before the conclusion and then slam on the brakes for fear of falling into the gulch of subjectivity" (Kinsley, 2006, p. 1).

The Internet has significantly increased both the volume of information and the variety of voices that are reaching the public. In 1997 an online gossip column written by Matt Drudge reported rumors that President Bill Clinton had had sex with a White House intern. That led to Clinton's impeachment and aquittal (Blumenthal, 2003). In 2004 bloggers successfully proved that CBS and *60 Minutes* had been duped in their story reporting that President George W. Bush years before had lied to get out of going to Vietnam. CBS apologized, fired the producer and eventually removed Dan Rather as the anchor of its evening news program ("CBS," 2005).

While these new websites and blogs have broadened and diversified news sources, they have also made it more difficult to assess the credibility of what information is in the marketplace. The standards set by traditional news organizations should be clear, and they aim to be accurate and fair. While this chapter highlights examples of inaccurate or biased reporting, such stories are the exception. For stories to get on television news or major newspapers, they first have to go through a long vetting process to make sure they have complied with that objective. Environmental organizations, such as the Sierra Club and industry groups such as the American Chemical Society, also have clearly defined, but different principles. But how can people judge the credibility or accuracy of

Taking sides

For months arsonists had been setting fire to a series of luxury houses under construction in the Phoenix Mountain Preserve in Arizona. A group called CSP, which stood for Coalition to Save the Preserves, had taken credit for the fires. In January, 2001 James Hibberd of the *Phoenix New Times* wrote a story sympathetic to the arsonists. Hibberd wrote in the alternative weekly newspaper that not enough was being done to preserve open space in the area. Shortly afterwards, the newspaper got an anonymous message from one of the purported arsonists. It began "Thou shall not desecrate God's creations" (Epler, 2001, p. 24). Eager to talk to him, the newspaper in its next edition put a teaser across the top addressed "To Thou Shall Not" and included Hibberd's direct phone line. The next day Hibberd received the call he expected and soon met with the purported arsonist. His story, titled "An Exclusive Interview with the Preserves Arsonist," led the next edition of the *New Times* and was picked up by other media in Phoenix, which had already made the arsons a major local story. The unidentified arsonist explained that his group was composed of mountain bikers upset about how open space in the Preserves area was vanishing (Epler, 2001).

While other news organizations covered the story, many also criticized *New Times* for consorting with a group that was breaking the law and for the newspaper's failure to turn over information to police. Both the *Arizona Republic* and KPNX-TV also received letters, turned them over to police, and agreed with the investigator's requests to publish only limited excerpts. The *Republic*'s story quoted a journalism professor who criticized the decision to run the interview and the Phoenix mayor said that the *New Times* was assisting the arsonist. Talk shows were also generally critical (Epler, 2001).

Journalism has a long history of consorting with a wide range of characters, from whistleblowers to convicted felons. In 1971 many major news organizations knowingly and willingly accepted stolen documents from a former Department of Defense official, Daniel Ellsburg. The documents produced during the Vietnam war described the origins of the conflict and many had been classified. The news organizations successfully fought in the courts the Nixon administration's attempts to prohibit news stories about what became known as the Pentagon Papers (Ungar, 1989).

As portions of the environmental movement have become more radical, journalists increasingly face risks in covering their activities.

Besides engaging in arson, radical activists have been known to destroy animal labs, disrupt logging operations, and attack Hummers. Such organizations are secretive and journalists say often they can only get the full story about what a group is doing by joining them on a mission. In such situations journalists must walk a fine line between observing and participating. Sometimes, the initial step of joining is unacceptable to authorities. In 1999 a reporter for the *Colorado Daily* in Boulder joined activists who entered a ski resort and chained themselves to a truck. Even though the reporter did not join the protest, he was still arrested for trespassing (Powers, 2004). Such situations are even more difficult for alternate news organizations and those whose advocacy is well documented. When a journalist is a known advocate it can be difficult to distinguish between his role in pushing the cause and his work as a journalist. In the case of the Phoenix arsons, was the writer openly advocating in favor of arson or was he simply giving the side of the arsonist? The First Amendment openly grants protection to both advocates and reporters. But credibility has to be earned.

news online from sources that can easily disguise their motivations, funding sources and hidden agendas? Studies were showing that news consumers were increasingly wary of many online news sites because readers were unable to distinguish truth from rumor on them (Project for Excellence in Journalism, 2006).

Defining the task

The term objectivity may be contributing to the confusion and the date. The term itself can be misleading. Objectivity begins to break down the moment a journalist starts selecting what will be reported. Christy George, a producer for Oregon Public Broadcasting, said, "Let's be honest – the most subjective editorial decisions are *what* to cover, *where* the story is placed and how much time or space it gets," she said. "Use your gut and your heart to decide *what* stories to pitch, then report them according to the principles of good journalism" ("Are we," 2003, p. 22). While story selection, reporting, writing, editing and story presentation are all selective, good journalism still demands that environmental reporters follow certain tenets on each aspect of the story. These include:

Sustainable Journalism

In the 1990s a new journalism movement called Civic or Public Journalism developed. The idea behind the concept was that journalists should report on issues but also become involved in them with readers or viewers. Stories should be built around the concept of public interaction and discussion, space should be reserved for readers and viewers to talk back to journalists, readers should be helped in finding ways to solve community problems and help journalists broaden their diversity of sources. Begun as an experiment in many communities, critics called it a gimmick and a last gasp effort by a profession that technology was irrevocably changing. The future for the concept remains uncertain (Witt, 2003).

Similar ideas have been expressed about a comparable movement for environmental journalism. Called Sustainable Journalism, it was first proposed by author Carl Frankel and it has been endorsed by Jim Detjen, the director of the Knight Center for Environmental Journalism at Michigan State University. Frankel said the concept would combine traditional journalism of accurate reporting and writing while striving to educate people about finding a way to balance the needs of nature with sound economic development. He said it would also support a dialog with the public in an effort to find solutions to environmental problems and that it would bridge the divides between objectivity and advocacy. Detjen said that too many journalists tended to shy away from the really big problems that threatened the planet such as consumerism, overpopulation and growing global water shortages. He said that if Sustainable Journalism was pursued some of the components would include:

- Increased access to information by opening freedom of information laws.
- Expanded coverage of international environmental issues, especially climate change.
- Steps to make the multinational corporations that own much of the news media more accountable to their own environmental track records.
- Increased coverage of complex environmental issues with the stress on potential solutions (Detjen, 2004).

The idea is admirable, at least in its desire to move reporters away from entertainment and titillation and towards a more meaningful discussion of fundamental problems troubling the world. However, just like Public Journalism, its prospects for moving forward remain in doubt.

Accuracy

The story must be factual. Sources must be properly identified, their quotes correct, their comments clearly attributed. The battle begins to be lost when names are misspelled. The war is lost when facts are manufactured (Gillmor, 2005). The line between these two is not that distant. Many critics of Stossel's reporting felt validated in their concerns when he had to make an on-air apology for his reporting about organic produce (Coen, 2003). Sometimes the distinction in getting it correct is not as clear. Both Shabecoff and Schneider were environmental reporters at the *New York Times* who were accused of bias, one to the left, the other to the right. But the distinction was that in Schneider's situation the criticism did not just come from environmental advocates but from many in the science community. Kevin Carmody, a longtime environmental journalist who wrote about Schneider's dioxin reporting in 1995, said Schneider's articles "were mostly accurate, judged fact by fact, but they led readers to conclusions that were, in truth, highly debatable" (Carmody, 1995, p. 2).

Thoroughness

In the PBS story "Trade Secrets," Bill Moyers let the facts speak for themselves in the documents he collected about the chemical industry and its efforts to keep important facts from the public. He said it was too difficult to track down the authors of those documents. Also, he was afraid that if he disclosed what he had found to the chemical industry, that those officials would distort the message. Such selective reporting is a problem (Gillmor, 2005). The result of that decision by PBS and Moyers was that it opened up an opportunity for the chemical industry to move the focus away from the facts in the story to the ethics of the reporting and editing.

Balance

Environmental journalists must know the science of a particular issue and be aware when controversies and disputes are factual and when they are manufactured. They also have an obligation to educate their editors who will be reading the copy, writing the headlines and deciding on a story's display or placement. At the same time, journalists need to be open to criticism. That does not mean they need to accept it. Journalism has a place for reporting that goes against conventional views. However, when the vast number of peers reach an opposite conclusion based on the facts, then journalists need to go back, review their reporting, and make sure they are right.

Fairness

While it is important to report accurately about the science of an environmental issue, journalists also write about the political and public policy issues related to environmental initiatives. There are many elements to being fair. Reporters need to tell sources the purpose of the story. Questions can be tough and demanding but they need to be fair. "Ambush journalism" may be a hallmark of some television reporting, but it is more entertainment than journalism. Titillating but relatively meaningless facts should not be hyped (Gillmor, 2005).

Transparency

A century ago bylines were extremely rare in newspapers. Today the profession is festooned with personalities, primarily on television, but also in radio, publications and the Internet (Gillmor, 2005). Increasingly news organizations are trying to acquaint readers and listeners with those who are giving them the news, by providing email addresses, biographies and blogs. Journalists need to gather the facts and then write with authority. That allowed Dan Fagin of *Newsday* to write about cancer clusters on Long Island, Dina Cappiello of the *Houston Chronicle* to warn of toxic air pollution, Candace Page of the *Burlington Free Press* to describe environmental land conflicts, Matt Hammill of WQAD-TV to report about urban sprawl in the nation's heartland and Tom Meersman of the *Minneapolis Star Tribune* to warn of invasive species altering the Great Lakes. But journalists also need to spend more time explaining to their readers and listeners how and why they wrote and report these stories.

Passion

This last tenet may ultimately be the most important. Many go into journalism because they believe they can make a difference through their profession. Environmental journalists have a passion for the environment, the same way good sports reporters care about sports, education writers believe in learning, and business journalists thrive on the events of economic commerce. No one is in favor of pollution. SEJ has a t-shirt. It says "we are not environmental journalists; We are reporters who cover the environment" ("Are we," 2003, p. 19).

Study guide

1 Numerous news organizations have established programs on ethics or ethical codes. The Poynter Institute has a special program in ethics at www.poynter.org. Codes and their sites include The Society of Professional Journalists Code of Ethics, www.spj.org/ethics_code.asp; American Society of Newspaper Editors Statement of Principles, www.asne.org/kiosk/archive/principal.htm; and Associated Press Managing Editors Code of Ethics, www.apme.com/about/code_ethics. shtml. Review these codes and standards. What are their chief attributes? What are their major limitations?

2 When, if ever, would you include your own opinions in a news story, broadcast, or Internet report?

3 The Bill Moyers' "Trade Secrets" story was criticized for not going far enough in getting industry's side of the story even though the documents were decades old. What is the obligation of a reporter to get the other side in a story like that?

4 John Stossel has been called an entertainer/political commentator more than a journalist. Do some research on Stossel's career. Do you agree with that label? Are television programs such as 60 Minutes and 20/20 inherently more entertainment than journalism?

5 Did the Phoenix New Times cross an ethical line when it solicited an interview with an arsonist and published his comments? How far should journalists go in observing or participating in illegal actions in order to get the story?

6 The chapter briefly mentioned Jayson Blair of the New York Times and how he fabricated and plagiarized facts in news stories. What are the details about Blair? Have there been journalists who have engaged in similar ethical lapses since Blair? Name them and spell out their misdeeds.

7 For further reading, consider Michael Frome's Green Ink (1998), Stephen Glass, The Fabulist (2003) and The News About the News by Leonard Downie Jr. and Robert G. Kaiser (2002).

Chapter 16

The future of environmental journalism

In August, 2005 the future of journalism and the environment appeared to arrive in New Orleans with terrifying suddenness. Even before Hurricane Katrina struck both the environment and journalism were being shaken by impending change. Media experts say that in the coming years newspapers and television news stations may die and be replaced by online news sources. Meanwhile scientists warned that climate change may melt the polar ice caps, causing increased coastal flooding and possibly more violent storms.

New Orleans is very much a coastal city, residing at an elevation as much as ten feet below sea level even though it is 110 miles from the Gulf of Mexico. In the aftermath of the storm the levees that keep back the Mississippi River collapsed, flooding better than half of New Orleans. The day after the storm passed, Tuesday, August 30, 2005, three of the city's four television stations were off the air and the *Times-Picayune* staff had evacuated the city.

What happened next was remarkable. While the lessons learned in New Orleans do not guarantee the future of journalism or the environment, they are certainly worth examining as an indication of what may be ahead.

Even during the storm the normal means of communicating news had begun to breakdown and change. When the *Times-Picayune* lost its power and was unable to publish it continued to produce news stories that it fed to its sister website, *NOLA.com*. The website had been known not for news, but for its entertainment offerings including a live webcam on Bourbon Street that sometimes produced unusual images during Mardi Gras (Glaser, 2005b).

Its new role had begun during the storm when it set up two emergency blogs. One was from the *Times-Picayune* city desk and it featured news and stories from the staff. The second blog was run by Jon Donley, editor of *NOLA.com*, who stationed himself near a police scanner radio and transcribed what he was hearing. "I could actually hear phone calls patched through, and you could hear the water going up in someone's attic, and you could hear the cops crying 'I can't get to them, they're dropping off the roof one at a time'" (Glaser, 2005b, p. 4).

Then others started sending messages requesting help through *NOLA.com*. Donley said emails were coming in from places like Idaho reporting about someone who was trapped at a New Orleans address. "It was weird because we couldn't figure out where these pleas were coming from," he said (Glaser, 2005b, p. 5). Eventually they realized that people even in the poorest neighborhoods had cell phones and that they were sending out text messages to family or friends who were emailing them to the website. Soon rescue missions were underway based on the information flowing into *NOLA.com*.

Donley said he never anticipated the storm would be that strong, or that the newspaper would lose electricity, and that the flooding would eventually force his operation to Baton Rouge. But as far back as 1998 when Hurricane Georges had prompted a massive evacuation of the Gulf Coast he had seen the power of the Internet and *NOLA.com*. He found that once people got to a safe location they immediately went online and tried to find information about what was happening back home. That pattern continued in subsequent years and escalated after Katrina. The website that averaged about 800,000 page hits a day was getting ten million the day before the storm struck, 17 million the next day and 30 million by the end of the week when final evacuations were completed (Glaser, 2005b).

Broadcasters also turned to their websites and to other stations in the Gulf region to reach their viewers. Television station WDSU produced broadcasts from stations in Jackson, Houston and other locations. WWL produced news stories, which it permitted any station in the country to broadcast (Thomas, 2005). Radio also adapted to a changed environment. Fifteen stations owned by Clear Channel Baton Rouge and Entecom New Orleans joined to create a 24-hour news station. The station became a community bulletin board, allowing officials a communication voice and individuals to send messages to loved ones.

Mark Schleifstein, the environmental reporter for the New Orleans *Times-Picayune*, listened to the station as he and his colleagues were leaving New Orleans on August 30. Local officials were explaining that the flooded city had to be evacuated. Schleifstein took notes in the truck and then wrote a story during the two-hour drive from New Orleans to Houma, LA. The local daily newspaper, the *Houma Courier*, had agreed to provide space to the *Times-Picayune*. The staff only spent a day in Houma before transferring its operations to space at Louisiana State University in Baton Rouge. Within two days the *Times-Picayune* was producing a paper edition, printed by the *Houma Courier*, and later by the *Mobile Register*. By November the staff and the paper were back in New Orleans (Thomas, 2005).

Besides overcoming technical and production difficulties, hometown reporters and the national press also produced great journalism in the weeks after the storm. The evidence of journalism's power to be a watchdog of government was showcased as reporters described the tens of thousands of people, primarily poor and minorities, who were left stranded in the city. For days television networks described the many who continued to wait, without food or water, at the convention center. Michael Brown, director of the Federal Emergency Management Agency, kept telling reporters that he was only learning of those problems. Finally, ABC's Ted Koppel exploded: "Don't you guys watch television? Don't you guys listen to the radio?" (Thomas, 2006, p. 26). Two weeks later Brown was fired. Newspaper coverage was just as thorough, resulting in Pulitzer Prizes for Katrina coverage for both the *Times-Picayune* and the *Biloxi-Gulfport Sun Herald* (Pulitzer.org, 2006).

Despite such achievements, the future of journalism was less than secure in the aftermath of the storm. As costs soared for local news organizations and advertising disappeared, rumors started that the owners would shut them down. Executives at the *Times-Picayune* repeatedly tried to dispel rumors that the paper would fold. Many residents were not returning to New Orleans. That threatened the paper's circulation and advertising base. Editors struggled to determine how the paper would cover a drastically different city. Schleifstein, of the *Times-Picayune*, was worried. He spoke during a discussion sponsored by the Society of Environmental Journalists about the future of environmental journalism. "I'm caught in a microcosm of everything that has happened over the past 10 years," said Schleifstein. "We are now downsized. We're trying to figure out what type of newspaper we are while trying to figure out everything else that is occurring" (Miller *et al.*, 2005).

SEJ and New Orleans were not the only ones wondering about the future of journalism. As the first decade of the twenty-first century moved forward, journalism was undertaking a re-examination of what was ahead. The Project for Excellence in Journalism, which is affiliated with the Columbia University Graduate School of Journalism, issued an annual report called "The State of the News Media." It concluded that the profession of "journalism was in the midst of an epochal transformation, as momentous as the invention of the telegraph or television" (Project for Excellence in Journalism, 2005, p. 1). The Carnegie Corporation joined with five major journalism schools to examine the future of journalism education in light of what was occurring in the profession (Connell, 2006). Merrill Brown, a former editor-in-chief of MSNBC.com, participated in that review and warned that "a radical revolution (is) taking place in the news business today" (Brown, 2006,

Figure 16.1 The Superdome in New Orleans has been repaired in the aftermath of Hurricane Katrina and is a symbol of the rebirth occurring in the Louisiana city (source: courtesy Federal Emergency Management Agency).

p. 42). David Zeeck, president of the American Society of Newspaper Editors, called a conference at the Poynter Institute on the future of journalism. Rusty Coates, general manager of TBO.com, told the editors at the conference that "tomorrow is our permanent address" (Favre, 2006, p. 1).

Polls showed working journalists were concerned. One said that reporters believed that business pressures were making their product less substantial and advertisers and owners seemed to have an increasing reach into the newsroom. At the same time audiences were declining and jobs were disappearing. The pollsters reported:

> News people are not confident about the future of journalism. Overall, they appear split over whether journalism is headed in the right or wrong direction. At the national level a slim majority are pessimistic. At the local level a slim majority are optimistic. Broadcasters are more pessimistic. Print people are more optimistic. Internet journalists are the most optimistic of all.
>
> (Kovach *et al.*, 2006, p. 2)

Why the gloom?

The Internet and online news has increasingly been impacting journalism, clearly affecting the negative attitudes and patterns of both news professionals and news consumers. Technological transformations were taking place 500 years ago with Gutenberg and the invention of moveable type. The real difference now is how quickly these cycles of new inventions and change occur. The telegraph was supplanted by the radio, then television, cable and now the Internet. Each has been remarkably resilient and adaptable to change. The exception may be the Morse code and paper telegrams, but they were replaced more by individual communication modes, such as the telephone, rather than by mass media (Kovach *et al.*, 2006).

Development of new business models that controlled news organizations and the reluctance of new owners to invest in news budgets fueled the pessimism. The trend toward publicly-traded large corporations owning strings of newspapers, radio and television stations have accelerated through much of the twentieth century. News organizations can be enormously profitable. Newspapers can produce pre-tax profit margins of 20 percent while that figure can soar to 40 to 50 percent for many local television news stations (Project for Excellence in Journalism, 2005). The problem has been trying to maintain the relative balance for owners between the bottom line and public service responsibilities. Chain ownership resulted in less of a commitment to local communities.

Pressures appeared greatest with newspapers. In 1960 four out of five households read a daily newspaper. In 2005 that figure was one in two. Much of that decline came from competition from new technologies, especially television. Still, while the American population has risen, newspaper circulation has fallen from around 62 million in 1990 to 54 million in 2005. Losses have been the greatest with the newspapers' future readers – the young (Project for Excellence in Journalism, 2005). A study by the American Newspaper Association found that the percentage of people ages 30 to 39 who read a newspaper every day fell from 73 percent in 1972 to 30 percent in 1998. Meanwhile the percentage of even younger readers, 14 to 24, who said they read newspapers dropped by 14 percent (Brown, 2006). At the same time overall newspaper advertising revenue declined. Newspaper monopolies for classified advertising have been threatened by online competitors such as Monster.com and Craigslist.com. One study just confined to the San Francisco Bay area newspapers showed they were losing $50 million to $65 million a year in job listing revenue (Brown, 2006). The response by many newspaper executives has been to cut budgets and staffs. While the overall number of newsroom jobs rose from 43,000 in 1977 to 54,000 in 2004, significant reductions were being made at major newspapers in the early 2000s. Between 2000 and 2004 newsrooms lost 2,000 positions (Kovach *et al.*, 2006).

The picture for television was not as clear. Evening network television viewing has declined with some switching to cable news programs and others possibly to morning news shows. Ratings for evening news programs, which count the number of television sets in the U.S. tuned to a specific program, was 50 percent in 1969. Meanwhile market share, which measured the number of sets turned on, was 85 percent in 1969. By 2004 the ratings for network news had fallen to 20.2 percent and the market share was 38 percent (Project for Excellence in Journalism, 2005). Some of those viewers have been captured by cable news programs including Fox News, CNN and MSNBC. Fox in 2005 was still gaining in audience but the numbers were falling at the other two

Figure 16.2 Fishermen cast for salmon under an early evening moon with Mount Rainier in Washington in the background. An ideal environment is everyone's dream for the future (source: courtesy National Oceanic & Atmospheric Administration).

news stations (Project for Excellence in Journalism, 2006). Meanwhile, ratings and shares at local evening newscasts were also down in the early 2000s, although viewers were increasing at morning network and local broadcasts. The resulting cutback in staffing and budgets was most severe at local television news organizations. Reporters said they were increasingly being asked to do more to satisfy investors' need to maintain earnings (Project for Excellence in Journalism, 2005). That was worrisome. "The question is whether local stations are risking their future by continuing to insist on such huge profit margins and year-to-year growth in earnings when the audience is stagnant" (Project for Excellence in Journalism, 2006, p. 1).

The future would appear the brightest for online news organizations. Growth in the first years of the 2000s was strong, especially as more people switched over to broadband Internet access and technology advancements continued for wireless transmissions and downloading data and video to portable telephones and receivers (Project for Excellence in Journalism, 2006). The audience reading online newsblogs grew in the first six months of 2004 to 32 million, a 58 percent increase (Project for Excellence in Journalism, 2005). Advertising revenue also grew and an increasing number of websites were financially profitable (Project for Excellence in Journalism, 2006).

Weblogs were also changing how news was gathered and collected. Individuals were being transformed "from passive consumers of news produced by professionals into active participants who can assemble their own journalism" (Project for Excellence in Journalism, 2005, p. 1). Unlike other journalists, online reporters were extremely pleased with their work, with 85 percent of those in the business offering high ratings for the websites of national news organizations. Rich Gordon, director of new media programs at the Medill School of Journalism at Northwestern University, said "I think that when we look back on the early years of the 21st Century, we will recognize it as a period of exploding opportunity for journalists and the start of an exciting new era for journalism" (Gordon, 2005, p. 1).

Environmental journalism options

With the growth of online news organizations should come more opportunities for environmental reporters. National newspapers and the television networks in the early 2000s were building their websites and staffs. Several major newspapers in 2005 had moved to 24-hour online news desks. The *New York Times* and the *Washington Post* were among the leaders. Also in 2005 newspaper online revenue was producing 3 to 5 percent of all revenue coming in to newspapers. At that rate it would take a dozen years before that funding stream grew to a point where it reached parity with traditional advertising and circulation revenue (Project for Excellence in Journalism, 2005). Meanwhile CBS, with its CBSNews.com, was the most aggressive as it shifted much of its content online. Particularly innovative was the Public Eye weblog which was designed to provide more understanding of how the network made news decisions by taking such steps as offering webcasts of editorial meetings (Project for Excellence in Journalism, 2006).

Blogs and other entrepreneurial opportunities were another potential avenue for environmental reporters. The Internet has broken down an important barrier. For decades the cost of beginning even a small weekly newspaper or radio station in a rural area was too costly for anyone except the extremely wealthy. The Internet offered even entry-level journalists an opportunity to be creative and find a niche in a specialized area without that financial gamble. Individuals with very little cash could create their own websites or blogs and over time develop them into financially sustaining enterprises. Merrill Brown suggested journalism schools should become more active in encouraging students not to assume they needed to work for a large news organization. "I think what we need to do in our profession is to train all of us, especially those of us in school, to think about our careers differently," he said. "I think journalists have to think about controlling their destiny, when the opportunities arise, to think about the entrepreneurial opportunities that ubiquitous distribution makes available" (Miller et al., 2005).

Newspapers and television stations that want to survive the future will need to be more relevant to their readers. To do that many likely will be more locally oriented. That would mean more coverage of city zoning to greater reporting on local youth sports. "This is your strongest position," Tom Rosenstiel of the Project for Excellence in Journalism told editors at the Poynter forum on the future. "It requires boots on the ground" (Zeeck, 2006, p. 2). If news is going to get more local, a paramount concern would seem to be the quality of one's water, land and air resources.

Environmental reporters might also want to consider a way that their expertise could be better recognized by consumers. With so many sources of information, consumers may have difficulty evaluating the reliability of news. Philip Meyer, who wrote *Precision Journalism*, suggested that specialized journalists consider a certification program. Meyer indicated he was not talking about licensing, but a way to identify journalists who had demonstrated their ability to accurately cover complex issues ("Reporter Certification," 2005). It is unclear whether journalists would ever agree to such a concept, because journalists generally have been wary of such measures.

All future opportunities for environmental reporters are not tied to changes in the profession or technology. The growth of environmental

reporting in the past has always been tied to the interest news consumers have had in the environment. Bud Ward, the publisher of
Environment Writer and a longtime observer of the beat, said that
environmental coverage is cyclical. He recalled when ABC White House
correspondent Sam Donaldson left his beat in the late 1980s. Donaldson was confident he would still find important assignments. "No one's
carrying me out or shifting me to the ecology beat," said Donaldson (B.
Ward, 2004, p. 59). Shortly afterwards the *Exxon Valdez* oil spill
occurred and by 1990 environmental stories were constantly on page
one or leading local newscasts. "Want to know when the next boom
cycle for environmental coverage will begin?" asked Ward. "Determine
the time and place of the next environmental disaster" (B. Ward, 2004,
p. 59).

Ward spoke before Hurricane Katrina struck in 2005. The hurricane
was clearly the type of environmental disaster he had forecast. For a
two-week period it dominated news coverage. In was an especially big
story on national television. Jeanne Meserve of CNN described a boat
ride into neighborhoods that had just been flooded, and of hearing cries
of help from those trapped in flooded attics. When the government
recovery efforts began to fumble, Anderson Cooper of CNN was on the
air asking "Where's the help?" (Thomas, 2005, p. 26). And Ted Kopple
of ABC expressed outrage when federal officials said they did not know
people were marooned at the New Orleans Convention Center. "Don't
you guys watch television? Don't you guys listen to the radio?" he
asked (Thomas, 2005, p. 26). "This was a television story," said Jay
Harris, a professor at the University of Southern California journalism
school. "Television took people there, it showed an undeniable truth to
the people, it held the government up to ridicule" (Miller *et al.*, 2005).

After several weeks the camera crews left New Orleans, the story
faded from the front pages of America's newspapers and traffic fell at
NOLA.com. Katrina was the type of story that should have spurred
more interest in news of the environment. The problem was that too
often the stories centered on the tragedy and drama of the disaster.
While that story was compelling and important, reporters too often
ignored the underlying factors that caused the calamity. Dale Willman,
an independent radio reporter who covers the environment, said the
press spends too much time describing environmental processes and not
enough on substance. As an example he cited a public radio story he
had heard about the process of coal gasification and its implications in
producing cleaner air emissions. Willman said that the story was good,
but it concentrated on the bureaucratic obstacles developers were
encountering in building such plants. Willman said that he wanted to
know whether such plants actually worked, did they actually produce
cleaner air emissions and by how much? He said too many journalists

fall into that process trap. It became a habit in the grind to get news out. "We have to implement new habits and change the way we are looking at some of these stories," he said. "We have to go from processes to substances" (Willman, 2006).

Andrew Revkin of the *New York Times*, who covered climate change issues, had a slightly different take on the situation. He predicted that the disasters of the twenty-first century will not be the Bhopals, but issues such as climate change. They will not be oil spills from a tanker that went aground, but from nonpoint pollution dripping into the environment from a million sources. "There are 1.5 *Exxon Valdez* going into our ecosystem every year but it is not caused by some drunk sea captain," he said (Miller *et al.*, 2005).

Return to New Orleans

Over time the future was becoming clear in New Orleans.

In the aftermath of the storm New Orleans struggled to recover. A year afterward about half of the residents of this once thriving metropolis of 475,000 had returned. It took months to find all of the dead bodies, to get the infrastructure of government and commerce running, to return electricity and other vital services. Mark Schleifstein, the environmental writer of the *Times-Picayune*, suspected it would take years for the city to recover. Schleifstein remembered when Hurricane Camille struck in 1969. "The gulf coast did not recover until the gambling industry arrived, and that was in the 80s. The newspaper will be dealing with this for at least the next five years, if not the next 10 or 15" (Schleifstein, 2006).

The *Times-Picayune* had earned two Pulitzer Prizes for its coverage of the storm and Schleifstein found himself covering one aspect of the environmental beat – the levees. In a city where the levees had failed, perhaps nothing was as important as knowing how safe those flood barriers would be in the future. "That isn't going to change anytime soon," he predicted (Schleifstein, 2006).

The *Times-Picayune* was making a comeback. Donald E. Newhouse, president of Advance Publications, which owned the newspaper, had made it clear that the company had no plans to abandon New Orleans. The daily paper's circulation was more than 200,000 and rising towards its pre-Katrina figure of 260,000. Still, it was a different newspaper. For a while staffing had been allowed to fall, through attrition, but by summer of 2006 the newspaper was hiring again. With the city smaller and many of its residents now living in the suburbs, editors were trying to decide where to set their priorities in coverage (Schleifstein, 2006).

NOLA.com had also changed. Also owned by Advance but independent of the newspaper, the website's traffic had fallen significantly since the days after the storm. Still, its ability to cover the news was far stronger than before Katrina struck. While retaining its separate leadership, it had moved inside the *Times-Picayune*'s newsroom. Reporters for the newspaper were posting more stories online, producing more video and working closer with the online staff.

Despite surviving the most devastating hurricane to strike the U.S. in a century, Schleifstein said that residents had not developed a greater appreciation for the environment. They already appreciated the fragile ecosystem they called home. "New Orleans and South Louisiana are so closely tied to the environment that there is no way they could not already have been concerned about them," said Schleifstein (2006). All of the region's major industries, from oil and gas to shipping to the fisheries, all have been concerned about everything from the weather to coastal erosion.

As the new hurricane season began each June, Schleifstein suspected that others would begin to realize that they too lived in a fragile environment. In the aftermath of Katrina issues such as flood protection and additional insurance, subjects that always worried New Orleans, had spread along the Gulf Coast and up the eastern seaboard. Awareness of the threat of greater storms and flooding was rising.

New Orleans really was not that much different from anywhere else. No matter where people live, they cannot avoid the environment. If it were not storms and flooding, it was earthquakes and forest fires, development and erosion, dirty water and foul air. It also could be a renewed environment of new growth and habitat, restored rivers and lakes, clear skies, nature and beauty. No matter how much technology may transform the media and even the nature of the news, there will always be a need in New Orleans and elsewhere to understand what is happening in the environment.

Study guide

1 The future of journalism will largely be determined by future news consumers. Interview at least one dozen people between the ages of 18 and 24 about where they go to obtain news on a daily basis. Accumulate quotes. Write a story, supplementing it with the facts in the chapter or with new information about 18-to-24 year olds.

2 What local innovative changes, if any, has the local newspaper done to improve its news product? Have local television or radio stations made similar changes? Are there Internet sites or blogs that have made changes?

3 Philip Meyers believed a voluntary certification program for specialists, such as environmental reporters, would be beneficial and

reassuring to news consumers. Do you agree? What are the pros and cons?

4 The information about the study by Carnegie Corporation regarding the future of journalism education can be found at www.carnegie.org and the Project for Excellence in Journalism's reports on the State of the News Media can be found at www.stateofthenewsmedia.org. Write a news story on the latest findings by either of these two groups about the state or future of journalism.

5 Some believe journalists in the future need to be more entrepreneurial. Do you agree? How could you develop a website or blog that was financially self-sustaining?

6 For further reading consider Philip Meyer's *The Vanishing Newspaper* (2005), Bill Bryson's *A Walk in the Woods* (1999), Jared Diamond's *Collapse: How Societies Choose to Fail or Succeed* (2004) and Jonathan Harr's *A Civil Action* (1996).

Glossary

7Q10 A water quality measurement involving the lowest stream flow for seven consecutive days that occurs on average once every ten years.

A-wire Primary news service wire of The Associated Press that carries the most significant national and international stories.

Acid On a scale of 0 to 14, an acid is a compound that has a pH of less than seven. Acids neutralize a base and have a high concentration of hydrogen ions. Corrosive acids are closer to 0 on the scale. The closer to seven on the scale, the weaker the acid.

Acid rain Clean rain has a pH of 5.6. Any precipitation with a lower pH is acid rain.

Active voice When the sentence structure is organized in order of subject, verb and object.

Acute dose This is a toxicology term meaning a large exposure in less than a week. Some may be hazardous, and are utilized to test chemical mixtures in a protected setting.

Acute effect The effect of an acute dose.

Add Each subsequent page of a news story written. In hard copy, the second page of a story is the first add, the third page is the second add. In electronic wire copy an add is additional information to a story.

Advance This is news or a story disclosing a coming event.

Aerosol A suspension of insoluble particles in a gas.

Agent Agents can be biological, physical or chemical, and are the cause of a particular effect or disease. Causation can be one or more agents acting together.

Ambient The surroundings, usually outdoors.

Anaerobic This means containing no oxygen.

Analysis piece A background story that adds meaning or interpretation to current issues in the news by explaining them further.

Anchor On-camera reporter who reads the script for a broadcast news show. Some anchors write their own scripts, some read from scripts supplied by others.

Aquifer   A reservoir of water underground.

Assignment editor   Editor who coordinates all assignments in a newsroom. At a broadcast station the editor has key responsibilities. Editors make assignments and keep track of reporters in the field.

Associated Press   The world's oldest cooperative news-gathering service, often called AP.

Background   Information in a news story that explains or provides technical information or details that were reported in earlier stories.

Background level   The normal level of physical or chemical substances found in the environment, both with and without the influence of humans.

Beat reporter   Reporter who covers a specific geographic or subject area, such as covering the environment, science or medicine.

Best Available Control Technology (BACT)   An air emissions regulation that sets the degree of emissions based on the availability of technology. This allows the regulatory agency to make changes in the air emission if a permit holder makes changes or improvements to its facility.

Bioaccumulate   The build up of a substance in the body over time due to the ingestion of small amounts.

Biodiversity   Living organisms from all sources. Measured within ecosystems, between ecosystems, and within a region.

Biological Oxygen Demand (BOD)   A measure of the amount of oxygen consumed in the biological process. Large amounts of organic waste use up large amounts of dissolved oxygen. The greater the degree of BOD, the greater the degree of pollution.

Blog   Also called a weblog. A blog is an Internet site, generally run by an individual or organization, that reports and provides news and opinion. Some personal blogs have been called a new type of citizen journalism.

Boldface   A printing term for dark type that is thicker and blacker than ordinary text type.

Breaking news   News that is available for publication or broadcast and that reporters try to provide quickly.

Brownfields   This is a term for sites where concern about contamination has hindered redevelopment, and they have become abandoned.

Bulletin   Priority news report developed by the wire services. A bulletin of one publishable paragraph alerts newsrooms that a major story is developing.

Bureau   Geographically removed extension of a news medium's headquarters. The *New York Times*, for example, has its headquarters in New York, but it has bureaus in many states and countries.

Buried lead   Term for a news story's most important point that usually has been accidentally placed lower in the story than warranted.

Byline   Identification of the author of a news story, usually in a line at the top of the story.

Cancer cluster   A high incidence of cancer in a certain area.

Carbon dioxide (CO_2)   A colorless, odorless nonpoisonous gas that is a product of fossil fuel combustion and that is believed to be causing a build-up of atmospheric temperatures.

Carbon monoxide (CO)   A colorless, odorless highly toxic gas that is a byproduct of incomplete fossil fuel combustion. It is one of the major air pollutants and can be harmful in small amounts if breathed over a certain period of time.

Carcinogen   An agent shown to cause cancer.

Cardiovascular disease   Disease of the heart and/or blood vessels.

Case-control study (also retrospective study)   Research that compares people who have a condition with similar people who do not have the condition. The most well-known of this type are the tobacco/lung cancer studies.

Chlorofluorocarbon – (CFC)   Compounds containing chlorine, fluorine, and carbon that are used in aerosol cans and insulators. CFCs enter the atmosphere as greenhouse gas.

Chronic dose   Exposure to small amounts of a substance over a period of time (more than a year for humans).

City editor   Editor who runs the city desk and is in charge of local coverage. The city editor is responsible for local general assignment, beat and specialty reporters.

Cluster   A high number of events in a given area that appear to have a pattern. They may or may not have a common cause.

Cohort study   (also concurrent study, follow-up study, incidence study, longitudinal study, prospective study). A type of research that follows a group (cohort) over time.

Communicable disease   This describes diseases that are contagious.

Computer-assisted reporting   The gathering of information through the retrieval and sorting of information on the Internet or computer databases.

Concentration   The amount of material to a given substance.

Confounding factor   A confusing factor in a study that complicates the results.

Contrast lead   Lead that compares or contrasts one person or thing with one or more other people or things.

Control group   A scientifically valid study has a comparison (control) group; that is, a group that is statistically identical to the study group except that it does not receive the condition that is being studied.

Copy News story or written material produced by journalists.

Copy desk Newsroom desk where copy editors edit copy and then write headlines.

Copy editor Editor who checks stories to make certain that they follow proper style, usage, spelling, and grammar rules. The copy editor also makes certain that a story is well-organized and not libelous. After editing the story, the copy editor writes a headline for it.

Correction Material that corrects information in a previous news story.

Correlation A number ranging from one to −1 that shows the extent to which two variables are related increase or decrease together. It is a statistic that shows the strength of the relationship between variables, regardless of causation.

Dateline An opening word in a story that provides the geographic designation of where the reporting for the story occurred. Many news organizations only use a dateline when a reporter has physically visited that location.

Delayed lead Opening paragraph of a news story where the most important elements of the story are purposely withheld. Instead, a delayed lead features a narrative, description, quote or other writing device.

Direct-address lead Lead that communicates directly with a reader, sometimes including the word "you."

Dose A measurement of an amount of exposure.

Double truck Story or advertisement that covers two facing pages of a publication.

Ecology The relationship between living organisms and the environment.

Ecosystem A system of nature's communities and the surrounding environment that interacts as a unit.

Editor Manager in charge of the editorial function of a news organization.

Editorial news hole Designation of how much news space exists on a particular page or throughout the publication. The ads are laid out on the page first; the editorial news hole consists of the remaining column inches.

Effluent Usually liquid waste products from a manufacturing or treatment plant, and often toxic.

Embargo An understanding between a news source and a journalist that information will be released with the agreement that the news organization will not disseminate it until a later, agreed upon date. Academic journals often release upcoming articles on an embargoed basis.

Endocrine disrupters Chemicals that interfere with the function of the endocrine system and hormones that could be a change that may lead to harmful health effects.

Enterprise story Stories that require reporters to use initiative. For example, a routine story would be to cover a press conference where an announcement was made. An enterprise story would examine why that announcement occurred, and it would require multiple sources, statistical information and extensive quotations.

Environment Everything external to a person. Environment includes biological and physical factors.

Epidemic An occurrence of cases of health-related events in excess of what is normal.

Epidemiology The study of patterns and causes of diseases, and how to control them.

Estuary Inland marine waterway where the tide meets the current that is dominated by grass or grass-like plants.

Expository story Nonfiction prose that sets forth facts, ideas and arguments. The inverted pyramid is an example of expository writing.

Exposure Contact, either internal or external, with a substance or agent.

Feature story Story that provides a human interest element and that may not have a strong time element. Such stories entertain; or describe people, places or things that are in or out of the news.

Follow Sometimes called a second-day story because it is produced after the first news story on an event. A follow provides the latest news in the lead or early in the story, but it also repeats the major news that was reported earlier.

Foreign editor An editor who supervises news reporters based in bureaus or locations outside the country.

Freedom of Information Act This is generally referred to as the FOI Act, the law that provides access to federal or state records and access to many public gatherings. Laws will vary between states and the federal government.

Freelance A reporter who produces news stories for several news organizations, none of which is a full-time employer.

Gatekeepers Editors or reporters who make news decisions. News personnel, on a story-by-story basis, decide what information to include and what angles to emphasize.

Gene Pieces of DNA; the physical unit of heredity.

General assignment reporter A reporter with no assigned beat who covers a range of issues and stories assigned by an editor.

Graph A journalism term for paragraph. Also spelled graf.

Greenhouse gases These are gases that trap heat and cause global warming in the troposphere.

Groundwater Water beneath the earth's surface, in the space between soil and rock.

Habitat The location, climate, vegetation, and physical element of a species.

Hard copy Computer term for a story composed and printed out by a computer.

Hard news Information that is timely and fact-based. A speech by a high public official is an example.

Hazard Exposure to a substance that could cause harm. The severity of an environmental hazard often depends on its concentration and exposure.

Hazardous waste A waste that may significantly contribute to a threat to human health or the environment if it is not under control.

Health Physical, social and mental well-being.

Heavy metals Metallic elements such as mercury, lead, zinc and cadmium that are of environmental concern because they do not degrade over time. In high concentrations they can be toxic.

Hourglass style Form of writing in which the major facts of a story are written in the first few paragraphs and then a transitional paragraph introduces a chronology of the details of the story.

Human interest story News feature story that emphasizes a subject's unusual, emotional or entertainment value.

Hypothesis A scientific guess that might lead to a research study.

Incidence The number of new events in a given time period, usually one year.

Insert Copy that is placed, or inserted, into a story to clarify or make the story more complete.

Internet A communications medium that connects supercomputers, mainframes, workstations and personal computers so that they can exchange information.

Inverted pyramid A form of writing in which the key points of the story are put in the opening paragraph with less important news in succeeding paragraphs in order of descending importance.

In vitro Outside the body.

In vivo Inside the body.

Journalists' privilege A legal term asserting that journalists have a right, under certain conditions, not to reveal information supplied by a source.

Jump When a story continues from one newspaper page to another.

Layout To position stories and art elements on a publication page. An editor uses a diagram, or dummy, to plan how the page will look when it is printed.

Lead A journalism term for the opening paragraph of a story. Also spelt lede.

Lead   A metal that does not biodegrade or break down with other substances, and is a toxic metal present in the atmosphere in large concentrations.

Linear story   An Internet term for an online story with a beginning, middle and end which lends itself to scrolling.

Listserv   Composed of people who are linked by the Internet or email and who share a common interest.

Longitudinal study   A research study that takes place over time.

Managing editor   The editor responsible for getting the paper out on time each day and that manages the budget. Also responsible for hiring and firing newsroom personnel and helps in selecting stories, photos and graphics.

Masthead   Box that appears inside a publication identifying its top executives.

Material Safety Date Sheets (MSDS)   Product safety information prepared by manufacturers of products containing toxic chemicals.

Mercury   A stable-occurring toxic trace metal refined from cinnabar to form a variety of compounds.

Metals   A class of chemical elements that do not break down or degrade.

Morbidity   The incidence of a disease.

More   Message at the end of a page of a story that is being written that indicates another page will follow.

Morgue   Traditional name for a newspaper library where clippings-files and reference books were kept. Many of the functions have been replaced by electronic databases of news stories.

Mortality   Death.

Mugshot   Head-only photograph of a person named in an accompanying story, usually one column or less in width.

Multiple-element lead   Opening paragraph that provides two or more of the primary elements of a news story. The lead signals to readers that more than one major event is occurring.

Mutagen   An agent that can cause a mutation, altering genetic material.

Narrative lead   A feature or anecdotal lead that uses narrative to draw people into a story. The lead is popular with feature or non-breaking news stories.

Narrative story   Nonfiction prose that attempts to tell a story. Narrative includes set scenes, characters, action that unfolds over time, the interpretative voice of a narrator, a sense of relationship to the reader and a tale that leads the reader to a point, realization, or destination.

National editor   Editor who supervises reporters based in bureaus around the nation.

News director Top person in a television newsroom, who reports to a station manager, general manager or both. The news director does many of the jobs that a managing editor of a newsroom does, including deciding what goes on the air, the newsroom budget and news personnel issues.

News meeting Daily meeting of a newspaper's editors to discuss and then decide which of the top foreign, national, state and local stories and photographs and graphics will go on page one or other news sections.

News peg Information that identifies the news in a story.

Nitrogen oxides (NOx) Produced from burning fuels, including gasoline and coal, that can cause ground-level ozone or smog. A recognized air pollutant by the EPA.

Nonpoint source pollution Pollution where the source is broad and cannot be easily pinpointed.

Nuclear fission The process of splitting atomic molecules.

Nut graph Explanatory paragraph in a story that follows a delayed or feature lead and explains the significance of a story.

Obit Short for obituary, a report about someone who has died. Once a news story, an obit increasingly is becoming a paid advertisement in many newspapers.

Off the record Agreement between a reporter and a source before an interview that prohibits use of the material revealed. Often, reporters are wary of accepting such terms, choosing instead to try to obtain the information from another source.

On background Agreement between a reporter and source made before an interview that the material can be used, but without attribution to the source.

On deep background An agreement between a reporter and a source before an interview that the material can be used but not in direct quotations or with attribution.

Online A computer term for information that is available on the Internet. Increasingly the term is used interchangeably with Internet and Web.

On the record Agreement between a reporter and a source before an interview that the material can be used without any restrictions.

Op-ed page Page that runs next to an editorial page, providing a mix of opinion columns and illustrations. John Oakes of the *New York Times* is credited with beginning the concept.

Organic Derived from living organisms.

Outrage A risk communication phrase that describes how people often react to perceived hazards not through a clinical and organized study, but through a set of psychological or physiological factors.

Ozone   A colorless gas with a pungent odor it can be found in two layers of the atmosphere. Ozone is found naturally in the stratosphere and it provides a protective barrier shielding the Earth from harmful ultraviolet radiation. In the lower atmosphere or troposphere it is a chemical oxidant and major component of smog.

Pagination   Electronic layout process in which news stories, photographs, graphics, cutlines and headlines are assembled on a computer screen.

Paraphrase   Information about what a source said, but not the source's precise words.

Particulate matter   A very small particle which can be toxic and is regulated by the EPA.

Passive smoke   Nonsmoker's exposure to smoke.

Passive voice   Term describing the verb form used when the subject of a sentence is acted upon by the object.

Pathogen   An organism capable of causing disease.

Pesticide   A chemical control of unwanted plants, insects, rodents, or other pests, including herbicides, insecticides, and fungicides.

pH   The measure of strength of acids and bases, measured on a scale of 0 to 14, where seven is neutral (neither acid or base). Acids measure less than seven on the scale, and bases measure greater than seven on the scale.

Pharmacology   The study of the uses and effects of drugs.

Photo editor   Editor who supervises a newspaper's photographers. This editor may also select and crop photos as well as write the captions that run with the photos.

Podcast   An audio broadcast disseminated over the Internet.

Point of entry   A typographical device using a headline, pull quote, cutline or sidebar as a design element with a story or news page, and is a tool designed to attract readers.

Precision journalism   Use of social science research methods, including using sampling procedures and computer analysis, to gather facts. Philip Meyer, a longtime editor and educator, is credited with popularizing the reporting technique.

PPB (parts per billion)   The occurrence relative to a base of one billion. One part per billion is five people out of the total world population (five billion) or four drops of water in an Olympic size pool (64,000 gallons).

PPM   Parts per million.

Prevalence   How widespread a disease is in a certain population at a certain time, including both new and old cases.

Pull quote   A typographical term for using a sentence or quote from a story, increasing its type size, and using it as a display mechanism on a news page.

Quantitative risk assessment   An evaluation process used to measure how biological, chemical and physical substances affect health.

Question lead   Lead that uses a question to begin the news story. The question must be particularly powerful to succeed in attracting the reader to continue the story.

Radiation   Energy generated through space in the form of waves or particles. Examples are microwaves, light and heat.

Relative risk   (also risk ratio). A comparison of a group exposed to a disease and a group not exposed.

Release date   Date at the top of a press release, wire story or other information that informs the media of the earliest time that they can use the information. Many press releases are stamped for immediate release. Others are embargoed and the information cannot be used until the agreed release date. Embargoes are common for many scientific journals.

Risk   The chance of injury or harm to life, health or property.

Risk assessment   The evaluation of the risk of a hazard, and its possible implications.

Risk communication   The process of providing information about health or environmental risks by risk assessors to the public, news media and special interest groups.

Risk management   The process of evaluating and then acting on potential environmental hazards through public policy initiatives.

Second-day story   Secondary information reported after the breaking news has been disseminated.

Shield laws   Statutes (existing in many states) that allow journalists and other specified people to protect the identity of their sources under certain circumstances.

Shovelware   Text, photos, audio and/or video that are taken from newspapers and TV stations and put directly on their website. News organizations sometimes augment shovelware with original material.

Sidebar   Story that runs with the main story. A sidebar isolates a person, place or thing usually mentioned in the main story, often in a feature approach.

Slot editor   Person responsible for the copy desk who supervises copy editors. The slot editor distributes stories to copy editors and reviews their work.

Slug   One- or two-word label for a story that is often the computer file name for the story.

Soft news   Events that are usually not considered immediately important or timely but are still of interest to a news audience. An environmental soft-news story could be about the efforts of wildlife biologists to save the life of one snake that was endangered.

Solvent   A liquid that dissolves a substance.

Source   Written material or a person that provides information to a reporter.

Spot news   Breaking news event covered by reporters.

State editor   Editor who supervises reporters in bureaus throughout the state, but usually outside of the newspaper's metropolitan area.

Statistical significance   A numerical value that shows the probability that an observation occurred by chance.

Story budget   List of stories that are planned and includes a short summary of what each will say. The wire services move international, national and state budgets that contain overviews of the most important stories on each day's cycles.

Stratosphere   The atmosphere above the troposphere.

Stringer   Part-time reporter. Column inches used to be called string, and these reporters were paid by the number of column inches they produced.

Sulfur dioxide (SO)   A gas, often given off by power stations or boilers, that burn coal. Regulated by the EPA. Depositions of SO can lead to acid deposition or acid rain.

Sulfur oxides (SOx)   Formed from the combustion of fossil fuels, highly toxic and regulated by the EPA.

Summary lead   Opening paragraph that provides the most important elements of the story. Such leads are especially common for hard news or breaking stories.

Supplemental news services   Services that supply, for a fee, news media with materials ranging from cartoons to in-depth political analysis. Usually separate from the Associated Press.

Surface water   Water at the surface of the earth (not underground).

Thermal pollution   Atmospheric contamination caused by heat that may cause a condition in water that results in a fish kill.

Threshold   The minimum amount needed for a given effect to occur.

Threshold Limit Value (TLV)   A regulatory term involving the concentration of airborne substances that a healthy person can be exposed to for a 40-hour work week without adverse effect.

Time element   The "when" of the news story. Generally, the time element is included in the lead paragraph of a print story but may be ignored in a broadcast script.

Total Maximum Daily Load (TMDL)   The most pollutants a body of water can handle and still meet quality standards.

Toxic   A poisonous substance.

Toxicologist   Scientists who study how chemicals interact with the body.

Transition   A writing technique that uses a word, phrase, sentence or paragraph to move readers from one subject area of a story to another. Broadcasters may use sound or visuals as transitions.

Troposphere The part of the atmosphere closest to earth, where clouds and weather patterns are.

Visuals Non-word elements, including photographs, illustrations and graphics. Especially important in television.

Vital records Governmental records of births, deaths, marriages, divorces etc.

Voice A writing device that allows a writer to provide a signature or personal style to a story. Voice may reveal a reporter's personality.

Volatile Having the ability to change into a gas quickly.

Volatile Organic Compounds (VOC) Types of organic chemicals that often are used in solvents, degreasers, paint thinners and fuels. They can quickly evaporate into the atmosphere and can contribute to smog and health problems.

Watershed A drainage area where water not absorbed into the ground finds its way to a water source.

Water soluble The ability of a substance to be dissolved in water.

World Wide Web An Internet device that allows users to use a computer browser to view text, photographs, art, videos, sound and animation at the same time.

X-rays A form ionizing radiation, x-rays are electromagnetic waves similar to light but with a higher frequency.

(West *et al.*, 2003; Itule & Anderson, 2007; EPA, 2006e)

References

Abbott, K. & Bristow, J. (Producers). (2006, July 16). *Global warming: What you need to know* [Television broadcast]. New York and London: BBC, Discovery Channel and NBC News.

About Grist. (2006). *Grist Magazine.* Retrieved July 18, 2006, from www.grist.org.

ActivistCash. (2006). *At ActivistCash.com, we follow the money.* Retrieved May 18, 2006, from http://activistcash.com.

Adler, J. (2006, July 17). Going green. *Newsweek.* 43–52.

Allen, W. (2007, January 11). Personal communication.

Are we fooling ourselves? (2003, Spring). *SEJournal, 12(4)* 1, 19–24.

Arledge, R. (2003). *Roone.* New York: HarperCollins.

Arnold, A. (1990). *Fear of food.* Bellevue, WA: Free Enterprise.

Barry, D. (2002, November 24). Pouch potatoes. *Washingtonpost.com.* Retrieved July 3, 2006, from www.washingtonpost.com.

Barry, D. (2003). *Boogers are my beat.* New York: Random House.

Best newspaper writing. (Yearly, 1977–2005). St. Petersburg, FL: Poynter Institute.

Bilger, B. (2002). Braised shank of free-range possum. In T. Folger (Ed.), *The best American science and nature writing, 2002.* (pp. 10–23). Boston: Houghton Mifflin.

Blum, D., Knudson, M., & Marantz Henig, R. (Eds.). (2006). *A field guide for science writers.* New York: Oxford University Press.

Blumenthal, S. (2003). *The Clinton wars.* New York: Farrar, Staus and Giroux.

Borenstein, S. (2001, April 18). High gas prices is spurring development of "clean coal technology." *McClatchy Washington Bureau* (former Knight Ridder/Tribune News Service). Retrieved February 8, 2006, from www.realcities.com/mld/krwashington.

Borenstein, S. (2002, December 19). Life of elderly less valuable in White House cost benefit analysis. *Pittsburgh Post-Gazette.* Retrieved August 18, 2006, from https://www.lexis-nexis.com.

Borenstein, S. (2005, January 3). As tsunami reminds us, "Mother Nature will win when she wants to." *Pittsburgh Post-Gazette.* Retrieved August 18, 2006, from https://www.lexis-nexis.com.

Borenstein, S. (2006, February 24). Personal communication.

Bosso, C. (1994). After the movement: Environmental activism in the 1990s. In N.J. Vig & M.E. Kraft (Eds.), *Environmental policy in the 1990s.* (pp. 31–50). Washington, DC: Congressional Quarterly.

Bowles, D. & Borden, D. (2004). *Creative editing.* Belmont, CA: Thomson Wadsworth.

Boykoff, M. & Boykoff, J. (2004, July). Balance as bias: Global warming and the U.S. prestige press. *Global Environmental Change, 14(2)*, 125–136.

Bradbury, R. (1997, April 20). Downtown fires intensify crisis. *Grand Forks Herald.* Retrieved August 10, 2006, from www.pulitzer.org.

Brady, J. (1977). *The craft of interviewing.* New York: Vintage.

Brodeur, N. (2006, April 2). Grist keeps on growing and green. *Seattle Times.* Retrieved February 3, 2007, from http://web.lexis-nexis.com.

Brodeur, P. (1989). *Currents of death.* New York: Simon and Schuster.

Brooks, B., Kennedy, G., Moen, D., & Ranly, D. (1996). *News reporting and writing.* New York: St. Martin's.

Brown, M. (2006). Abandoning the news. In C. Connell, *Journalism's crisis of confidence.* (pp. 42–55). New York: Carnegie Corporation.

Brown R. (1991, June 3). Newsrooms hit paydirt with environment. *Broadcasting, 120(22), 56.* Retrieved November 3, 2005, from http://find. galegrop.com.

Bruggers, J. (1998, Fall). Our beat is a different ball game. *SEJournal, 8(3)*, 7.

Bruggers, J. (2003, Fall). Louisville's year of breathing dangerously. *SEJournal, 13(2)*, 16–21.

Bryant, P.J. (2002). *Biodiversity and conservation: A hypertext book.* Retrieved February 13, 2006, from http://darwin.biog.uci.edu.

Bryson, B. (1999). *A walk in the woods.* New York: Random House.

Buffalo news's MacClennan ends column after 27 years. (1998, April). *Environment Writer.* Retrieved July 3, 2006, from www.environmentwriter.org.

Bullard, R. (1996–2006). *Environmental justice in the 21st century.* Environmental Justice Resource Center. Retrieved June 23, 2004, from www.ejrc.cau. edu/ejrcmile.html.

Burkett, D. (1973). *Writing science news for the mass media.* Houston, TX: Gulf.

Calvert, S. (2001, July 19). Hidden historical asset of Baltimore was born of necessity. *Baltimore Sun.* Retrieved November 1, 2005, from www.baltimoresun.com.

Cappiello, D. (2005a, January, 16). Troubled neighbors: People who live nearest to the area's refineries and petrochemical complexes have little idea what's in the air that blows across industry's fence line and into their lives. *Houston Chronicle.* Retrieved November 1, 2005, from http://chron.com.

Cappiello, D. (2005b, January 17). Making it easy? The state of Texas' science for monitoring air toxics is difficult to explain, even for experts. *Houston Chronicle.* Retrieved November 1, 2005, from http://chron.com.

Cappiello, D. (2005c, January 19). Unseen dangers: The sum of invisible leaks – Called fugitive emissions – Can be more hazardous to communities than other sources of air pollution. *Houston Chronicle.* Retrieved November 1, 2005, from http://chron.com.

Cappiello, D. (2005d, Winter). What's in the air? Conduct your own air pollution study. *SEJournal, 15(3)*, 9, 27.

Cappiello, D. (2006, May 30). Personal communication.

Carbone, G. (1994, January 22). Personal communication.

Carmody, K. (1995, May/June). It's a jungle out there. *Columbia Journalism Review*, 40–45.

Carson, R. (1941). *Under the sea-wind*. New York: Oxford University Press.

Carson, R. (1951). *The sea around us*. New York: Oxford University Press.

Carson, R. (1962). *Silent spring*. Boston: Houghton Mifflin.

CBS ousts four for Bush guard story. (2005, January 10). *CBS News*. Retrieved August 14, 2006, from http:www.cbsnews.com.

Center for the Defense of Free Enterprise. (2005–2006). *Undue influence: Tracking the environmental movement's money, power and influence*. Retrieved May 18, 2006, from http://undueinfluence.com.

Ceppos, J. (2000, November 1). Accepting the blame. *Poynteronline*. Retrieved April 13, 2006, from www.poynter.org.

Chapman, C. (2003). A skeptical look at September 11th. In E. O. Wilson & B. Bilger (Eds.), *The best science and nature writing, 2003*. (pp. 15–24). Boston: Houghton Mifflin.

Chappell, R. (2004, Summer). Whom do we believe? A scientist's advice on assessing the science. *SEJournal, 14(1)*, 4, 24–26.

Cherrington, M. (2001). To save a watering hole. In R. Dawkins & T. Folger (Eds.), *The best science and nature writing, 2001*. (pp. 8–14). Boston: Houghton Mifflin.

Cheves, J. (2004, April 11). Kentucky citizen-lobbyist campaigns to improve poverty, environment. *Lexington Herald-Leader*. Retreived July 28, 2006, from http://web.lexis-nexis.com.

Clark, R.P. (1996, February). Three little words. *St. Petersburg Times*. Retrieved August 7, 2006, from www.poynter.org.

Clark, R.P. (2002, May 15). Shrinking the A-head. *Poynteronline*. Retrieved June 17, 2006, from www.poynter.org.

Clark, R.P. (2004, December 21). Writing tool #36: Write a mission statement for your story. *Poynteronline*. Retrieved June 17, 2006, from www.poynter.org.

Clark, R.P. (2005, March 1). Tool #46: Storytellers, start your engines. *Poynteronline*. Retrieved June 17, 2006, from www.poynter.org.

Clayton, M. (2007, January 5). New prospect for U.S.: Glut of ethanol plants. *Christian Science Monitor*. Retrieved January 13, 2007, from http://web.lexis.nexis.com.

Coen, R. (2003, March/April). The Stossel treatment. *Extra!* Retrieved August 14, 2006, from www.fair.org.

Cohn, V. (1989). *News & Numbers*. Ames, IA: Iowa State University Press.

Cohn, V. & Cope, L. (2001). *News & numbers*. Ames, IA: Iowa State University Press.

Colborn, T., Dumanoski, D., & Meyers, J.P. (1997). *Our stolen future*. New York: Plume.

Columbia University. (2006). *John B. Oakes award: About John B. Oakes*. Retrieved July 2, 2006, from www.jrn.columbia.edu.

Connell, C. (2006). *Journalism's crisis of confidence*. New York: Carnegie.

Contributors to Gannett Center Journal try to define environmental journalism. (1990–1991, Winter). *SEJournal, 1(2)*, 6–8.

Cooper, A. (2002, Fall). SEJ survey finds EPA information policies vary by region. *SEJournal, 12(2)*, 12–13.

Cooper, J.F. (1959). *The pioneers*. (First published 1823). New York: Rinehart.

Cooperman, J. (Producer). (2004, April 20). *Clearing the air* [Television broadcast]. New York: NBC.

Court denies challenge on abortion for teens. (1996, April 30). *USA Today*. Retrieved July 28, 2006, from http: web.lexis-nexis.com.

Cox, B. & Carmody, K. (Eds.). (1992, Winter). Editor's note. *SEJournal, 2(1)*, 7.

CSG (Council of State Governments). (2001). *Environment and energy: Interstate compacts*. Retrieved May 16, 2006, from www.csg.org.

CSPI (Center for Science in the Public Interest). (n.d.). *Integrity in science project*. Retrieved May 18, 2006, from http://cspinet.org/integrity.

Davis, J. (2001, April/May). Trade secrets raises issues about industry, media. *Environment Writer*. Retrieved June 13, 2006, from www.environmentwriter.org.

Davis, J. (2005, Spring). Recent government actions close off more information. *SEJournal, 15(1)*, 20.

Davis, J. (2006, February 6). Personal communication.

Dawson, B. (2004, June). Bitter power struggle dominates Sierra Club election coverage. *Environment Writer*. Retrieved May 21, 2006, from www.environmentwriter.org.

Dawson, B. (2005, August). CNN's environment unit: End of the road for what remained. *Environment Writer*. Retrieved June 22, 2006, from www.environmentwriter.org.

Detjen, J. (1991). The traditionist's tools (and a fistful of new ones). In C.L. LaMay & E. Dennis, *Media and the environment*. (pp. 91–102). Washington, DC: Island.

Detjen, J. (2003, Summer). The beat's basics: A primer on taking over the environmental beat. *SEJournal, 13(1)*, 1, 22–23.

Detjen, J. (2004). A new kind of environment reporting is needed. In M. Ludke (Ed.), *Nieman Reports*. (pp. 56–57). Cambridge, MA: Nieman Foundation at Harvard University.

Detjen, J., Fico, F., Li, X., & Kim, Y. (2000, January 1). Changing work environment of environmental reporters. *Newspaper Research Journal, 21(1)*, 2–12.

Diamond, J. (2004). *Collapse: how societies choose to fail or succeed*. New York: Viking.

Digg.com. (2007). *What is Digg?* Retrieved February 3, 2007, at http://digg.com.

Dillard, A. (1974). *A pilgrim at Tinker Creek*. New York: HarperCollins.

Downie, L. & Kaiser, R. (2002). *The news about the news*. New York: Knopf.

Dugger, C. (2006, June 28). Push for new tactics as war on malaria falters. *New York Times*. Retrieved August 1, 2006, from http://web.lexis-nexis.com.

Duncan, H. (2004, Winter). Get the story talking. *SEJournal, 14(3)*, 1, 21–22.

Dunne, M. (2001, Winter). Poison in your backyard. *SEJournal, 11(4)*, 1, 22–24.

Dunne, M. (2002a, Spring). Exploring the cost of mining the West. *SEJournal, 12(4)*, 1, 17–18.

Dunne, M. (2002b, Summer). Moyers: Did Ida Tarbell seek industry response? *SEJournal, 12(1)*, 1, 15–17.

Dunne, M. (2002c, Summer). Veteran journalist unravels emerging issue. *SEJournal, 12(1)*, 1, 22–23.

Dunne, M. (2002d, Winter). It's best to prepare for the worst. *SEJournal, 12(3)*, 1, 13–15.

Dunne, M. (2003, Fall). Lessons from newspaper's The Nature Conservancy probe. *SEJournal*, 13(2), 1, 23–25.

Dunne, M. (2004, Spring). It's best to trust the numbers, not the politicians. *SEJournal, 13(4)*, 1, 18–20.

Dunne, M. (2005a, Spring). In harm's way details Houston's air-pollution problems. *SEJournal, 15(4)*, 1, 16–19.

Dunne, M. (2005b, Summer). Testing a family for pollutants yields startling results. *SEJournal, 15(1)*, 1, 19–22.

Dunne, M. (2005c, Fall). The lesson: You must get some answers on your own. *SEJournal, 15(2)*, 1, 17–20.

Dunne, M. (2005d, Winter). Carbon black report shows impacts on Native Americans. *SEJournal, 15(3)*, 1, 21–24.

EIA (Energy Information Administration). (n.d.). Energy kids page, ethanol made from corn and other crops. Retrieved January 13, 2007, from www.eia.doe.gov.

Egan, D. (2005, July 8). $20 billion estimate for Great Lakes: EPA advisory group delivers cleanup plan. *Milwaukee Journal Sentinel*. Retrieved April 18, 2006, from http://web.lexis-nexis.com.

Eggington, J. (1980). *The poisoning of Michigan*. New York: Random House.

EPA (Environmental Protection Agency). (2006a). *Budget*. Retrieved April 13, 2006, from www.epa.gov.

EPA (Environmental Protection Agency). (2006b). *Clean water act*. Retrieved April 13, 2006, from http:www.epa.gov.

EPA (Environmental Protection Agency). (2006c). *Major environmental laws*. Retrieved April 13, 2006, from www.epa.gov.

EPA (Environmental Protection Agency). (2006d). *The plain English guide to the clean air act*. Retrieved April 13, 2006, from www.epa.gov.

EPA (Environmental Protection Agency). (2006e) *Terminology reference section*. Retrieved January 15, 2007, from http:://epa.gov.

Epler, P. (2001, Winter). Eco-terrorist chat lights a fire. *SEJournal, 11(4)*, 1, 24–26.

Ettlin, D. & Wilber, D.Q. (2001, July 19). Train fire, toxic cargo shut city. *Baltimore Sun*. Retrieved November 1, 2005, from www.baltimoresun.com.

Fagin, D. (2002a, July 28). What went wrong? A $30-million study of breast cancer and pollution on LI has disappointed activists and scientists alike. *Newsday*. Retrieved February 8, 2006, from http://susanlovemd.org.

Fagin, D. (2002b, July 28). Study in frustration – The ambitious search for links between pollution and breast cancer on LI was hobbled from the start, critics say. *Newsday*. Retrieved February 8, 2006, from http://susanlovemd.org.

Fagin, D. (2002c, July 29). Still searching – A computer mapping system was supposed to help unearth information about breast cancer and the environment. *Newsday*. Retrieved February 8, 2006, from http://susanlovemd.org.

Fagin, D. (2002d, August 11). Poorly designed, superficial studies means the state can't answer key questions about cancer clusters on Long Island. *Newsday.* Retrieved February 8, 2006, from http://susanlovemd.org.

Fagin, D. (2002e, August 12). Flaws in the system: The anatomy of a cancer cluster probe: Why can't anyone figure out what's going on? *Newsday.* Retrieved February 8, 2006, from http://susanlovemd.org.

Fagin, D. (2002f, August 13). New approaches in cluster hunting: New computer-aided methods may help researchers identify the hidden causes of cancer clusters. *Newsday.* Retrieved February 8, 2006, from http://susanlovemd.org.

Fagin, D. (2006, February 24). Personal communication.

Favre, G. (2006, January 21). The future of news: New relationships, new pressures, new potential. *Poynteronline.* Retrieved June 22, 2006, from www.poynter.org.

Fedler, F., Bender, J., Davenport, L., & Drager, M. (2005). *Reporting for the media.* New York: Oxford University.

Feldstein, D. (2005, January 18). Too little research: Many people believe hazardous air pollutants on the Texas Gulf coast are a deadly public health problem. *Houston Chronicle.* Retrieved November 1, 2005, from http://chron.com.

Flattau, E. (2000, January 13). Gulf of Mexico's "dead zone" is not a figment of regulators' imagination. *St. Louis Post Dispatch.* Retrieved July 3, 2006, from http://web.lexis-nexis.com.

Fleishman, E. (2002, December). The error of judgment: Struggling for neutrality in science and journalism. *Conservation Biology, 16(6),* 1451–1453.

Fleming, P. (2006, January 2). Personal communication.

Flippen, J. (2000). *Nixon and the environment.* Albuquerque, NM: The University of New Mexico.

Foundation Directory Online. (2002). *Choose the plan that's best for you.* Retrieved August 3, 2006, from www.fconline.fdncenter.org.

Fox, M. (2004). Climate change experts despair over U.S. attitude. *Reuters News Service.* Retrieved June 24, 2004, from www.news.google.com.

Fox, S. (2004). *John Muir and his legacy.* Boston: Little Brown.

Franklin, J. (1994). *Writing for story.* New York: Plume.

Franklin, J. (1998, October). A death in the family. *Raleigh News & Observer.* Retrieved June 17, 2006, from http:www.nieman.harvard.edu.

Freedom of Information Center. (2005). *Freedom of Information Center, Access: A guide to local public records.* Retrieved August 11, 2006, from http://foi.missouri.edu.

Friedman, S., Dunwoody, S., & Rogers, C. (1999). *Communicating uncertainty.* Mahwah, NJ: Erlbaum.

Friedman, S. (1991). Two decades of the environmental beat. In C.L. LaMay & E. Dennis (Eds.), *Media and the environment.* (pp. 17–28). Washington, DC: Island.

Friedman, S. (2004). And the beat goes on: The third decade of environmental journalism. In S. Senecah (Ed.) *The environmental communication yearbook,* Vol. 1. (pp. 175–188). Mahwah, NJ: Erlbaum.

Friedman, S. & Rogers, C. (1991, February). Environmental risk reporting: The science and the coverage [Proceedings of a workshop]. Department of Journalism. Bethlehem, PA: Lehigh University.

Friendly, F. (1967). *Due to circumstances beyond our control*. New York: Vintage.

From Jekyll to Hyde – John Stossel's brand of libertarian journalism. (1995, January). *Environment Writer*. Retrieved June 13, 2006, from www.environmentwriter.org.

Frome, M. (1992, November/December). Snapshot – Michael Frome, writer, teacher, outdoorsman. *The Courier, 37(10)*, 13.

Frome, M. (1998). *Green ink: An introduction to environmental journalism*. Provo, UT: University of Utah.

Fumento, M. (2004, August 16). The "dead zone" fish story. *Fumento.com*. Retrieved July 3, 2006, from www.fumento.com.

Gahran, A. (2005a, September 28). Blogs, feeds, wikis and podcasts: Links for SEJ. *Contentious*. Retrieved May 26, 2006, from http://blog.contentious.com.

Gahran, A. (2005b, September 29). Some great environmental podcasts. *Contentious*. Retrieved July 17, 2006, from http://blog.contentious.com.

Gahran, A. (2006, September 1). Wiki journalism experiment: Wired news. *Poynteronline*. Retrieved February 2, 2007, from http://poynter.org.

Gahran, A. (2007, January 30). Personal communication.

General Accounting Office. (2002, April). Tax exempt organizations, improvements possible in public, IRS and state oversight of charities. GAO-02-526, Report to the Chairman and Ranking Minority Member, Committee on Finance, U.S. Senate.

George, C. (2006, July 26). Personal communication.

Gillmor, D. (2005, January 20). The end of objectivity [Weblog]. Retrieved June 30, 2006, from http://dangillmor.typepad.com.

Giorgianni, S.J. (Ed.). (2004). Vital link in telling the stories of health care science. *Pfizer Journal*. (pp. 4–9). New York: Pfizer.

Glaser, M. (Ed.). (2005a, July 28). Video journalists: Inevitable revolution or way to cut TV jobs? *Online Journalism Review*. Retrieved July 17, 2006, from www.ojr.org.

Glaser, M. (2005b, September 13). NOLA.com blogs and forums help save lives after Katrina. *Online Journalism Review*. Retrieved July 17, 2006, from www.ojr.org.

Glass, S. (2003). *The Fabulist*. New York: Simon & Schuster.

GLRC (Great Lakes Radio Consortium). (2006). *Story Archives*. Retrieved August 3, 2006, from www.grlc.org.

Gordon, R. (2003). *Digital journalism: Emerging media and the changing horizons of journalism*. Lanham, MD: Rowman & Littlefield.

Gordon, R. (2005, October 27). Online opportunities make journalism's future bright, despite gloomy feelings. *Online Journalism Review*. Retrieved June 22, 2006, from www.ojr.org.

Grant, S. (1991, June/July). Canoeing the Connecticut: A log of life on the river [Special Issue]. *Hartford Courant*, 1–20.

Grant, S. (2004, June 24). Where life and beauty abound, Bartholomew's Cobble offers diversity of habitats, species. *Hartford Courant*. Retrieved June 29, 2006, from www.courant.com.

Grant, S. (2006, June 28). Personal communication.

Gray, B. (1990a). City water supply said to be hazardous. In T. Wills (Ed.). *The Pulitzer Prizes 1990*. (pp. 7–25). New York: Simon & Schuster.

Gray, B. (1990b). State office installs bottled water dispensers. In T. Wills (Ed.). *The Pulitzer Prizes 1990*. (pp. 9–10). New York: Simon & Schuster.

Gray, B. (1990c). State: City cancer risk could be 1-in-250. In T. Wills (Ed.). *The Pulitzer Prizes 1990*. (pp. 18–21). New York: Simon & Schuster.

Grimaldi, J. (2002, Fall). Make that FOIA officer your key source. *SEJournal*, *12(2)*, 11.

Grow, G. (1999). Seven types of paragraph development. Retrieved June 19, 2006, from http://longlef.net/ggrow.

Guernsey, L. (2005, September 5). Reporting and living out a calamity. *New York Times*. Retrieved November 10, 2005, from http://web.lexis-nexis.com.

GuideStar.org. (2006). *Using GuideStar*. Retrieved May 22, 2006, from http:www.guidestar.org.

Hafner, K. (2006, June 17). Growing Wikipedia revises its "Anyone can edit" policy. *New York Times*. pp. A1, B9.

Hafner, K. & Lyon, M. (1996). *Where wizards stay up late: The origins if the Internet*. New York: Simon & Schuster.

Hammill, M. (2006, July 30). Personal communication.

Hampel, C. & Hawley, G. (1965). *Glossary of chemical terms*. New York: Van Nostrand Reinhold.

Hand, G. & Ballman, C. (Producers). (2001a, May 4). Tongass I. *Living on Earth*. Boston: Public Broadcasting System.

Hand, G. & Ballman, C. (Producers). (2001b, May 18). Tongass II. *Living on Earth*. Boston: Public Broadcasting System.

Hansen, J. (2006, May 5). Through hell and high water. *Atlanta Journal Constitution* [Audio podcast]. Retrieved August 10, 2006, from www.ajc.com.

Harr, J. (1996). *A civil action*. New York: Vintage.

Harris Interactive. (2005, October 13). *Three-quarters of U.S. adults agree environmental standards cannot be too high and continuing improvements must be made regardless of cost*. Retrieved October 28, 2005, from www.harrisinteractive.com.

Harrison, B. (1993). *Going green: How to communicate your company's environmental commitment*. Homewood, IL: Business One.

Hartz, J. & Chappell, R. (1998). *Worlds apart: How the distance between science and journalism threatens America's future*. Nashville, TN: First Amendment Center.

Hauserman, J. (2001, March 11). The poison in your backyard. *St. Petersburg Times*. Retrieved June 15, 2006, at www.sptimes.com.

Hebert, J. (2003, July 1). False fronts: Consider the source – If you can identify it. *San Diego Union-Tribune*. Retrieved May 21, 2006, from http://web.-lexis-nexis.com.

Heinzerling, L. (1998, September–October). The perils of precision. *The Environmental Forum*. Retrieved August 20, 2006, from www.law.georgetown.edu/faculty/heinzerling/articles/htm.

Hiaasen, C. (1995). *Stormy weather*. New York: Knopf.

Hiaasen, C. (2006). *Nature girl*. New York: Knopf.

Hofstader, D. (1985). *Mathematical themas.* New York: Basic Books.

Hohenberg, J. (1959). *The Pulitzer Prize story.* New York: Columbia University Press.

Hohenberg, J. (1974). *The Pulitzer Prizes.* New York: Columbia University Press.

Hohenberg, J. (1980). *The Pulitzer Prize story II.* New York: Columbia University Press.

Holtcamp, W. (2006, Spring). The joy of a personal blog or becoming a "blog mama." *SEJournal, 16(1),* 24–25.

Holtcamp, W. (2006, July 17). Personal communication.

Houston, B., Bruzzese, L., & Weinberg, S. (2002). *The investigative reporter's handbook.* New York: St. Martin's.

Houston, B. (2003). *Computer assisted reporting: A practical guide.* New York: St. Martin's.

Howarth, W. (Ed.). (1976). *The John McPhee reader.* New York: Farrar Straus Giroux.

Howe, J. (2006, November 3). Gannett to crowdsource news. *Wired News.* Retrieved February 3, 2007, from http://wired.com.

Huizenga, J. (1993). *Cold fusion: The scientific fiasco of the century.* New York: Oxford University Press.

Hunter, M. (2006, May 19). Deaths of evacuees push toll to 1,577. *New Orleans Times-Picayune.* Retrieved July 31, 2006, from www.nola.com.

IBrattleboro.com. (2007, February 2). *Welcome to IBrattleboro.* Retrieved February 3, 2007 from www.ibrattleboro.com.

Icerocket.com. (2007). *Icerocket.com blogs, every search is a direct hit.* Retrieved February 3, 2007, from www.icerocket.com.

Idealbite. (2007). About us. Retrieved February 3, 2007, from www.idealbite.com.

IFEJ (International Federation of Environmental Journalists). (2001). *About us.* Retrieved January 2, 2006, from www.ifej.org.

IPCC (Intergovernmental Panel on Climate Change). (2007, February 2). *Climate change 2007: the physical science basis.* Retrieved February 2, 2007, from http://ipcc.ch.

IRE (Investigative Reporters and Editors). (2006). *The Arizona project.* Retrieved August 7, 2006, from www.ire.org.

ISI Web of Knowledge. (2007). *ISI web of knowledge – take the next step.* Retrieved January 8, 2007, from http://scientific.thompson.com.

Itule, B. & Anderson, D. (2007). *News writing and reporting for today's media.* New York: McGraw Hill.

Iyer, P. (2004). Introduction. In P. Iyer (Ed.), *The best American travel writing, 2004.* (pp. xvi–xxiv). Boston: Houghton Mifflin.

Janofsky, M. (2005, May 20). New EPA chief says budget is sufficient. *New York Times.* Retrieved April 18, 2006, from http://web.lexis-nexis.com.

Jenkins, M. (2004). The ghost road. In P. Iyer (Ed.), *The best American travel writing, 2004.* (pp. 129–148). Boston: Houghton Mifflin.

Jenkins, M. (2006). Nature. In D. Blum, M. Knudson & R. Maranz Henig (Eds.), *A field guide for science writers.* (pp. 229–235). New York: Oxford University Press.

Johnson, D. (2006, June). *Service assessment: Hurricane Katrina August 23–31, 2005.* Silver Spring, MD: National Oceanic and Atmospheric Administration.

Johnson, S. (2006). *The ghost map.* New York: Riverhead Books.

Jones, S. (Producer). (2001, March 26). *Trade secrets* [Television broadcast]. Washington, DC: Public Broadcasting Services.

Judge dismisses apple growers' suit against CBS. (1993, September 14). *Associated Press.* Retrieved July 28, 2006, from http: web.lexis-nexis.com.

Kamrin, M., Katz, D., & Walter, M. (1994). *Reporting on risk: A journalist's handbook.* Ann Arbor, MI: Michigan Sea Grant Communications.

Keith Schneider's environmental journalism evolution: From friend to foe with property rights activists. (2004, March). *Environment Writer.* Retrieved June 22, 2006, from www.environmentwriter.org.

Kelley, D. (2005, October 29). Agency is weak but flexing muscle. *Los Angeles Times.* Retrieved April 18, 2006, from http://web.lexis.nexis.com.

Kendrick, A. (1969). *Prime time: The life of Edward R. Murrow.* Boston: Little Brown.

King, L. (2000, Fall). Fiery aftermath: Dump inferno leaves legacy of suffering, death, payoffs. *SEJournal, 10(4),* 16–17.

Kingsolver, B. (2000). *Prodigal summer.* New York: HarperCollins.

Kinsley, M. (2006, March 31). The twilight of objectivity. *Slate.* Retrieved June 30, 2006, from http:www.slate.com.

Klaidman, S. (1991). *Health in the headlines.* New York: Oxford University Press.

Knudson, T. (2001a, April 22). Fat of the land: Movement's prosperity comes at a high price. *Sacramento Bee.* Retrieved May 18, 2006, from http://sacbee.com.

Knudson, T. (2001b, April 29). Environmental groups stay green. *Ventura County Star.* Retrieved May 18, 2006, from http://web.lexis-nexis.com.

Knudson, T. (2001c, July 29). Audubon's membership at crossroads. *Sacramento Bee.* Retrieved May 19, 2006, from www.sacbee.com.

Kolbert, E. (2006). *Field notes from a catastrophe: man, nature and climate change.* New York: Bloomsbury USA.

Kovach, B., Rosenstiel, T., & Mitchell, A. (2006). Commentary on the survey findings. *Journalism.org.* Retrieved July 10, 2006, from www.journalism.org.

Kovarik, W. (1997). *Environmental history timeline.* Retrieved October 24, 2005, from www.radford.edu/~wkovarik/envhist/index.html.

Kraft, M.E. & Vig, N.J. (1994). Environmental policy from the 1970s to the 1990s: Continuity and change. In N.J. Vig & M.E. Kraft (Eds.), *Environmental policy in the 1990s* (pp. 3–29). Washington, DC: Congressional Quarterly.

Kunreuther, H. & Patrick, R. (1991, April). Managing hazardous waste. *Environment, 33(3),* 13–14; 31–35.

LaMay, C.L. & Dennis, E. (1991). *Media and the environment.* Washington, DC: Island.

LeDoux, J. (1998). *The emotional brain: The mysterious underpinnings of emotional life.* New York: Simon and Schuster.

Leopold, A. (1966). *Sand County almanac.* (First published 1949). New York: Oxford University Press.

Lester, J. (1994). A new federalism? Environmental policy in the states. In N.J. Vig & M.E. Kraft (Eds.), *Environmental policy in the 1990s* (pp. 51–68). Washington, DC: Congressional Quarterly.

Little, A. (2006a, January 26). Mass backward. *Grist.* Retrieved August 19, 2006, from http:www.grist.org.

Little, A. (2006b, April 12). Don't discount him. *Grist.* Retrieved August 19, 2006, from http:www.grist.org.

Little, A. (2006c, June 14). *Environmental reporting on the Internet.* Paper presented at the University of Rhode Island Narragansett Bay campus, Narragansett, RI.

Little, A. (2006d, June 16). Labor gains. *Grist.* Retrieved August 19, 2006, from www.grist.org.

Little, A. (2006e, June 30). Ag reflex. *Grist.* Retrieved August 19, 2006, from www.grist.org.

Little, A. (2006f, July 19). The writing on the Wal-Mart. *Grist.* Retrieved August 19, 2006, from www.grist.org.

Living on Earth. [Radio script]. (1991–2006). Retrieved August 4, 2006, from www.loe.org.

Loftis, R. (1992, Winter). The tough times. *SEJournal, 2(1),* 1, 6–7.

Lomborg, B. (2001). *Skeptical environmentalist.* New York: Cambridge University Press.

Lord, P. (2001a, May 13). Another generation caught in a sad cycle. *Providence Journal.* Retrieved August 11, 2006, from www.projo.com.

Lord, P. (2001b, May 14). Unsafe at home. *Providence Journal.* Retrieved August 11, 2006, from www.projo.com.

Lord, P. (2001c, May 15). No sanctuary in America. *Providence Journal.* Retrieved August 11, 2006, from www.projo.com.

Lord, P. (2001d, May 16). Struggling for the right words. *Providence Journal.* Retrieved August 11, 2006, from www.projo.com.

Lord, P. (2001e, May 17). We're on the side of angels. *Providence Journal.* Retrieved August 11, 2006, from www.projo.com.

Lord, P. (2001f, May 18). Enact new laws, enforce the old. *Providence Journal.* Retrieved August 11, 2006, from www.projo.com.

Lord, P. (2005a, June 5). Not for sale. *Providence Journal.* Retrieved August 11, 2006, from www.projo.com.

Lord, P. (2005b, June 6). Coming aboard. *Providence Journal.* Retrieved August 11, 2006, from www.projo.com.

Lord, P. (2005c, June 7). Rescue mission. *Providence Journal.* Retrieved August 11, 2006, from www.projo.com.

Lord, P. (2005d, June 8). Like father, like son. *Providence Journal.* Retrieved August 11, 2006, from www.projo.com.

Lord, P. (2005e, June 9). One of the last great places. *Providence Journal.* Retrieved August 11, 2006, from www.projo.com.

Lord, P. (2005f, June 10). All together now. *Providence Journal.* Retrieved August 11, 2006, from www.projo.com.

Lord, P. (2006, May 30). Personal communication.

Luechtefeld, L. (2004). *Covering pollution: An investigative reporter's guide.* Columbia, MO: Investigative Reporters and Editors.

McCabe, C. (2006, June 5). Personal communication.

MacClennan, P. (2004, February 29). Environmental movement fading away. *Buffalo News*. Retrieved July 3, 2006, from http://web.lexis-nexis.com.

McClure, R. (2003a, Winter). The risks and benefits of reporting on risk. *SEJournal, 13(3)*, 5, 24.

McClure, R. (2003b, Summer). Tips on interviewing from some of the best. *SEJournal, 13(1)*, 1, 24.

McClure, R. (2006, Spring). From ink to Internet, journalists write the blogosphere. *SEJournal, 16(1)*,1, 23.

McConnaughey, J. (2004, Summer). Making numbers real, or how do I show how little 12 parts per billion is? *SEJournal, 14(1)*, 8.

McCormick, J. (2003, February 7). Deconstructing an editorial. *Poynteronline*. Retrieved June 17, 2006, from www.poynter.org.

McGrath, J. (2006). *Frank Norris, a life*. Urbana, IL: University of Illinois Press.

McGuire, M., Stilborne, L., McAdams, M., & Hyatt, L. (2002). *The Internet handbook for writers, researchers, and journalists*. New York: The Guilford Press.

McNeil, D. (2006, June 27). An iron fist joins the malaria wars. *New York Times*. Retrieved August 1, 2006, from http://web.lexis-nexis.com.

McQuaid, J. (1996, March 24). Way of life threatened along with Gulf's vast bounty. *New Orleans Times Picayune*. Retrieved November 1, 2005, from www.pulitzer.org.

McQuaid, J. & Schleifstein, M. (2006). *Path of destruction*. New York: Little Brown.

Mansur, M. (2005, Spring). A FOIA state of mind. *SEJournal, 15(4)*, 1, 20–22.

Marsh, G. (1965). *Man and nature*. (First published 1864). Cambridge, MA: Belkamp.

Marston, B. (2005, November 28). *Heard around the west*. Highcountrynews.org. Retrieved July 2, 2006, from www.highcountrynews.org.

Martin, A. (2005, September 24). Paper keeps head above water. *Irish Times*. Retrieved November 10, 2005, from http://web.lexis.nexis.com.

Media Resource. (2005). *Media resource, linking journalists and scientists*. Retrieved July 27, 2006, from www.mediaresource.org.

Meersman, T. (1990–1991). The advocacy debate. *SEJournal, 1(2)*, 1, 5–6.

Meersman, T. (2004, June 13–15). Invaded waters. *Minneapolis Star Tribune Special Report Reprint* (pp. 1–14).

Meersman, T. (2006, June 15). Personal communication.

Mejia, R. (2003, winter). Interviewing scientists: A primer on finding and building a stable of science sources. *SEJournal, 13(3)*, 1, 22.

Meyer, P. (1972). *Precision journalism*. Bloomington, IN: Indiana University Press.

Meyer, P. (2005). *Vanishing newspaper*. Columbia, MO: Missouri University Press.

Michaels, P. (Ed.) (2005, March 15). *World climate report*. Retrieved August 3, 2006, from http:www.worldclimatereport.com.

Miller, J., Harris, J., Bailey, R., Brown, M., Revkin, A., Crouse, B., & Schleifstein, M. (2005, September 30). *Is journalism – environmental or otherwise – a dying idea?* [Panel presentation]. SEJ 15th Annual Conference, Opening Plenary. Austin, TX: University of Texas Press.

Miller, S. (2003, Winter). Environment on TV: Tips from a TV veteran on getting more play and airtime. *SEJournal, 11(4)*, 16–17.

Mohan, G. (2003, October 30). Trapped crew sits out a raging firestorm. *Los Angeles Times*. Retrieved October 31, 2005, from www.pulitzer.org.

Monks, V. (1993, March). See no evil. *American Journalism Review*. Retrieved December 12, 2005, from www.ajr.org.

Monks, V. (2005, January 21). Carbon black. *Living on Earth*. [Radio transcript]. pp. 1–8.

Monks, V. (2006, August 1). Personal communication.

Moon, W.L.H. (1983). *Blue highways*. New York: Little Brown.

Mooney, C. (2004, November/December). Blinded by science. *Columbia Journalism Review*. Retrieved December 12, 2005, from www.cjr.org.

Morley, C. (Ed.). (1938). *Familiar quotations by John Bartlett*. Boston: Little Brown.

Moro, J. & Lapierre, D. (2002). *Five minutes past midnight: The epic story of the world's deadliest industrial disaster*. New York: Scribners & Son.

Morris, E. (2001). *Theodore rex*. New York: Random House.

Mothers' group fights back in Los Angeles. (1989, December 5). *New York Times*. Retrieved May 22, 2006, from http://vpn. web.lexis-nexis.com.

MSNBC. (2005, June 21). *Los Angeles Times suspends wikitorials*. Retrieved July 17, 2006, from www.msnbc.com.

Muir, J. (1998). *First summer in the Sierra*. (First published 1911). Boston: Houghton Mifflin.

Murray, D. (2000). *Writing to deadline*. Portsmouth, NH: Heinemann.

Murray, D., Schwartz, J., & Lichter, S. (2001). *It ain't necessarily so, how media make and unmake the scientific picture of reality*. Lanham, MD: Rowman & Littlefield.

National Public Radio (Producer). (1999). *The best of NPR, writers on writing*. [Audio Tape]. New York: Warner Adult.

Nature Conservancy. (2006). *Nature Stories* [Podcast]. Retrieved July 17, 2006, from www.nature.org/podcasts.

NCCS (National Center for Charitable Statistics). (2006). *Largest organizations, environmental*. Retrieved May 18, 2006, from www.nccsdataweb.urban.org.

Nelkin, D. (1987). *Selling science*. New York: WH Freeman.

NESCAUM (Northeast States for Coordinated Air Use Management) (2004–2006). *Overview*. Retrieved April 24, 2006, from www.nescaum.org.

Neuzil, M. (2005, September/October). The great moon hoax of 1835. *The History Channel Magazine*, 34–37.

New Orleans Times-Picayune and NOLA.com. [Weblog]. (2005, August 29). Hurricane Katrina – the storm arrives. Retrieved January 1, 2006, from http://web.lexis.nexis.com.

Newsvine. (2007). *Using newsvine*. Retrieved February 3, 2007, from www.newsvine.com.

NICAR (National Institute for Computer Assisted Reporting). (2005). Retrieved August 11, 2006, from www.nicar.org.

NIEHS (National Institute of Environmental Health Sciences). (1999, May 4). NIEHS report on health effects from exposure to power-line frequency electric and magnetic fields.

Niles, R. (2006, April 23). Can newspapers do blogs right? *Online Journalism Review.* Retrieved June 7, 2006, from www.ojr.org.

NOAA (National Oceanic Atmospheric Administration). (2005, November 29). *NOAA reviews record-setting 2005 Atlantic hurricane season.* [Revised April 13, 2006]. Retrieved July 31, 2006, from www.noaanews.nozz.gov/storms.2005.

Norris, F. (1901/1986). *The Octopus.* New York: Viking Penguin.

O'Donnell, M. (2004, Spring). The value of CAR, when a regulator says "Don't worry," check it out. *SEJournal, 14(4),* 1, 21.

Olsen, L. (2003, Spring). Looking deep into data on water polluters pays off. *SEJournal, 13(4),* 8.

O'Neill, T. (1994). *All politics is local.* Holbrook, MA: Bob Adams.

Opie, J. (1998). *Nature's nation, an environmental history of the United States.* Orlando, FL: Harcourt, Brace.

ORSANCO (Ohio River Valley Water Sanitation Commission). (n.d.). *About ORSANCO.* Retrieved May 15, 2006, from www.orsanco.org.

Ottaway, D. & Stephens, J. (2003a, May 4). Nonprofit land bank amasses billions: Charity builds assets on corporate partnerships. *Washington Post.* Retrieved November 1, 2005, from http:web.lexis-nexis.com.

Ottaway, D. & Stephens, J. (2003b, May 5). How a bid to save a species came to grief. *Washington Post.* Retrieved November 1, 2005, from http:web.lexis-nexis.com.

Ottaway, D. & Stephens, J. (2003c, May 6). Nonprofit sells scenic acreage to allies at a loss. *Washington Post.* Retrieved November 1, 2005, from http:web.lexis-nexis.com.

Outing, S. (August 26, 2005). The source strikes back. *Poynteronline.* Retrieved November 25, 2005, at www.poynter.org.

Pace, D. (2005, December 13). More blacks live with pollution. *Associated Press.* Retrieved January 3, 2006, from http://web.lexis-nexis.com.

Page, C. (2003, March 16). Junkyard plans touch off classic development battle. *Burlington Free Press.* Retrieved February 7, 2006, from www.burlingtonfreepress.com.

Page, C. (2005a, October 6). Rare snake slithers home. *Burlington Free Press.* Retrieved February 7, 2006, from www.burlingtonfreepress.com.

Page, C. (2005b, November 9). Rehabbed snake found dead. *Burlington Free Press.* Retrieved February 7, 2006, from www.burlingtonfreepress.com.

Page, C. (2006, May 22). Personal communication.

Paine, T. (1964). *Common sense.* (First published 1776). Mineola, NY: Dover.

Parkman, F. (1943). *The Oregon trail.* (First published 1849). New York: Hermitage.

Patton, V. (2004, October 18). Hovering over a live volcano. *TelevisionWeek,* pp. 9, 12.

Patton, V. (2006a, summer). A dozen (or more) TV stories to sell your news manager for sweeps. *SEJournal, 16(2),* 1, 23–24.

Patton, V. (2006b). Personal communication.

Pawelski, N. (2004). Networks aren't tuned in to the environment. In M. Ludke (Ed.), *Nieman Reports Special Issue* (pp. 87–89). Cambridge, MA: Nieman Foundation at Harvard University.

Pawlick, T. (2001). *The invisible farm, the worldwide decline of farm news and agriculture journalism training.* Chicago: Burnham.

Pew Center on Global Climate Change. (2006). *What's new.* Retrieved August 18, 2006, from www.pewclimate.org/.

Phillips, S. (2004, April 20). *Clearing the air.* [Dateline NBC broadcast]. Retrieved August 2, 2006, from http://msnbc.com.

Philp, T. (2004a, August 23). The lost Yosemite. *Sacramento Bee.* Retrieved May 24, 2005, from www.pulitzer.org.

Philp, T. (2004b, August 29). Hetch Hetchy reclaimed: The dam downstream. *Sacramento Bee.* Retrieved May 24, 2005, from www.pulitzer.org.

Philp, T. (2004c, August 30). Hetch Hetchy reclaimed: San Francisco's paradox. *Sacramento Bee.* Retrieved May 24, 2005, from www.pulitzer. org.

Philp, T. (2004d, September 7). Yosemite on the cheap. *Sacramento Bee.* Retrieved May 24, 2005, from www.pulitzer.org.

Philp, T. (2004e, September 18). Hetch Hetchy reclaimed: Drain it, then what? *Sacramento Bee.* Retrieved May 24, 2005, from www.pulitzer.org.

Philp, T. (2004f, October 25). Lines in the sand. *Sacramento Bee.* Retrieved May 24, 2005, from www.pulitzer.org.

Philp, T. (2004g, November 14). The pendulum shifts. *Sacramento Bee.* Retrieved May 24, 2005, from www.pulitzer.org.

Philp, T. (2004h, Fall). Utterly boring, looking at the mundane agencies of your beat may startle. *SEJournal, 14(2),* 17–20.

Philp, T. (2006, June 21). Personal communication.

Pinker, S. & Folger, T. (2004). *The best American science and nature writing 2004.* Boston: Houghton Mifflin.

Pollan, M. (2002). *Botany of desire.* New York: Random House.

PollingReport.com. (2006). *Environment.* Retrieved July 28, 2006, from http://pollingreport.com/enviro.htm.

Population Reference Bureau. (n.d.). *Human population: Fundamentals of growth, population growth and distribution.* Retrieved June 24, 2004, from www.prb.org.

Power of Words. (2001, August 2). *How to make a major project work.* Retrieved October 31, 2005, from www.projo.com/powerofwords.

Powers, A. (2004, May 4). When reporters accompany activists, do they get the story, or do they become part of the story. *Los Angeles Times.* Retrieved June 25, 2004, from http://web.lexis-nexis.com.

ProfNet. (1995–2005). *ProfNet experts, where the media and sources connect.* Retrieved July 27, 2006, from http:www.profnet.org.

Project for Excellence in Journalism. (2005). *The state of the news media 2005.* Journalism.org. Retrieved November 1, 2005, from www.stateofthenews media.org.

Project for Excellence in Journalism. (2006). *The state of the news media 2006.* Journalism.org. Retrieved July 9, 2006, from www.stateofthenewsmedia.org.

Prwatch. (n.d.). *Center for media and democracy.* Retrieved May 19, 2006, from www.prwatch.org/.

Puchalla, D. (1994, March). Radiation redux. *American Journalism Review.* Retrieved December 12, 2005, from www.ajr.org.

Pulitzer.org. (2006). *The Pulitzer Prize winners.* Retrieved August 8, 2006, from www.pulitzer.org.

Quammen, D. & Bilger, B. (Eds.). (2000). *The best science and nature writing 2000.* Boston: Houghton Mifflin.

Rachel Carson dies of cancer; 'Silent Spring' author was 56. (1964, April 15). *New York Times.* Retrieved October 24, 2005, from http:www.rachelcarson.org.

Reading Rack: More Blacks live with pollution. (2006, January). *Environment Writer.* Retrieved August 11, 2006, from www.environmentwriter.org.

Reddit (2007). *Never reddit before? Here's how.* Retrieved February 3, 2007, from http://reddit.com.

Redmond, J., Shook, F., Lattimore, D., & Lattimore-Volkmann, L. (Eds.). (2005). *The broadcast news process.* (7th ed.). Englewood, CO: Morton.

Reporter certification: Professionalism seen as antidotes for ailing mainstream news. (2005, June). *Environment Writer.* Retrieved June 22, 2006, from www.environmentwriter.org.

Revkin, A. (2004a, May 21). Nothing comes easy on an ice cap. *New York Times.* Retrieved August 5, 2006, from www.nytimes.com.

Revkin, A. (2004b, May 22). Seeking clues in a vast frozen mystery. *New York Times.* Retrieved August 5, 2006, from www.nytimes.com.

Revkin, A. (2004c, May 23). Heading for home. *New York Times.* Retrieved August 5, 2006, from www.nytimes.com.

Revkin, A. (2006). The environment. In D. Blum, M. Knudson & R. Marantz Henig (Eds.), *A field guide for science writers* (pp. 222–228). New York: Oxford University.

Rich, C. (2005). *Writing and reporting news* (4th ed.). Belmont, CA: Wadsworth Thomson Learning.

Rieder, R. (2003, January). The Jayson Blair affair. *American Journalism Review.* Retrieved August 14, 2006, from www.ajr.org.

Riffenburgh, B. (1993). *The myth of the explorer.* London: Belhaven Press.

Roe, S. (2000, Spring). The beryllium story: How one tip led to expose. *SEJournal, 10(1)*,14.

Rogers, P. (1999, Winter). Ranking NGOs: SEJ members list likes and dislikes. *SEJournal, 9(4)*, 4–5.

Rogers, P. (2004). Complexity in environment reporting is critical to public decision-making. In M. Ludtke (Ed.), *Nieman Reports Special Issue* (pp. 50–52). Cambridge, MA: Nieman Foundation at Harvard University.

Ropeik, D. (2004). Journalists can be seduced by aspects of risk. In M. Ludke (Ed.), *Nieman Reports, Special Issue* (p. 69). Cambridge, MA: Nieman Foundation at Harvard University.

Ropeik, D. (in press). Risk communications, an overlooking tool for improving public health. *Public Health and Preventive Medicine.*

Ropeik, D. (2006a, January 10). Personal communication.

Ropeik, D. (2006b, February 1). *Risk perception* [Lecture]. Storrs, CT: University of Connecticut.

Ropeik, D. & Gray, G. (2002). *Risk.* Boston: Houghton Mifflin.

Rosenbaum, R. (2005, February 21). Tape it, baby, tape it! Scrawled interviews are a risky romance. *New York Observer*, pp. A1, A4.

Rosenbaum, W. (1994). The clenched fist and the open hand: Into the 1990s at EPA. In N.J. Vigs & M.E. Kraft (Eds.), *Environmental policy in the 1990s* (pp. 121–143). Washington, DC: Congressional Quarterly.

Rosenberg, T. (2004). What the world needs. now is DDT. *New York Times Magazine.* Retrieved July 1, 2004, from http://nytimes.com.

Rosenthal, E. & Revkin, A. (2007, February 3). Science panel says global warming is unequivocal. *New York Times,* pp. A1, A5.

RTNDA (Radio, Television, News Directors Association, Producer). (2003). Best practices in environmental journalism [Educational video]. (Available from the RTNDA, 1600 K St. Washington, DC 20006).

Russell, C. (2006). Risk reporting. In D. Blum, M. Knudson & R. Marantz Henig (Eds.), *A field guide for science writers.* (2nd ed., pp. 251–256). New York: Oxford University Press.

Rutledge, R. (2006, December 26). Progress: Investing in a rural future. *Milwaukee Journal Sentinel.* Retrieved January 13, 2007, from http://web.lexis-nexis.com.

Rutten, T. (2005, September 2). Katrina's aftermath: A warning sent but not heeded. *Los Angeles Times.* Retrieved November 10, 2005, from http://web.lexis-nexis.com.

Saar, M. (2006, December 20). Reporting mass appeal; amateurs working as journalists are giving rise to a new wave of "citizen journalism." Results are mixed. *Los Angeles Times.* Retrieved February 2, 2007, from http://web.lexis-nexis.com.

Sachsman, D., Simon, J., & Valenti, J. (2006). Regional issues, national norm: A four-region analysis of U.S. environmental reporters. *Science Communication, 28:1,* 93–121.

Sandman, P. (1994). Mass media and environmental risk. Retrieved January 3, 2002, from www.fplc.edu.

Scanlan, C. (1995, July 1). Writers at work: The process approach to newswriting. *Poynteronline.* Retrieved June 17, 2006, from www.poynter.org.

Scanlan, C. (2003, September 29). What is narrative anyway? *Poynteronline.* Retrieved June 17, 2006, from www.poynter.org.

Scanlan, C. (2006, July 6). Voicing the story: The art and craft of podcast narration. *Poynteronline.* Retrieved July 7, 2006, from www.poynter.org.

Schleifstein, M. (2005a, August 28). Katrina bulks up to become a perfect storm. *New Orleans Times-Picayune.* Retrieved November 9, 2005, from http://web.lexis-nexis.com.

Schleifstein, M. (2005b, November 10). Personal communication.

Schleifstein, M. (2006, July 6). Personal communication.

Schleifstein, M. & McQuaid, J. (2002, June 23). The big one. *New Orleans Times-Picayune.* Retrieved October 11, 2005, from www.nola.com/hurricane/.

Schmid, R. (2006, March 16). Experts argue over ivory-billed woodpecker. *Associated Press,* p. 1. Retrieved July 31, 2006, from www.usatoday.com.

Schulte, H. & Dufresne, M. (1994). *Getting the story: An advanced reporting guide to beats, records and sources.* New York: Macmillan College.

Schwartz, D. (2001, Winter). The Hudson River: A cybernews lesson. *SEJournal, 11(4),* 9, 11.

Science citation index. (2007). *Science citation index (SCI)*. Retrieved January 8, 2007, from http://scientific.thomson.com.

Science communications and the news media: Workshop, W. Alton Jones Campus, University of Rhode Island. (2003, November). *Environment Writer*. Retrieved October 11, 2005, from www.environmentwriter.org.

Science communications and the news media: Scripps Institute of Oceanography, LaJolla, CA. (2004a, March). *Environment Writer*. Retrieved October 11, 2005, from www.environmentwriter.org.

Science communications and the news media: University of Washington, Seattle, WA. (2004b, November). *Environment Writer*. Retrieved October 11, 2005, from www.environmentwriter.org.

Science communications and the news media: Columbia University Lamont-Doherty Earth Observatory. (2005, June). *Environment Writer*. Retrieved October 11, 2005, from www.environmentwriter.org.

Seattlepi.nwsource.com. (2002). Our troubled sound. *Seattlepi.com*. Retrieved August 19, 2006, from http:seattlepi.nwsource.com.

SEJ (Society of Environmental Journalists). (2003). *Winners: SEJ 2nd annual awards for reporting on the environment*. Retrieved August 3, 2003, from www.sej.org.

SEJ (Society of Environmental Journalists). (2005a). *Winners: SEJ 4th annual awards for reporting on the environment*. Retrieved August 10, 2006, from www.sej.org.

SEJ (Society of Environmental Journalists). (2005b, June 7). *SEJ's history*. Retrieved September 2, 2006, from www.sej.org.

Shabecoff, P. (1993). *A fierce green fire*. New York: Hill and Wang.

Shabecoff, P. (2004). The environment beat's rocky terrain. In M. Ludke (Ed.), *Nieman Reports Special issue* (pp. 52–54). Cambridge, MA: Nieman Foundation at Harvard University.

Shafer, J. (2006, June 24). The incredible shrinking newspaper. *Slate*. Retrieved July 5, 2006, from http://beta.slate.com.

Shiffer, J.E. (1998, fall). Seeking the muse along the neuse. *SEJournal*, *8(4)*,14–15.

Siegfried, T. (2006). Reporting from science journals. In D. Blum, M. Knudson & R. Marantz Henig (Eds.) *A field guide for science writers*. (2nd ed., pp. 11–17). New York: Oxford University.

Sill, M. (2005, June 3). Case study: The News & Observer changes the face of hog farming. *Poynteronline*. Retrieved January 13, 2007, from http://poynter.org.

Sims, N. & Kramer, M. (Eds.). (1995). *Literary journalism*. New York: Ballantine.

Sipress, A. & Goodman, P. (2004, December 26). Sea surges from massive quake kill over 13,000 across South Asia. *Washington Post*. Retrieved October 31, 2005, from www.asne.org.

Sivak, M. & Flanagan, M. (2004, July–September). Consequences for road traffic fatalities of the reduction in flying following September 11, 2001. *Transportation Research Part F, 7 (4–5)*, 301–305.

Slovic, P. (1991, February). Perceptions of risk: Paradox and challenge. In S. Friedman & C. Rogers (Eds.), *Environmental risk reporting: The science and the coverage.* (pp. 7–12). [Proceedings of a workshop]. Bethlehem, PA: Department of Journalism, Lehigh University.

Snyder, L. & Morris, L. (1962). *A treasury of great reporting: Literature under pressure from the sixteenth century to our own time.* New York: Simon & Schuster.

Soennichsen, O. (2004, November 29). An interview with Jon Franklin. *Nieman narrative digest.* Retrieved June 17, 2006, from www.nieman. harvard.edu.

Sonner, S. (2002, October 2). Convoy of western ranchers, farmers press property rights. *Associated Press.* Retrieved July 28, 2006, from http://web.lexis-nexis.com.

Soroos, M. (1994). From Stockholm to Rio: The evolution of global environmental government. In N.J. Vig & M.E. Kraft (Eds.), *Environmental policy in the 1990s* (2nd ed., pp. 299–321). Washington, DC: Congressional Quarterly Press.

Sptimes.com. (2001). Our vanishing wetlands. *Sptimes.com.* Retrieved August 19, 2006, from http:www.sptimes.com.

Srinivas, S. (2005, January 7). Online citizen journalists respond to South Asian disaster. *Online Journalism Review.* Retrieved July 18, 2006, from www.ojr.org.

Stauber, J. & Rampton, S. (1995). *Toxic sludge is good for you.* Monroe, ME: Common Courage.

Steffens, L. (1931). *The autobiography of Lincoln Steffins.* New York: Harcourt, Brace.

Stephens, M. (1980). *Three Mile Island: The hour-by-hour account of what really happened.* New York: Random House.

Stovall, J. (2004). *Web journalism: Practice and promise of a new medium.* Boston: Pearson Education.

Stowe, H.B. (1981). *Uncle Tom's cabin.* (First published 1852). New York: Penguin.

Streater, S. (2001, February 18). Hidden hazard. *Pensacola News-Journal.* Retrieved July 28, 2006, from www.pensacolanewsjournal.com.

Stuebner, S. (1992, Winter). Reporters watch out: Are you too green for your boss? *SEJournal, 2(1),* 7.

Sunstein, C. (2002). *Risk and reason: Safety, law and the environment.* New York: Cambridge University Press.

Swords, P., Bjorkund, V., & Small, J. (2003). *How to read the IRS form 990 and find out what it means.* Nonprofit Coordinating Committee of New York, 1–19. Retrieved May 22, 2006, from www.npccyn.org.

Syndicated columnist Ed Flattau recaps 40-year "intellectual journey." (2004, February). *Environment Writer.* Retrieved July 2, 2006, from www.environmentwriter.org.

Tarbell, I. (1904). *The History of the Standard Oil Company.* New York: McClure, Phillips.

Taubes, G. (1994, November). Fields of fear. *The Atlantic Monthly,* 94–108.

The best American science and nature writing. (2000–2006, Yearly). New York: Houghton Mifflin.

The best American travel writing. (2000–2006, yearly). New York: Houghton Mifflin.

The human toll. (n.d.). *United Nations Office of the special envoy for tsunami recovery.* Retrieved July 31, 2006, from www.tsunamispecialenvoy.org/country/humantoll/asp.

Theroux, P. (1995). *The great railway bazaar.* New York: Penguin.

Thevenot, B., Spera, K., & MacCash, D. (2005, August 31). Old west has nothing on Katrina aftermath. *New Orleans Times-Picayune.* Retrieved August 10, 2006, from www.pulitzer.org.

Thomas, L. (1978). *Life of a cell.* New York: Penguin.

Thomas, R. (2005, Winter). Hurricane Katrina jolts journalism – and New Orleans. *SEJournal, 15(3),* 1, 25–26.

Thoreau, H.D. (1930). *Walden.* (First published 1854). London: Dent & Sons.

Time. (1989, January 2). Planet of the year, endangered earth. Cover.

Treehugger. (2007). About us. Retrieved February 3, 2007, from www.treehugger.com.

UNFCCC (United Nations Framework Convention on Climate Change). (n.d.). *Essential background.* Retrieved August 5, 2006, from www.unfccc.int.

Ungar, S. (1989). *The papers and the papers.* New York: Columbia University Press.

USDA (U.S. Department of Agriculture). (2005). Agriculture, biotechnology. Retrieved January 10, 2007, from http://usda.gov.

U.S. Forest Service. (2003). *May 18, 1980 eruption of Mount St. Helens.* Retrieved January 8, 2007, from www.fs.fed.us.

Wallace, J. (1997). *Overdrive: Bill Gates and the race to control cyberspace.* Hoboken, NJ: John Wiley & Sons.

Ward, B. (Ed.) (2003). *Reporting on climate change: understanding the science* (3rd ed.). Washington, DC: Environmental Law Institute.

Ward, B. (2004). Environmental journalists don't get much respect. In M. Ludke (Ed.), *Nieman Reports Special Issue.* (pp. 58–60). Cambridge, MA: Nieman Foundation at Harvard University.

Ward, K. Jr. (2005a, July 1). DEP approves Massey permits near school Manchin had promised to hear complaints. *Charleston Gazette.* Retrieved April 6, 2006, from www.wvgazette.com.

Ward, K. Jr. (2005b, July 16). DEP halts Massey silo project: Maps show facility outside site's original permit area. *Charleston Gazette.* Retrieved April 6, 2006, from http://wvgazette.com.

Ward, K. Jr. (2005c, July 17). DEP criticized over Massey silo: Complaints of proximity to school ignored, boundary advances overlooked, Raleigh residents say. *Charleston Gazette.* Retrieved April 6, 2006, from www.wvgazette.com.

Ward, K. Jr. (2006, May 30). Personal communication.

Ward, K. Jr. (2007, January 8). Personal communication.

Ward, K. Jr., Wall, D. & Bruggers, J. (2005, September 30). *FOI session: Fighting to keep public information public.* SEJ 15th Annual Conference. Austin, TX: University of Texas.

Warrick, J. & Stith, P. (1995, February 19). New studies show that lagoons are leaking. *Raleigh News & Observer.* Retrieved January 13, 2007, from http://web.lexis.nexis.com.

Watson, B. (2003). Sounding the alarm. In E. O. Wilson & B. Bilger (Eds.), *The best American science and nature writing, 2003* (pp. 248–253). Boston: Houghton Mifflin.

Weaver, J. (2002). *What are the odds: The chances of extraordinary events in everyday life.* Amherst, NY: Prometheus.

Weiss, R. (2006, December 7). U.S. uneasy about biotech food. *Washington Post.* Retrieved January 14, 2007, from www.washingtonpost.com.

Welch, C. (2004, December 13). *Exxon Valdez,* other spills taught Alaskans to be ready. *Seattle Times.* Retrieved August 10, 2006, from http://web.lexis-nexis.com.

Welsome, E. (1999). *The plutonium files: America's secret medical experiments in the cold war.* New York: Dial.

West, B., Sandman, P., & Greenberg, M. (2003). *The reporter's environmental handbook* (3rd ed.). New Brunswick, NJ: Rutgers University Press.

Wheeler, T. (2003, September). The trouble(s) with covering population. *Environment Writer.* Retrieved August 11, 2006, from www.environmentwriter.org.

Wheeler, T. (2006, February 13). Personal communication.

Whitney, D. (2003a, September 8). KMOV pollution expose has far-reaching results. *Television week,* 45.

Whitney, D. (2003b, September 8). Weather staff pull double duty. *Television week,* 33, 36, 39.

Whitney, D. (2003c, September 8). Ferreting out the environmental angle. *Television week,* 38.

Whitney, D. (2004a, October 18). Environmental blues: Financial pressures keep stations scrambling for ways to strengthen coverage. *Television Week,* 9–10.

Whitney, D. (2004b, October 18). Pollution story results in changes at city hall. *Television Week,* 18–19.

Whitney, D. (2005, September 26). Katrina: A new light on the environment. *Television Week,* 23, 33–35.

Williams, B. & Werve, J. (2004, July 15). *Gimme shelter (from taxes).* The Center for Public Integrity. Retrieved December 5, 2005, from www.publicintegrity.org.

Willman, D. (2005, January). Will overnight ratings replace broadcast consultants in driving TV coverage of environment? *Environment Writer.* Retrieved June 22, 2006, from www.environmentwriter.org.

Willman, D. (2006, July 11). Personal communication.

Wills, T. (Ed.). (1990). *The Pulitzer Prizes 1990.* New York: Simon and Schuster.

Wilson, D. (2002). *Freedom of Information Act fundamentals.* Society of Environmental Journalists. Retrieved May 16, 2006, from www.sej.orgo.

Wilson, E.O. (1998). *Consilence: The unity of knowledge.* New York: Knopf.

Wilson, E.O. (2001). Introduction: Life is a narrative. In R. Dawkins & T. Folger (Eds.), *The best American science and nature writing 2001* (pp. xiii–xx). Boston: Houghton Mifflin.

Wikinews. (2007, February 3). *Welcome to Wikinews.* Retrieved February 3, 2007, from http://en.wikinews.org.

Witt, L. (2003, November). This movement won't be buried. *American Journalism Review.* Retrieved June 30, 2006, from www.ajr.org.

Woods, K. (2003, February 7). Seven strong steps to a strong opinion. *Poynteronline*. Retrieved July 2, 2006, from www.poynter.org.

Wyss, B. (2003a, August). Population/wildlife. *Environmental Writer*. Retrieved August 11, 2006, from www.environmentwriter.org.

Wyss, B. (2003b, September). Population and water II. *Environment Writer*. Retrieved August 11, 2006, from www.environmentwriter.org.

Yergin, D. (1991). *The prize*. New York: The Free Press.

Zeeck, D. (2006, June 21). Keys to the future: News as watchdog, as trusted agent, as useful tool. *Poynteronline*. Retrieved June 22, 2006, from www.poynter.org.

Zinsser, W. (1988). *Writing to learn*. New York: Harper & Row.

Index